91

se Buying,
ing and
nveyancing

Bradshaw

nd updated by Georgia Bedworth, Barrister

A fine
after
item
he
Rep
da
w

House Buying, Selling and Conveyancing
by Joseph Bradshaw; revised and updated by Georgia Bedworth, barrister.

Published by
Lawpack Publishing Limited
76–89 Alscot Road
London SE1 3AW

www.lawpack.co.uk

First edition 1999
Second edition 2001
Third edition 2003
Fourth edition 2004
Fifth edition 2006

Land Registry forms reproduced with the permission of HM Land Registry.

ISBN: 1-905261-35-7
ISBN: 978-1-905261-35-2

Exclusion of Liability and Disclaimer

Contents

Important facts

This book contains the information and instruction for buying and selling registered and unregistered houses without a solicitor. This book is for use in England or Wales; it is not suitable for use in Scotland or Northern Ireland. The law is stated as at 1 July 2006.

The information it contains has been carefully compiled, but its accuracy is not guaranteed, as laws and regulations may change or be subject to differing interpretations.

Neither this nor any other publication can take the place of a solicitor on important legal matters. As with any legal matter, common sense should determine whether you need the assistance of a solicitor rather than rely solely on the information and forms in this book.

We strongly urge you to consult a solicitor if:

- you do not understand the instructions or are uncertain how to complete and use a form correctly;

- what you want to do is not precisely covered by this book.

Introduction

It isn't true that only those who have gone through a long, expensive and involved training can possibly understand the intricacies of house buying, selling and conveyancing.

Anyone can set up as, and take on the title of, estate agent. No qualifications or licences are required.

Traditionally, trained and qualified solicitors have done conveyancing. Not because their training qualified them to do it, but because a nineteenth century government, grateful for their support in collecting some taxes, gave them a legal monopoly of conveyancing for a fee. That leaves doing a conveyance for no fee, which means that you can do a conveyance for yourself or anyone else for whom you wish to do a favour. The only skills required are reading, writing and an ability to count your money.

People do far more for themselves than ever before. From painting and decorating to car maintenance, people are having a go themselves. And it isn't only practical things that are tackled.

A few years ago, the technicalities for obtaining a divorce were simplified and a little later the government withdrew the provision of legal aid for parties to divorces that were not defended. The increasing popularity of divorce and the bankrupting nature of solicitors' fees for doing the transaction have between them produced thousands of do-it-yourself divorcees who have done their own divorces, and saved themselves over £500 by expending a little time and effort.

Moreover, during the process of doing their own divorces, people have found that what hitherto they thought was a thoroughly legal process is only judicial in so far as a judge has to give a nod over their papers, and all the rest is an administrative matter.

In this book, I hope to show that housing transactions have even less of the law about them than divorce actions. Nowadays, transferring a house from one owner to another is done, in most of England and Wales, by filling in simple forms – that is the legal side of it. The bit that can be complicated is when you are using money from the sale of one house to pay for the purchase of another. But that is not a legal problem, it is a business transaction. You don't hare off to a fully trained legal man when you are trading upmarket from a Bentley to a Rolls; settling the Hire Purchase on one and taking out a new loan on the other. In most straightforward cases, you no more need to know the relevant housing Acts of Parliament inside out when you buy a house than you need to know the Road Traffic and Consumer Credit Acts when buying or selling a car. Whether it is a house or car that is being dealt with, you need to know about honesty and fair dealing and if you meet up with someone who sells you an unroadworthy car or seriously misrepresents a property to you, the laws are there to punish the offender; it is then that you really need a lawyer – a good one.

Just because you might have a legal remedy against wrongdoers, this does not mean to say you should not be prudent within your competence. If you are considering buying a car that has done a fair mileage, you put it through some stringent tests, and if you are not sure about it, but are still interested, at a price, you get a qualified mechanic to give you a report on it. If you want to make sure there is no Hire Purchase on it, go to the local Citizens Advice Bureau (don't ring, there's a form to fill in) and for little more than the cost of a stamp they will check it out for you. So there you are, the legal owner of a bigger and better car, and you need know no more law at the end of the transaction than at the beginning. But look at what you have accomplished: you have satisfied yourself that the car is what it is cracked up to be and checked that the person offering it for sale owns (has good title to) it. 'Ah!' you say, 'houses are not like cars. Surely it's more complicated, and doesn't the rule *caveat emptor* (let the buyer beware) apply in full force to a housing transaction? Isn't the whole business a splendid opportunity for scoundrels to practise their wicked ways?'

My answer is: certainly houses are not like cars. Cars can be stolen, repainted, engine and number plates swapped. You can't very well shift a whole house. As for 'let the buyer beware', in its application to housing it is, in the main, a reference to the purchaser making sure that the vendor has good title (can prove he owns and has the power to sell) and as you will learn from these pages, you obtain this assurance by sending a simple form (no fee payable) to the Land Registry. Other potential flies in the ointment can also be discovered from the Land Registry entries.

Most Land Registry forms mentioned can be found on the Land Registry website, www.landregistry.gov.uk, where they can be filled out and printed off (but, currently, not saved, so check before printing), others from law stationers, still others from HM Revenue & Customs Stamp Office (www.hmrc.gov.uk/so).

No solicitor has a better method than that given here, and if, when you last bought a house, any precautions were taken to make sure that you did get vacant possession before the money was handed over (and vice versa when you sold) the odds are that it was you who did the legwork. Solicitors rely on the general law, together with the basic honesty of the absolute majority of house owners on these practical points. On the legal point of proving ownership, where the ownership is registered, they rely on the state-backed guarantee provided by Her Majesty's Land Registry. I invite you to do the same.

HM Land Registry was established at the end of the nineteenth century, the Land Transfer Act which set it up having finally made its way through Parliament after centuries of attempts had failed. If you read what the sponsors of the Act had to say in its support, you will see that they intended to make dealing in land as simple as dealing in, to use their nineteenth century words, 'stock and chattels'. To that end the Land Registry was established, and of course someone has to pay for its upkeep. Who better than those who benefit. The public? Today, the buyer of the average house pays nearly a hundred pounds to the Registry – but who has had the dealing simplified for him? The lawyer.

It is ironic that an Act passed a century ago to benefit the general public, at a time when most people had left school at 11 years of age or earlier, has been made to appear so complicated that the vast majority of house buyers and sellers, who will have had at least 11 years of schooling, are being persuaded to pay solicitors to do something they could well do for themselves. It tells us something, either about our education system or about the lawyers' propaganda machine; I think it is the latter. Indeed, the propaganda is so effective it has even convinced lawyers themselves that they really are protecting their clients from a thousand and one things that can go wrong.

Since 1984, governments have laboured mightily to bring about competition in the conveyancing business. According to the Council for Licensed Conveyancers there are now approximately 750 licensed conveyancers in the UK (including both fully and limited licensed) to compete with more than 38,000 lawyers. So throughout we will refer to fee-taking conveyancers as solicitors, under the generic surname of Skinner.

I have done my own little survey. I put this question, 'What do you think a solicitor does for you that you could not do for yourself?' Invariably the answer is, 'All those searches'. This answer is usually spoken with such reverential awe, it seems that ordinary trusting people have come to believe that every time they buy a house their solicitor has worked his way through reference after reference, file after file, and book after book in office after office and cellar after cellar, emerging with the scrolls into the light of day, covered in dust and with a cold wet towel round his head.

In reality, the searching consists in sending off a few forms, which have ready-printed questions, to the authorities who answer them for you. If you really find this difficult to believe, at least have a look at the said forms. When you see them, I am sure you will agree that of all the forms you have ever had the misfortune to struggle with, those used in housing transactions suffer least from officialese and gobbledegook. If you have already bought or sold a house, you will have found that the only thing about the whole transaction which struck you as truly professional was the sheer size of the bill at the end of it. It doesn't matter whether your conveyance was done by qualified solicitors or their clerks, you got the same job done and the same breathtaking bill.

Another thing that really seemed to puzzle the respondents to my survey was: how did one manage to use the money from the sale of Flitsville for the purchase of Newsville, when it is well known that you actually have to flit from Flitsville before you get your money for it? As you will learn, it can be done when you can get all the parties or their representatives together at the same time. But where that is not possible it is done by the simple expedient of taking a bridging loan for a few days. The interest is at about 3 per cent over base rate, so on £30,000 the charge is a mere £10.46 per day with a minimum of £15, plus an arrangement fee which will depend on the moneylender you go to. To bridge a day, you can even leave your furniture in the van overnight and get bed and breakfast somewhere.

Because those who cut out estate agents can choose their own buyers and control the pace, they seldom need a bridging loan and never need to give four or five thousand pounds to the chain-breakers.

The high costs of moving house do deter many people from changing their abode, particularly those people with young growing families. The older end, having seen it all before, cannot face the anxieties generated by the selling and conveyancing system. To them, the opportunity to do their own and cut out the middlemen has proved a godsend.

Over the years I have, as a property owner, conveyed shops, offices, houses and the like for myself – nothing has ever gone wrong. Never have I regretted my choice, and neither have I ever met any other person who does his own conveyancing who has any regrets. Sorting out the problems that house buyers and sellers have has convinced me that it would have been far better for many of them had they tackled the job themselves from the beginning.

Transferring property is nowhere near as difficult as it has been made out to be, but that does not mean to say that the technical work can be done by a two-year-old chimpanzee suffering from brain damage. If in a few of the pages that follow it seems rather complicated, take courage and keep going, remembering it's all new to you. It might even be shock that is stopping your brain functioning; shock at the simplicity, and shame as you realise how in the past you have been so easily persuaded that it was all so fantastically difficult.

Though it is hoped that this book makes an interesting and useful read in itself, it is intended to be kept at the learner estate agent's and conveyancer's elbow for reference as he picks his way through buying and selling and conveyancing for himself.

On the way he will notice that strategies and tactics are given so that purchasers pay less and vendors get more. This inherent paradox can only make life more interesting all round where both vendor and purchaser have invested in the book. So if you spot from your opposite number's tactics a fellow reader, keep the knowledge to yourself, turn back to the book and check up on how to cope. Why let the professionals have all the fun? Do the job yourself and take a pride in it!

A word about forms

One word of warning regarding form numbers, which this book refers to frequently. These numbers come from a variety of sources. All Land Registry forms and Land Charges Department forms are numbered by the Land Registry and the numbers are used by all law form publishers. The same principle applies to HM Revenue & Customs forms. There are also forms which are produced by commercial firms that use the name and number of the originating party, such as the local search forms.

However, other forms are given their number by the publisher of the form and, frequently, different publishers use different numbers. Plus, over the years solicitors have got used to using general conveyancing expressions. For example, 'preliminary enquiries' and 'Enquiries before Contract' are the questions to be asked in writing before exchange of contracts; the publishers will name and number them according to their own preference. So when asked to answer preliminary enquiries if you are selling, do not be surprised to find that the form has a different name. In the old days, the buyer's solicitors sent these to the seller's lawyers; they still do if they do not accept the Seller's Property Information Forms.

The various Property Information Forms. These were introduced in an attempt by the legal profession to create a seller's property information pack and the idea was that the seller's solicitors would complete and send these to the buyer or his solicitors, along with a local search, draft contract, title information and so on. These forms have generally been replaced by standard Property Information Forms, which are used in most residential conveyancing transactions. These forms are available online.

Do not be surprised to find that when you sell your home you may be asked to volunteer replies to the Property Information Forms, or you may be sent the buyer's solicitors' preferred version of preliminary enquiries. When you buy your new house, do not be surprised if you are sent replies to Property Information Forms, or are invited to send in your preliminary enquiries. This confusion simply represents the distinction between solicitors who prefer the old way and those who prefer the new.

A similar confusion in names and numbers applies to the Requisitions on Title, questions posted by the buyer to the seller's solicitors after contracts have been exchanged. Even more confusion may arise once the Home Information Packs come into force, but more about that later.

CHAPTER 1

Buying

First of all, you must find something to view. Answering estate agents' and private vendors' advertisements in local papers is one obvious way, and touring round finding 'For Sale' boards is another. But there are also the not so obvious, such as placing your own advertisements in newspapers and even shop windows in the locality you have decided is the one for you. There is also the direct approach of knocking on doors and asking 'Is this house for sale?' to which you might be lucky enough to get the answer, 'No, but that one over there is.' In any case, such an approach can often lead to a useful conversation about the area and its qualities and problems.

The internet is becoming an increasingly useful tool in searching for property. Websites such as www.findaproperty.com, www.propertyfinder.com or www.hotproperty.co.uk, to name but a few, have made the process of finding a property that you want to buy even easier. These websites contain flexible search engines which allow you to search in your chosen area, even if it is many miles away from where you currently live.

When you have viewed a number of houses within a short period of time it is sometimes, at the end of the day, difficult to remember which had what – the address alone is not always sufficient to bring the memories flooding back. So try to pick on some salient feature – the more ridiculous the better, such as 'the one with the surly butler', 'the one with the circular pink mirrors on the bathroom walls', 'the one to suit mother-in-law', etc., and make a note accordingly on the particulars if you have got some from an agent. Why not take your video camera (though the owners might think you are a burglar's agent, or worse a reporter!)? Remember, when viewing property to which you have been introduced by an agent, that he gets his commission from the vendor – he owes very little, if any, duty to a purchaser. The higher the price he gets for the vendor, the more his commission, but he's got to be a bit of a dullard if the only reason he is sticking out for the extra couple of hundred pounds is because it will push his commission from £500 to £505.

Having found a house to view your main consideration is: can I make a home here? I suggest that there are two additional criteria to which you should pay attention. The first is already at the back of your mind: is it structurally sound? The second sounds a bit daft when you haven't yet bought, but old hands who have often been moved up, down and across the country for one reason or another will testify to its importance: will it be easy to sell if ever I need to move? We will look at each in turn.

Whether you can make a home in the house you are about to view is a highly personal question. Nevertheless, there are a few points that are common to many people. For instance, if you are getting on in years you have to consider whether children screaming at all times of the day and night are easily tolerated. Even if you are young, you might well find other people's kids too much to bear. A new, neat and tidy development where there is just a bunch of nice newly married couples but very few children is no guarantee of a quiet life for those who want one. Noisy, late-finishing house-warmings, followed by every conceivable sort of party, followed by slamming of car doors can disturb the sleep just as effectively as the screaming children the newly weds will soon produce!

If you are buying a semi or terrace (town/mews/cottage style) house, get to know as much as you can about who will be doing what at the other side of that joint and party wall, and if the vendors have the television, radio or CD player going full blast when you call, have it switched off and listen. When there are neighbours' drives that you look out over, try to make sure there will not be a boat or caravan blocking your view.

Vendors who insist on viewing 'strictly by appointment' often do so because they want to manipulate the situation – for example, if they have at one side a neighbour who takes his bagpipe band off every weekend in his caravan, while the young mariner at the other takes his boat and yapping dog away at the same time, who can blame such a vendor for insisting on weekend viewing? And it's a certainty that any vendor, if questioned, will only vouchsafe that the neighbours are quiet people who keep themselves to themselves, but are of sterling worth if called upon in a crisis. And if he thinks you have an inkling that a band next door is trying to perfect its line-up and gets it all together on Mondays, Wednesdays and Thursdays, he will laugh that off with: 'Oh, it's quite lively, we quite enjoy it – keeps us young, you know. Actually, we've heard that they are splitting up – pity, really'.

If vendors don't mention why they want to sell and where they are moving to, ASK! If the answer doesn't have the ring of truth, you have been warned.

If you are a non-gardener or simply can't find the time for Britain's major hobby, don't be persuaded to buy just because the garden looks so well established, so neat and tidy already, and only appears to need a minimum of maintenance. All gardens need constant attention if they are to look as though they need no attention. A shower of rain just after you have viewed can germinate a thousand weeds.

Any objection from any member of your family should be listened to before you finally decide. Teenagers might say of an open-plan house that there is nowhere for them to go. Open-plan houses seem to suit the very young and the very old, but situations near rivers don't suit either. They are too wet for non-swimmers and too damp for the arthritic.

Before you go out viewing, it is a good idea to get into your head what hectares, yards, feet and metres look like. When told a room is 20 feet by 14 feet or 6 metres by 3 metres, can you visualise it in your mind? Is the bath at your present abode of such a size that you can enjoy a long, lazy soak in it? Whether it is or not, measure it, and use the size as a comparison. Will your furniture fit? If it will, fine. If it won't then you have to choose – furniture or house.

Having made your first visit during the week, make your second at the weekend (or vice versa), so as to get a different perspective of the neighbours and the neighbourhood. Park your car some distance away and walk – you will see a lot more of the district that way.

With a bit of luck, there will be heavy rain before you move in, so while you're around, look for damp, and you never know, there might have been a burst pipe or a fire to ruin the decorations. Even if contracts are signed you may still say, 'You didn't tell me about this lot. To be fair you must put it right', but that very much depends on the contract, as you will see from chapter 9.

You are not really entitled to make these subsequent visits (but why should the sellers object?), and maybe the first thing you must really persuade yourself of is that though you are going to the house to poke around in somebody else's private domain, you must not be embarrassed about it. The vendors knew you and others were likely to do this from the moment they thought about putting the house on the market, and they have had ample time and opportunity to hide any dirty linen and to empty the cupboard of skeletons.

A lot can be learned while walking up the path. A gate that is falling to bits isn't a very good introduction. Is the path itself cracking and subsiding? Is the drive likely to help or hinder when you have a flat battery? Will icing cause problems in the winter? Can you see any cracks in the stucco or brickwork? If there is a lot of zig-zag cracking around the windows and doors they are signs of old or new subsidence. If the cracks have been filled in some time ago and have not re-appeared, all is no doubt well.

All houses subside a little after being built and it usually expresses itself in no more than cracked plaster. But if the cracks have been filled and parted again, or, worse still, bricks have cracked vertically, there is real trouble, as there is if a wall is starting to lean or taking on the shape of a saucer. You don't need to start digging around the foundations or paying a surveyor to do so to know that this one is not for you – unless it can be bought for the price of the land.

While still walking slowly up the garden path, have your first look at the downpipes, roof and chimney if there is one. Have another look up from the back garden later, and if it is a tall house bring along your binoculars so that you can inspect the chimney stack and pot. A swift look at the TV aerials in the vicinity will tell you about TV reception. If there are a lot of tall fancy ones about, reception is likely to be poor.

Damp

Once again, you are looking to see if the structure is doing the thing that a house is supposed to do: shelter you from the elements. Damp is the indicator of most structural problems in a house. Water tries to get in from the top, ends, sides and bottom. As if that were not enough, we bring it in via pipes, and builders use thousands of gallons of water in the building of a house. Houses are built of such things as bricks, mortar and wood, all of which are porous, and the soil in Britain seldom dries out, so the fabric of a British house is always damp to some extent. It is when that dampness passes an unacceptable level that things begin to rot and owners have to start paying out.

Blocked, overflowing gutters and cracked downpipes can be a source of water which will penetrate in sideways, as also can badly pointed chimney stacks. Driving rain can find its way in through cracks around doors and windows. Otherwise, sideways penetration of water is very rare as modern houses are almost certainly constructed with two outside walls roughly two inches apart and pinned together by metal wires or straps. The two-inch gap, called a cavity, forms an insulation barrier ensuring that water can penetrate only as far as the cavity and no further. However, in the building process careless builders have been known to drop mortar down the cavity and allow it to accumulate on the ties.

In this case the mortar build-up can form a bridge to convey water from the outer to the inner wall. If you are buying a house in the course of construction take your torch to have a look and tell the foremen if you find his brickies are laying up problems, as well as bricks, for the future. Once a house is completed and there is no internal evidence of damp from this cause you can be pretty sure there is none. If you really want to be sure, there is only one way to find out and this applies to much else – take the house down brick by brick!

In all modern, indeed in nearly all, houses, there will be a damp-proof course. This is needed because the ground in Great Britain is nearly always damp, the brickwork in the foundations will soak it up, and it will quickly spread round the house. A damp-proof course is a water-tight skin of some sort.

The old system was to set slates on the third or fourth brick course above the ground, and below the level of the floor joists. Slate does not bend and the slight movements of a house can, over time, fracture parts of the slate course. For many years now, builders have used mineral felt or plastic sheet, both of which are flexible and can cope with anything but a really radical structural movement. What it can't cope with is the owner who piles soil up against the wall to a height above the course.

Count to the third or fourth course of bricks and you will see the slate or black, bituminous material protruding a little somewhere along the line.

Once you have found the height follow the line right round the house to see if your vendor has been silly. If he has, pay really particular attention to the plaster, skirting board and any other woodwork on the opposite side of that patch inside the house and give general attention to the whole of the ground floor woodwork if there are wooden floors, because damp does spread. If no real damage has been done, removal of the offending material from the outside wall is imperative. This done, check to make sure that the air bricks are clear and if the damp is only slight it will soon disappear.

What can be done when the damp course is damaged or the house was built without one? You could get a builder to go round the house knocking out a brick at a time and inserting a damp course as he goes. It might work – it will certainly be expensive. There are firms who specialise in various, what can loosely be described as, 'patent systems'. You can find them in the Yellow Pages and they will usually give a free estimate. Some of these systems have a good success rate. Most firms will give some sort of long guarantee. And here it is worth making a general point about 10-, 20-, 30- or even lifetime guarantees and it is this: it's easy for the firm to give the guarantee, but who will guarantee that the firm will still be in business if ever you need them?

So that's the base and sides dealt with; what about the roof? The most common form of construction for residential property is a pitched roof, covered with either slates or tiles. It is often difficult to gain access to roof space, but if you have any doubts about the construction, it is best to cope with the difficulty now. In the case of an old house, it is reasonable to assume that any fault in the construction itself will have developed already and your external examination will have told you whether the roof is bowing or not. If it is and has been bowed or buckled for a number of years and there is no internal evidence of damp, it is probably all right. However, if you decide to have a look in the roof space, take a good torch with you but keep switching it off to see if any daylight is coming in because of missing, broken or drifting slates or tiles. While you are up there you can check on insulation of ceiling, tanks and pipes, and if there is none or it isn't done up to modern standards, you have found another bargaining point or two.

Recent decorations can provide internal evidence of damp. Vendors do titivate their houses up ready for sale; and they also, sometimes, do it to cover up evidence. If you suspect this has happened, see if you can borrow a damp meter from your friendly DIY shop, but be careful that you are not tracing the run of a water pipe or drain and mistaking it for damp. The instructions that come with the meter will tell you about all that.

Flat roofs need special attention. If a pitched roof covered in slate or tile goes wrong, the replacement of a few slates or tiles will, more often than not, solve the problem. But the only remedy for a badly damaged flat roof is often the complete replacement of the covering. The most usual coverings are lead, asphalt roofing felt and sometimes zinc, and it is important that roofs be laid to a proper fall so that water does not gather in any depressions. If you can see any such pools then trouble is on its way – sooner or later.

As the covering is exposed to heat in one season and cold in another and sometimes both on the same day, and its expansion and contraction rate is not equal to the boards on which it is laid, you can often see the skeleton impression of the boarding showing through the covering. Now, that boarding should run at right angles to the gutter; if it is parallel to the gutter, water will gather in the depressions, which will have nothing on the depression that will settle over you when you get the builder's quotation (avoid estimates) for the repairs. Felt roofs last about ten years, asphalt up to 30 years. Evidence of downward damp can be seen on ceilings, upstairs walls and chimney breasts. The fault can often be located and dealt with by climbing a ladder and cleaning out the gutter. Where there are stains all round the upper walls, unless you are getting a real bargain, it might be as well to try elsewhere.

It is not always easy to examine floors, particularly when they are covered with lino or carpets. A vendor refusing to let you have a careful look might give grounds for suspecting his: 'Oh, the floors are all right, you can take my word for it.' It is particularly desirable to have a thorough examination made if there are any indications of springiness, such as ornaments rattling, when you walk across the floor, or you suspect that it is rotting joists that are allowing the floor to part company from the skirting board. The floor into a bay window is the favourite place for the rot to set in and by an outside door is runner up. If your vendor tells you that you can have every confidence in it, ask him to jump up and down on it for a while; after all, he knows the way round his cellars better than you do.

Timbers can be affected by dry rot, wet rot, beetle or woodworm. Dry rot is insidious. It is a fungus and it glories in finding a bit of damp wood to set up business in. It gets down between the fibres of wood and dries the wood out. Dry-rotted wood looks as if it has been dehydrated to a brown cracked appearance and crumbles to dust at a touch when in an advanced stage of development. Unfortunately, the damage is well under way before there is any external manifestation of it as mentioned above. But the conditions under which it thrives can be spotted: damp, smelly, unventilated corners.

Wet rot gets going when the wood becomes so saturated that the fibres break apart, weakening the wood. It tends to happen at the end of timbers (hence the attention to skirting board gaps) where water can get in between fibres, but of course, it can occur elsewhere; around sink, bath and WC wastes are likely areas. Depending on how far the wet rot has gone it can be cured, often quite inexpensively, by replacing the rotted timber and rectifying the fault that caused it. Take a strong torch with you into the cellar (if there is one), because the floor joists are more likely than not to be nicely exposed for your inspection. Poke around with a strong penknife – if you can slide it into the wood at right angles to the run of the grain you've found something.

The third ill that can affect timbers is beetle or woodworm. Woodworm is the caterpillar of the beetle. The flying beetle alights and injects her egg into timber and flies away until she is ready for a repeat performance. The egg develops into a worm which, feeding on the life-giving juices of the timber, transforms itself into a beetle in the image of its mother, and burrows out into the light of day leaving behind it a tunnel in the wood and a little pile of sawdust beside it. Which all goes to show that if you simply go round, no matter how meticulously, squirting things into the worm holes, you can't be sure you have got all the little beggars; that is why you need a specialist firm in to say whether the beetle is still active, and if it is, to give you a quote for pressure spraying the timbers.

To find out if the worm has been active enough to cause real danger, the penknife test is used. As with the wet and dry rot, badly affected timber can be replaced and your decision must be based on the amount of repair required; so if you find evidence of wood rot of any kind, call in one of the specialist firms who will give you a quotation and offer a guarantee. If the problems have been discovered early enough the cost need not be ruinous.

There are a lot of solid floors about nowadays, so if such a floor has parted from the skirting board the supporting fill has rearranged itself and that is why settlement has taken place – it can be rectified, but make sure there is no zig-zagging on the outer wall because in that case the foundations might be rearranging themselves too.

Electrics

Another point to cover is the electrical system. A sure sign of wiring that has had its day is the plug with round pins. The whole house needs re-wiring. In older houses during your inspections of the roof space and cellar, look out for any wires that pass across the joists. If you see two element wires twisted together and festooned along you can be pretty sure some re-wiring is necessary to bring the electrical system up to modern standards of efficiency, and, above all, safety.

Some electricity companies will be only too glad to make a visual inspection without charge and they will give a free quotation for any work required. If for any reason the supply is cut off, as it no doubt will be, if there is to be any gap between the time when the vendor leaves and you move in, no re-connection will be made if the whole system is not up to standard.

You should also be aware of recent changes to building regulations which require any recent changes to electrics to have been carried out by a qualified electrician. If you spot any new wiring, this might be something to keep in reserve to ask when it comes to enquiries before contract.

Decorations

Decorations can cover a multitude of sins, and are, of course, like sin, a matter of personal preference. Costs of decorating can be high particularly if you have tall ceilings, with fancy cornices or moulding. The rooms might look immaculate but always take the precaution of lifting a picture off the wall to find out if pale patches will remain when the vendor has gone. Incidentally, whether you redecorate because you dislike the colour scheme or because the place is a dirty tip, the cost will be pretty much the same, although, if the wallpaper is already peeling off it might be cheaper!

Plumbing

We've dealt with unwanted water getting into the house and causing damp – now we will have a look at the water that we do want in the house. If you are to get your water from a well, you will need someone to tell you if the well is sufficiently deep to avoid pollution of the water by any drains that might be or become defective. A well must also be situated at a reasonable distance from any possible source of contamination. In fact, before you go any further, a few words with the local authorities would be in order – they might already know the situation and have costly plans for the owner or his successor.

Find the tap at the highest point and try the pressure. Also try the hot water pressure to the bath – you don't want to wait all day for the bath to fill. Neither do you want to spend all day pulling on the WC plunger, so drop a piece of paper into the pan and see if you can send it on its way with one shot, and while you are about it note if the pan or the washbasin is cracked.

When you walk round the garden and find a portion that is squelchy or there is an ominous line of subsidence in the driveway it might be that the vendor is a bit of a stinker and is not levelling with you. However, you can square him up by getting a firm in to test the drains. If they use the water pressure system, they could cause damage so get the vendor's written permission first – as a matter of fact, if the firm has anything about them they will have a standard form intended to indemnify themselves, so have a word with them to make sure it isn't amended to land you in the …

I would like to instruct vendors not to read the next paragraph, but if they can't resist reading I implore them not to draw any guidelines from it to help them with their sales!

Central heating systems need examining. Ask to see last year's receipts for the fuel used. If it is a system such as gas, ask if it has been regularly serviced. Find a radiator at the highest point in the house and as you turn the air-release screw hold a lighted match to it. If you set up a lighted gas jet it isn't because gas has got into the system, it is the product of some corrosion that has started. It might only need some anti-corrosion fluid putting in the system – on the other hand that might not be sufficient. In any case, all the more reason to have a careful look round for leaks particularly at joints. Leaks also tend to make nasty stains on carpets.

If you remember most of the tips given above, a vendor will not notice how much you are noticing. A glance takes in that the electric socket on the skirting board has square holes, and the same glance tells you that the floor is well up to the skirting board, and as you walk over to the bay to admire the view your ears tell you that the presents from Blackpool and Malaga on the sideboard are not doing a clog dance accompanied by castanets. And while you are admiring the view, you might as well test the window to see if it opens.

Surveys

There might seem to be a lot to look at, but houses are big things and cost big money. You can't expect to get satisfaction if you buy one with the same nonchalance as when you buy a new light bulb.

Can you rely on a lender's surveyor's report thinking: 'Well, he will tell me if there is anything wrong with it'? Well, he will and he won't. His job is to tell the building society whether the land and buildings thereon (as the saying goes) is good enough security for the money they are thinking of lending you to assist you in your purchase. He has no obligation to you although he does owe you a duty of care; he will not stick his neck out telling you that the structure is perfectly sound, but you can be sure that he will let the building society know if the foundations or the roof are in danger of collapse, and that whereas they think they are getting a desirable residence as security, there is the distinct probability that in a year's time all that would be left for them to get their money back on would be a plot of land covered in rubble. (Incidentally, it does not necessarily work quite like that. When a borrower defaults, the building society does take and sell the property. In the extremely rare case where they do not raise sufficient money to cover the defaulter's indebtedness, and their own and their agents' and solicitors' costs, then the defaulting borrower can still be sued for the balance.)

A vendor of a property less than ten years old is apt to say that it is guaranteed by the National House Building Council (NHBC). Well, not quite! What a builder gets for his purchaser is a ten-year cover. It is sometimes called a 'ten-year structural warranty', but this is inaccurate. It covers more than just the structure, particularly for homes registered for cover since 1 April 1999. Since 1988, the scheme has been known as 'Buildmark'. An alternative to NHBC is Zurich Municipal.

You require the balance of the period of cover to be transferred to you, but NHBC and builders do not require it. Add a clause to the contract saying the vendor will assign it to you (using a Form CS12, or HB12).

The protection which NHBC gives is in two sections. First, the builder's obligations and second, NHBC's insurance cover. Under the first section, the builder has to put right at his own expense any defects that arise as a result of his failure to comply with the NHBC minimum standards of workmanship and material and which are notified to him in writing during the first two years of the house's life. Don't think that buying a recently built house means that you will get a repair-bill-free ten years - you won't. A house owner is not relieved of his normal maintenance responsibilities, and the agreement does not cover normal wear and tear, or normal shrinkage. Some items such as fences, white goods and lifts are not covered at all.

Under the second section, cover is in three main parts. First, against loss of deposit in the event of the builders' insolvency between exchange of contracts and completion. Second, against the costs of repairs that result from the builders' insolvency or failure to meet an arbitration award or judgment which arise during the period up to two years from the date of the NHBC certificate. Third, the cost of more serious items which arise during the third to tenth years from the date of the certificate (please note that the 'certificate' is also known as the 'Ten-Year Notice'). There is a fourth element of cover: the NHBC is the building control authority in place of the local council. This covers costs of putting right breaches of the statutory building regulations.

The NHBC cover saves you from the consequences of basic bad building and that's about it. That is to say, broadly, the cover is for such items as subsidence or settlement, and other major structural defects due to non-compliance with standards, such as collapse or serious distortion of joists or roof structure, or chemical failure of material affecting the load-bearing structure.

Since 1 April 1999, the cover has been expanded and includes, among other things, double glazing, defective flooring, defective flues and wet applied plaster. It also includes insurance against the cost of cleaning up contamination of the plot on which the house stands, if a statutory clean-up notice is served on the owner.

Since 1 April 2003, the Council of Mortgage Lenders (CML), the House Builders' Federation (HBF), the new home warranty providers (NHBC, Zurich and Premier Guarantee) and the Law Society of England and Wales have introduced a solution to the problem of home buyers reaching legal completion and moving into the newly built property before the property has been classified as satisfactorily complete, and in some cases, before the pre-handover inspection. It has been agreed that lenders will not release the mortgage funds for a new property until the buyer's conveyancer has received confirmation in the form of a cover note that the property has received a satisfactory final inspection and that a new full home warranty will be in place on or before legal completion.

If you are a second or subsequent buyer, you cannot claim on the NHBC for defects that the first purchaser reported to the builder, nor defects that were visible, on reasonable inspection (whatever that is), at the time of purchase.

During its existence, the National House Building Council has done sterling service for the owner-occupier, particularly the original purchaser from a builder, in raising minimum standards of building and finish. If you are thinking of buying a newly built house, see if the builder is on the NHBC Register. If he isn't, it might be that he has been kicked off. If he has, there may be problems with obtaining cover regardless of the fact that he may have hung on to the documents. On the other hand he might be a splendid, upright, entrepreneurial character who knows what he, like his father before him, is about and is determined not to have any 'pen-pushers' telling him what to do. Ask some of his previous buyers. They'll soon tell you how good he is. Mind you, he might be the salt of the earth, but he will never sell his house to anyone wanting to raise a loan on it and a cash buyer will never sell it to anyone wanting to raise money to aid the purchase. Fact is the absence of an NHBC Certificate for a new house renders it un-saleable unless something similar is in place which enjoys market recognition. Generally, this means insurance or the benefit of one of the other schemes recognised by the Council of Mortgage Lenders. See next section.

You will see from the necessarily brief description given above some of the things the NHBC is and isn't. When you are in any deal which involves the ten-year structural warranty, write off to their Council and get just as much information as you can. While we are dealing with newly built houses, it is as well to ask a vendor of a second-hand house whether he intends moving into one. Builders' dates for completion are seldom kept and can often be weeks, or even months, wide of the mark. Also, find out if you are likely to be tagging yourself into a chain and how long it is.

Given the climate in England and Wales, and the rarity of a long summer drought, the NHBC guarantees given in the past three or four years could well have expired before we experience a drying out of sub-soils, thus testing the foundations and possibly starting some nasty movements in many a dream home. So, the old hands will prefer to buy a house that is six or seven years old, where any weak spots have had time to show.

All the above might seem like a great song and dance production number, and if you employ a surveyor to make a full inspection of the property that is exactly what the vendor will tell you he did. Surveyors are responsible and can be held for cash damages at law if they put it down in writing that a house is sound, but experience proves otherwise. For example, when you move in together with a grand piano and a host of can-can dancing friends for a house-warming party and the floor is not strong enough to support the revelry, the surveyors could have to pay for new timbers for the floor, and wooden legs for you and your friends. So surveyors have to be very cautious, otherwise they don't get their insurance renewed. The premiums are high in any case and that, and the interminable time surveyors spend looking at property to make sure they are safe, is reflected in their bills. It is also reflected in their reports, which are sometimes splattered with gems of ambiguity.

If you opt for anything less than a **full structural survey** (very costly), all you will get are such masterpieces as 'from a head-and-shoulders inspection through the loft aperture the roof timbers appeared to be sound', or this page filler: 'the kitchen tiles are of a somewhat dated design'.

However, don't buy the idea that a full structural survey is a kind of insurance. If, after you move in, you spot things that the surveyor missed, don't think that a polite letter saying, 'Dear Mr Tape, please will you send me £2,000 to pay for repairing the woodrot that you did not warn me about' will take any tricks. It won't. It is not easy to sue for professional negligence, which is not the same as getting it wrong. You (on your own) have to prove that the surveyor (backed by his professional association and his insurance company, even into the House of Lords) did not use the level

Thornaby Central Library
Tel: 01642 528117
Email:
thornaby.central.library@stockton.gov.uk

Borrowed Items 03/01/2019 16:22
XXXXXX6030

Item Title	Due Date
* House buying, selling and conveyancing	24/01/2019

* Indicates items borrowed today
Thank you for using self service.
If your household voter registration info is
overdue a final reminder will arrive soon.
Reply ASAP!

Opening hours:
8:30 - 5:00 Mon, Wed, Fri
8:30 - 7:00 Tues and Thurs
9:30 - 4:00 Saturday

of skill and care that one would normally expect a qualified person to use. Not easy! Also, even if you do succeed, there is no guarantee you will get the costs of putting the problem right. The usual measure of damages is the difference between the amount the surveyor valued the house at and the actual value of the house with the defects.

A house which has been standing 50 years may be ready for a face-lift, but it isn't likely to fall down tomorrow, and though the finish on recently built houses might not be of the best, it is ridiculous to be frightened of what our builders have produced by the hundreds of thousands for private buyers. And there is always the National House Building Council guarantee.

CML Handbook

This is perhaps as good a place as any to make one cardinal observation. There are – in the estimation of solicitors and the banks, building societies and other organisations that lend money to aid a purchase – right ways and wrong ways of doing things.

Buying a new house from a builder who is the salt of the earth – as honest as the day is long sort of thing – who cannot offer NHBC or similar protection (see section 6.6 of the *Handbook* noted below) is something you are perfectly at liberty to do if you are not borrowing their money, but do not be surprised to find you may have trouble selling later.

There are other issues of a more technical nature, which will be referred to in the coming chapters; if you want to know what they are, have a look on the internet. Or ask a ten-year-old child to do it for you. (Perhaps the kid that got the new DVD player working!) Much of this 'lore' (not 'law') was published in 1999 as the Council of Mortgage Lenders' *Handbook for England and Wales*. You can find it at www.cml.org.uk. Check for updates (only available online as hard copies are no longer produced) as it has been changed on several occasions since first published.

Try to read Part I of the *Handbook*; it tells you what all the solicitors you will deal with ought to be doing. Part II sets out the special requirements of some of the main CML members. If you are buying and your lender is not named in the *Handbook*, ask them if they are members, and what their Part II requirements are. Then follow them to the letter! The CML *Handbook* is not the final word on what to do, but be warned, you can ignore all or any of it if you wish, if you are not borrowing money to aid the purchase, but if you gloss over some of the problems discussed in the *Handbook,* you may find you will have trouble selling later, or will be put to expense that perhaps your seller should have incurred when you bought the house.

Seven good questions

You can usefully look a vendor straight in the eye and ask him a few pertinent questions, the answers to which could determine whether you should spend further time and money on the project.

1. Is the property freehold? If it isn't, what is the ground rent and how long has the lease to run?

2. Does the owner have to pay any maintenance charges to anyone apart from builders, decorators, etc., to whom he himself has given specific orders?

3. Is the road and main drain taken over by the council or do the frontagers have to club up every now and then to have them repaired?

4. If you are in a business or profession, can you put up your brass plate and can your spouse hang out the washing or are there any restrictions?

5. Has anyone got the right to traipse across any part of your property? Ever?

6. If there is any evidence (extra cookers, sinks, etc.) of more than one family living in the property, what guarantee is there that they will all move out, thus ensuring that you get full vacant possession on completion?

7. Has the property ever been flooded or faced serious risk of flooding?

In case you are thinking of making alterations, ask if the vendor happens to know if there are any restrictions in the deeds on this point (this would particularly apply to leases) and if there aren't, whether there are any restrictions imposed by the local authority – such as a preservation order. A vendor might not declare all that he knows at this point, but don't worry too much as we have other ways of making him talk as you will learn later.

Think long and carefully about buying a house that will only fit your requirements if you make a number of structural alterations. Such alterations invariably cost more than the number you first thought of. It's the etceteras and extras that are costly. In any case, if you are buying a house on an estate, it will be a property of a certain class and by improving it you risk bringing it out of that class and making it difficult to sell, if and when you decide to move again.

This is the third criterion you must have in mind when you go viewing. Put the question: is it a good investment, in so far as I will be able to realise it without too much anguish, if ever I need to? You might think that, compared with similar properties, the one you are looking at is a snip. It no doubt has to be, to attract a viewer at all! You don't want to be in that vendor's situation ever, so you would be wise to avoid buying a house situated near any of the following: a fish and chip shop, a take-away cafe, a hospital, a public house, a church, a garage or repair shop, a fire station, or a public lavatory. All the foregoing, and a few more besides, can be anything from a nuisance to a serious disadvantage; even if you happen to be deaf and have no sense of smell, others are not so afflicted. Any estate agent who knows anything at all, knows that such badly located properties should only be put on the market at the height of a house-selling boom when, literally, anything will sell.

At the first whiff of any rumour about plans for any kind of non-residential development round about where you live, get together with your previously independent and apathetic neighbours and protest loud and long at any hint of intrusion by such property-price-debasers into what has previously been such a highly respectable area, unless, that is, you stand to make a vast profit because the property under discussion is your very own. In such a case, the protesters are dog-in-the-manger reactionary luddites opposed to all forms of progress which public spirited individuals (you) are slaving away trying to introduce.

Sometimes it takes ages to find a property that comes up to scratch and suits your requirements; sometimes it's a case of beginner's luck. In either case remember you are not the only bargain-hunter around, and the race goes to the swift. Don't go groggy when the finishing line is in sight – be ready with your own pack of conveyancing forms.

CHAPTER 2

New houses

For young people buying their first house, a brand new one has what can only be called a strong romantic attraction. Here they will make their attempt to create a home. Builders know what attracts – note how they advertise homes for sale, when what they are trying to sell is a plan, and more often than not, a half-finished house. But when the house is finished the starry-eyed home makers move in, secure in the knowledge that no one has been born, lived, loved, divorced or died in it. The aura of the past will not seep out of the brickwork. The dead hand of the past will not push them into outdated ways of living. It will all be new! It is all brave! But as in all romances, beauty is in the eye of the beholder – desire overpowers reason, and faults and blemishes are ignored. Another great attraction of a newly built house is that it promises to be repair-free for a number of years – if anything goes wrong it is likely to be because of a fault in manufacture for which someone else is responsible, and not wear and tear, which falls to the user to put right.

There is also the National House Builders' certificate, or one of the other schemes, the benefits and restrictions of which we have already noted. With this protection you have the warranty against ruinous subsidence, but some would say you can do without running the risk of a nightmare experience of subsidence in the first place. If you get subsidence from any other reason than climate it has to be because of bad building and that means solicitors, barristers and courts for you.

From an investment point of view, it is often the case that the last house to be completed on a development is the best buy. The romantic ideas and repair-free attraction of brand new houses militate against the resale of a house on an unfinished development. A vendor can have for sale a house to which he has added a number of refinements, is offering a fair list of extras and be only asking the same price as the builder is for a brand new house, yet the vendor has to search high and low for a buyer while the developer is signing buyers all the while, and he signs them up on a take-it-or-leave-it basis. Builders and their Skinners know how to take advantage of a situation where desire overpowers reason.

The developer appoints a solicitor who acts for him in the sale of each of the houses on the development. Except for the address or plot number, the contract and transfer (there are one or two things you need to know about contracts and transfers – all will be revealed in later chapters) are identical for all. It is almost unheard of for any purchaser's Skinner to persuade the developer's Skinner to change any detail in the contract or transfer and if this does occur, these changes will only cover minor issues. Layperson conveyancers get to see the papers with their own eyes, and if they see anything they don't like they can take it up with the builder face to face – whereas the Skinnerhood is deskbound and at best will only write a letter.

It is a common occurrence that builders and their agents will often try to pressurise buyers into signing a contract when a house has a substantial amount of work to be done on it, or even when the building has not been started. In such a case, you need to ensure that the contract is made subject to the house being completed in accordance with a set of plans and a specification. These would be attached to or referred to in the contract to ensure that the developer is under an obligation to carry out the work to a clearly described set of standards. The less of the house you can see when you sign the contract, the greater the risk. This is because the sale agreement will generally confer on the builder the right to change materials of construction and the design. Not necessarily to any material degree in his estimation, but it may be important from your standpoint!

Also try to tie the developer down to some kind of completion date. Houses are built in the open air, by people who are relying on others for supplies of material to arrive according to the hopes and dreams of a deviser of a critical path analysis, which pleased its creator when he put it on paper. But his Creator might send flood, storm, tempest, lightning and thunderbolt to thwart his plans, and deep down the developer knows about that. So, we are introduced to the almost meaningless phrases that abound in house sale and purchase transactions; a proviso for completion will be a slight variant on the well worn 'will use his best endeavours to complete the house with all due expedition'.

Sometimes builders will ask for stage payments. That is to say they will require a proportion of the purchase price to be paid when, say, the footings are in, followed by more money at window sill height, more when the roof is on, and a final payment on completion. This method can be costly, particularly if you are taking a mortgage, because at each stage the building society surveyor has to have a look, and you have to pay him a fee, and as soon as the stage payment is advanced you start paying repayments on the loan, even though you might not move into the house for many a month.

Your deposit money can also be at risk because the developer will usually want to use it to fund the later stages of his development and if the builder were to become insolvent before the completion of your purchase, your deposit could be lost.

First-time buyers

Some builders advertise as though there are some terms, prices, mortgages and services special to buyers of their houses. There are not. It is all put on the price of the house. The only help for first-time buyers is the government Home Loan Scheme. So tell the builder you will do your own conveyance, get your own mortgage, pay cash – how much discount for relieving them of all that worry? You could get a pleasant surprise provided you promise not to tell your new neighbours!

Last-time buyers

Now it's your turn. A plethora of advice to those about to retire pours forth from accountants, solicitors, estate agents, travel agents, stockbrokers, banks and building societies, all of whom claim to offer financial services.

Financial services hate stillness. Their motto is: Let's get them churning their money in my churn, and some of it will stick to the sides for me.

The death of a spouse or your retirement are not sufficient reasons to move house. It might be that you would save money on rates and heating in a smaller house, but just look at what the move will cost you. No matter where you live, you will pay some rates and heating bills. It could take you donkey's years to recoup the expense of moving.

If it's the cost of upkeep that bothers you, get down to your Citizens Advice Bureau (CAB) and find out what practical help is on offer from local charity organisations for someone like you who has spent a lifetime fighting and working for the country.

Elderly people sometimes fear a disabling fall and are attracted to living complexes where wardens, either resident or on call, can get an ambulance for them. The same reassurance could be gained by installing in one's present home a radio call signal; speak to the CAB or Help the Aged about it.

There is also the Department of Social Security. At long last the government is realising that though houses might be *privately* owned, they are part of the *national* stock of housing and wealth, and to those who can't cope financially, help should be given. Though less and less as time goes by.

Don't forget when doing your sums, to ask yourself a few 'comfort' questions:

- You have a garage of your own. Could you tolerate sharing? Is there a parking place for every resident and their visitors?

- You have, at worst, only had one wall through which noise could seep. Could you tolerate noise from the sides, above, below, and across the landing?

- When the sun shines you can sit in your own garden chair in your own garden, a few feet from your own door. Will you be able to do that?

- You have your own place for your own dustbin. Will the new compare favourably?

- You can choose your own odd-job man and your own time for the job to be done and, indeed, whether to have it done this year or at all.

Those who have never occupied a home under a lease usually only fully realise what they have committed themselves to when the bills come in. Leases inevitably have service charge provisions to provide for maintenance of the whole block. More about this later.

Part exchange

Find out 'what's the discount for cash?' It can be considerable. If you and the combined high-powered salesmanship of the local estate agency could not find a buyer for your house, neither can the builder … not at the price you were asking. So consider knocking your asking price down by the combined amount of the cash discount and the agent's fees and get the house sold yourself. You can then bargain with anybody anywhere and from then on get your sums right about how much your new house actually cost you and how much profit you made on the last one. No builder will be upset by the tactics recommended here. His advertisement drew you to the site, he has sold a house and that is what he wants … the sooner the quicker!

There are a lot of risks in buying and selling, but in order to get anything done one has to take some risks. The art is in drawing the line between acceptable and unacceptable risks and each person will decide for himself where that line is to be drawn when buying a new house, or for that matter in any of the other transactions outlined in this book.

CHAPTER 3

Sell first or buy first?

If you have never bought a house before, then the question answers itself. But if you are an owner who needs to move to a larger or smaller house, or needs to get away from the neighbours or in-laws, or needs to raise some money by buying a cheaper house, which way round you work is crucial. The decision has to be made in the light of both your personal needs and resources, and the general state of the housing market at the time.

You can, of course, go out viewing properties, and when you see one that suits you, say, 'Yes, I will buy this when I have sold my own.' And you might drag the vendors on for ages while you screw the last penny out of your sale. On the other hand, the vendor of your dream property may have read this book too, and the answer will be, 'I'll give you x number of weeks.' How many times have you heard of 'chains' breaking down? How many times have you seen the silly 'sold subject to contract' slips pasted onto and then taken off For Sale boards? Greed, slipshod estate agents and lawyers' bad timing are the usual causes.

Since the mid-1930s there has been a drift upwards in prices, but the movement goes in fits and starts, so spot the rising market and you can safely buy first, and be pretty sure of selling your own house swiftly and profitably. You can always tell when the housing market has reached its bottom and is about to rise. Similarly, you get a very clear signal that a boom is within six months or so of petering out: the mass media will tell you. When they make headlines out of the fact that young people are being priced out of the market, and when they have stories about people making fortunes in a few years out of houses, the market is at the top. Nevertheless, so as not to miss the bus, new buyers join in, and so keep the pot boiling a little longer. But the bus was just about to pull up at a compulsory stop.

On the other hand, when, on your telly, you see a lugubrious man standing in front of an agency For Sale board, which has obviously taken root, and he tells you that he has not had sign, sound nor smell of a viewer for over 18 months, then the market is about to pick up.

Houses adjacent to petrol stations, hotel car parks, fire stations and the like should always be sold when the market is on the boil, if they are to get sold at all.

February, March and April are the best months to sell. But life goes on 365 days a year. There are always some buyers about. Even Christmas can be good if a couple of your neighbours make you a present of having 'For Sale' boards planted in their gardens. Take advantage of their viewers who know all about their houses from the agent's particulars, so might drive past them, but if you have your own board – which will only cost you a few pounds, will knock on your front door, even if it is only to ask your price. Don't keep them on the doorstep in such poor weather – invite them in to discuss it.

CHAPTER 4

Estate agency

Insurance companies, building societies and brokers of all kinds have put together strings of house-selling shops, and distorted the business out of all recognition, but they still trade on the folk-memory of the personal service that independent estate agents took many years to establish in the minds of home owners.

Branch office after branch office has been opened. Every city and town centre is stuffed with them. Their numbers have increased out of all proportion to the increase in owner-occupied houses. Many offices are lucky to sell more than one house per week. Each office is staffed with a couple of receptionists who try to look busy for seven days a week, waiting for victims to give themselves up. The person who knows what estate agency is now about (possibly a chartered surveyor, more likely an insurance man) oversees a number of offices and can be called on the mobile on the golf course or in bed, when required.

If your name is Feather, and not Bold, and you give yourself up to an agent, the receptionist will make an appointment for the representative to call and 'survey' and value your house. It will no doubt happen on the same day as you applied. That's the last time you'll see any greased lightning in this transaction. Agents always have spent more of their own time and money on getting in houses for sale than in selling them, because, as you have already read, houses sell themselves – eventually, if you will let them.

Estate agents say they ...

1. make a survey of the house to be sold;

2. make a valuation;

3. prepare a set of particulars;

4. commission a photograph;

5. circularise the particulars using their computers and network of associated agents;

6. draft advertising and arrange for it to be displayed in their own monthly circular and in the press;

7. display a full-colour photo of your house in their shops;

8. negotiate with interested parties;

9. offer you and your purchaser a full range of financial services including using the money from one house to buy another;

10. liaise with your solicitor;

11. charge you according to their percentage scale, only if the house is sold.

Now for the facts ...

1. **Survey:** If it were a written structural survey that you could pass on to the prospective purchaser, that would be OK, but you won't get that. You are selling. What do you want with a survey? You check for subsidence every time you open a door or window. You check the drains every time you pull the plug, and if you haven't fallen through the floorboards into the cellar lately, the woodwork is good enough to be going on with, and you know without any help from them. Of course, if counting the number of rooms and jotting down their sizes is a survey, you get that. Big deal.

2. **Valuation:** When you have read chapter 7, you will be entitled to put the letters FBSPV (Fellow of the Bradshaw School of Property Valuers) after your name.

3. **Particulars:** If you can't go through your own house with a notebook and pencil, who can?

4. **Photographs:** Have you seen some of them? You've no doubt got better ones in your own album.

5. **Lists, computers and networks of agents:** Your postman, who sees your For Sale board every day, has more up-to-date news about who's looking for a house such as yours than any agent sitting in front of a computer 50 miles away. Having been a potential buyer, you will know what a fat lot of use the stuff is and it is nearly certain that your buyer will come from within 25 miles. Anyway, you too can use the internet to advertise your property and get that out-of-town buyer. www.houseladder.co.uk in particular provides such a service for private sellers together with advertisements on findaproperty.

   As far as matching people to houses, what has been your experience when you were looking for a house? New buyers come on the market every day, as they sell their own houses, having decided to get married, divorced or take promotion, all of which can necessitate a move.

   People drop off the lists when they get fixed up. You know how long they keep on sending you particulars after you have found a house. Sometimes they keep coming from an agency through whom you have just bought.

6. **Monthly magazine:** More junk mail. Newspapers: you will read the chapter on advertising and learn how much expenditure of time and expertise that requires. Do you think that what the agent does in this regard amounts to much?

7. **Shop window:** This is about the only thing that agents have that you can't have for yourself, and so 'anything you can do I can do better' doesn't apply. In this respect, property shops are worth considering because they do the display job at a fraction of the cost. Very few people buy houses they first saw displayed in an agency. The agency has already paid the rent, so putting up your photo costs next to nothing. If this is what works, why do they go in for all that costly advertising in the press, buying boards, paying signwriters to look after them, putting them up and taking them down; why not just use their own shop window (no prizes for even a polite answer)? Shop windows are used as much for attracting new vendors as for anything

else. But the pictures are of houses they have not sold. If they can't sell those, how can they sell yours?

8. **Negotiating** with a buyer usually amounts to persuading you to bring your price down and in getting you to wait till the buyer sells his house.

9. **Financial services:** There are so many agencies at it nowadays that selling commissions are not enough to keep them all going, so they have to look for other sources of revenue. So they try to sell you and your purchaser insurances, mortgages and, if things go badly enough, chain-breaking and bridging loans, so as to grab the commission amounting to thousands of pounds. This is where they come into their own, and yours as well, if you give them half a chance.

    Using the money from one house to buy another: the estate agent to whom you left it leaves it, in turn, to the solicitor, who in turn will often leave you with the problem of a bridging loan or a costly chain-breaking scheme.

10. **Liaison with your solicitor:** This amounts to the agent writing to your solicitor saying 'this is one of ours' and eventually, if ever, 'here is our commission bill'. If you do choose to use a solicitor, it is always better to keep in touch with him yourself, then you are in control, not the sharp suited agent.

11. **Advertising:** Historically, estate agents have written the most appallingly ambiguous rubbish when advertising the charming, deceptively spacious family property, in which, in real life, you can't swing a cat. Nowadays, this can be a criminal offence and so the agents will ask you to validate their claims and that can make you a criminal as well! They do the same when advertising briefly about their charges. 'No sale – no charge' sounds good enough, but it might mean that all you get is a mention of your house to anyone who enquires for a property such as yours. 'Free advertising' might mean: we put a few lines about it in our monthly bulletin which is given out to callers and distributed to the Skinners' waiting rooms where it takes its chance among a pile of magazines and other junk.

So after a little run-of-the-mill 'advertising' you will be expected to pay for your share of their full-page adverts, of which anything up to a quarter can be taken up in publicising their own outfit.

Now here's a little gem of business sense for you: if your name is Feather and you have been persuaded to use an agency and a Skinner, at least gird up your loins to write a letter to Skinner, Hand and Glove incorporating the following: 'do not pay the agent's commission out of the sale monies, but forward their account to me and I will deal with it'. You will then have some bargaining power if you have come to the conclusion that you have not had value for the money claimed, or charges have been made that you never agreed to. But if you do decide to do this, act very carefully and make sure that you read the contract before you refuse to pay the whole commission. Estate agents will think nothing of suing you for the commission – which could ultimately involve you in paying court costs. If you want to challenge the commission and it is less than £5,000, you could try pointing out that they will never recover their costs under the small claims track regime and negotiate for a discount.

Agency agreements do need looking at and studying before you sign; see what the agreement says about selling yourself or later through another agent. Don't be afraid to say to the representative, 'Leave it with me for my grandad or grandson, solicitor or nerve specialist to have a look at it.' Then calculate the likely bill, and ponder 1. to 11. above. Looked at in the cold light of day, the list of things agencies claim to do for you does not amount to much. Certainly not to the enormous commissions that get spirited away out of the price you get for your house.

If your local branch of Dick, Turpin & Co. only put a board in your garden and a picture in the shop window and then start charging for adverts, you can get that from a property shop at a fraction of the price.

Middlemen

Estate agents, solicitors, building societies, insurance people, and all the rest who are trying to amass a fortune as swiftly as possible out of the housing market, have needs of their own. From your own workplace you know that you do things not only for your customers, but also to keep the organisation going and see to your own creature comforts.

Trips abroad, cameras and other valuable prizes are offered on a local and regional basis to the 'representative of the month' by agency chains. The winners are those who get the most 'instructions' (houses for sale).

Competition is keen, not only within the firms, but also between agencies. Blows have been struck when a representative of one agency has gone poaching from another. Do not get caught in the crossfire. You could find yourself in court, at best as a witness, and, at worst, as a losing defendant who is refusing to pay two commissions because rival agencies are claiming to have been the effective cause of your sale.

So when you are dealing with these middlemen, recognise that much of the advice you get from them is not only what they think is best for you, but also what is best for them. For instance, they want to deal with as few people as possible for as much money as possible. Solicitors and agencies plead professional ethics as a reason for not dealing with more than one potential buyer – what miserable pleaders they are. An agency chooses a buyer with a house for sale so that it can swell the number of houses on its books – that buyer is not necessarily the best for you.

CHAPTER 5

The moneylenders

Bridging loans

You may have seen a house you particularly want, but have to exchange contracts quickly before you can organise your sale, or perhaps having made an acceptable 'subject to contract' offer to buy and having accepted an acceptable 'subject to contract' offer to sell, your purchaser has withdrawn at an embarrassingly late stage in the pre-contract game.

What are the options? One is obviously to lose your intended purchase, but bridging loans offer one way forward if you can afford to pay two mortgages – that on the house you wish to sell and that on the house you wish to buy.

If you are tempted to do this, ask yourself a question and make sure you get an honest answer. How quickly will your house sell and will you really get what you want for it? If you get it wrong and you still bridge, month after anxious month can pass before you get rid of your old home. One good tip is have the house you wish to sell structurally surveyed and if you are recommended to get specialist reports on the boiler, the electricity or whatever, get them. You will soon find out if there is a 'nasty' hiding under the floorboards that might have an adverse impact on your ability to sell, or to sell at the price you want or even need.

House exchanges

If you are buying a new house from a builder, you may find the builder will offer to take your own house in part exchange. He normally insists you buy a house with a higher market value, say 25 per cent, so this does not work if you are thinking of retiring and moving to a smaller house to release some capital for your old age.

This has the advantage for those who want a new house of taking you out of any chain. However, it seems that under the Stamp Duty Land Tax regime entering into an exchange will not save you any tax – although the builder may be eligible for relief on the purchase of your house, you will still have to pay Stamp Duty Land Tax on the value of your old house, plus the cash paid for the new one.

The builder's lawyers will generally carry out a cursory investigation of your title and will normally ask you to submit the barest minimum of paperwork. A formal Office Copy of your title (if registered), a copy of your title deeds if not, replies to the Seller's Property Information Forms and the Fixtures, Fittings and Contents Form, plus a local search, and that is about it.

You may still need to borrow on the new house, but if not, the deal can go through very quickly. Perhaps as soon as you get a reply to your local search, which can vary from a 24-hour turnaround with some councils to several weeks with others. Five to ten working days, however, is a comfortable 'norm'.

Mortgages

Many of you will have to borrow money to aid the purchase. Time was when the only serious options were the building societies and 'mortgage famines' were not unknown. If they did not know you, you joined a queue. Sometimes the queues were limited to first-time borrowers. In other cases, perhaps you got to jump the queue if you were an existing member. Perhaps you borrowed from them last time, or perhaps you were saving up for a deposit. Then the banks started to become involved, and then many building societies decided to convert to public company status and so on, and lack of money to lend has not been a major problem in recent years.

Time was also when the building societies operated prudent, if inflexible, rules. A sole buyer could not borrow more than two and a half times his salary. Couples could not borrow more than three times the higher salary. Other permutations were acceptable in some cases. If the surveyor selected to value the house for the building society felt it was worth less than you were paying, that did not always matter if you were providing a substantial contribution to the house. You are at liberty after all to lose your own money. But not theirs and so if they felt there was a risk, the answer was to insure. They took out, at your expense, a mortgagee protection policy. If the house was sold at a loss by the lender, they recouped the loss from the insurers. Unfortunately, they were their insurers not yours and so – invoking the insurance concept of 'subrogation' – the insurers would then chase the borrowers (if they had any money) for the loss.

In time, back in the 1970s, some institutions started to lend without asking for proof of ability to pay, particularly the secondary lenders. This worked well when prices were continually on the up, but when they fell they often recouped the loss by suing the surveyor or, if that failed, the solicitor. Sloppy file-keeping or inadequate procedures cost the legal profession a great deal, but at least the borrower was not chased for the loss!

In those days there were few payment options. A repayment mortgage involved the payment of interest and some capital each year. An endowment mortgage involved paying interest only. The capital came from an endowment policy that had to be paid for each month as well, but the theory was, at the end of the 20- to 25-year period, that the insurers would pay more than you needed to pay off the mortgage, and you would make a profit. Or you could rely on your pension insurance policy's lump sum to cover the capital. Unfortunately, your insurance salesman can only guess what the results are in the light of circumstances prevailing when you take out the endowment or mortgage. Unfortunately for many borrowers, a stable economy with low rates of inflation has resulted in a lower performance for these schemes than expected and there will be borrowers with endowment and pension mortgages who will have less than they need when the money becomes available to pay off the capital.

Nowadays there are so many different types of loan on offer that the best that can be recommended is to shop around. You will be expected to meet the costs of a valuation and the lender may or may not accept your nominee surveyor. The valuation is just that. It is not a structural survey and although the law requires a person carrying out a valuation to spot some of the more glaring faults, a large hole in the roof or major cracks suggesting subsidence, for example, there are limits to what the borrower can sue for.

Some lenders use in-house surveyors. That is, surveyors on the payroll. However, the norm is for a local firm to supply a report in a more or less standard form, so ascertain what levels of report are available (simple valuation or full structural survey) and what they will cost. Note also that surveyors frequently highlight problems for referral to others. If a major structural problem is highlighted, try a civil engineer; these can be relatively rare in any area and can be overworked folk and so do not expect them to rush around at the first sign of a cheque. Wiring, heating, rising damp, etc.: with all these problems, the surveyor is likely to recommend you hire an appropriate specialist.

If you hire someone to check on the damp course and timber, try to make sure you keep their survey and their guarantee (one without the other is useless) for when you come to sell, and try to select a contractor whose guarantee is backed by insurers. Contractors come and go and after a year or so it is not unknown for guarantees to become simply pretty sheets of paper with no legal or practical value whatsoever.

CHAPTER 6

No agents, please!

Why private vendors win

There are a lot of houses to be sold. In Great Britain there are nearly 12½ million owner-occupied houses. On average, spread over a year, close on a million houses change hands.

How, you may ask, can I compete in such a crowded market?

You must find some ways of drawing attention to your house; of marking it out from all others; of making potential buyers curious enough to come and view it. Not to worry.

You have already taken a decision that singles your house out as something different and especially attractive to any buyer. YOU HAVE DECIDED TO JOIN THE ONE IN THREE OF ALL VENDORS WHO SELL FOR THEMSELVES.

As soon as you announce the sale, you will signal to the whole wide world (particularly the twenty odd square miles that really matter) that your property is so good it is expected to sell itself. It does not need the wiles of a high-powered salesman to push it onto someone who doesn't really need it, at a higher price than they wanted to pay. It is also attractive to a lot of potential buyers who want to avoid agents because:

- They know that an agent's commission is added on to the price, so in effect it is the purchaser who pays it.

- An established agency cannot have avoided making enemies along the way. *You only need one buyer*, and that buyer might be so embittered by previous experiences with estate agents that never, ever, will that person have anything more to do with agents.

- Inexperienced buyers are afraid of smooth-talking salesmen, particularly those who, to hide the fact that they have no special expertise, overlay what they have to say with an inappropriately pompous language which hermetically seals off conceptual orientational realisation, and assails the unfortunate recipient's auditory structural system as a load of bull falling from a great height.

- Experienced buyers know that they can bargain directly with a private vendor. Quite rightly, they expect to get more sense out of the butcher than the block.

- Buyers are sick of collecting particulars from agents who, by describing the property in a different way, disguise the fact that every agent in town has the same rubbish for sale. The luckless viewer has wasted journeys. *When they come to a private vendor it is delightfully uncomplicated, and they will not get involved as witnesses in disputed commission claims.*

A quick look at the houses for sale pages of your local newspaper could easily lead you to believe that private sales are very few and far between. But, a recent survey found that only two-thirds of all house sellers used estate agents. That leaves a third who didn't. Over three hundred thousand vendors a year go it alone and win. Just keep your eyes open. Count the private adverts. Count the private For Sale boards – are they anywhere near a third of the total? Isn't that proof that a private sale does not have to be advertised again and again, and that a private For Sale board does not take root?

So, all in all, yours has the edge over the other properties with which you are in competition. You will get more viewers, and therefore sell quickly. That's another privately sold house off the market; buyers have to jump at an opportunity to buy privately or they miss out. **Private sales are prompt sales.**

Don't worry that by working on your own you will miss the one (in 20) potential buyer who comes from out of town. My experience is that he has always researched the market thoroughly. The internet has made this even easier for private vendors. They have to; they can't afford wasted journeys. They know what they are looking for, where it should be, and about what price it should be going for. They also know the districts in which they are likely to hunt down their quarry, and will be cruising past your house this weekend. When you put your For Sale board up they will see it. They know everything about every other house in the district from the agents' particulars. But there is something crucial that they don't know about your house just from the board: the price.

The car will have to stop. They will have to walk up your whitewashed path, stare at your dozzled-up front door, ring the bell and wait for you to come and offer to show them why yours is better than any of the rest, and if any mention is made about yours being higher priced than the others, 'Well, we can talk about that when you have looked round, can't we.'

There are two other situations which many think cannot be coped with unless an agent is brought onto the scene – they are wrong!

Just because you live alone and are fearful of having a stranger in the house does not mean to say you can't sell without an agent – you certainly can. You can certainly do without those who let it be known that they specialise in helping widows, orphans and the elderly.

When alone, you should follow your usual precaution of having the door on the chain. If you make a telephone appointment, get the name, address and telephone number of the caller and check identity by ringing back; also check with the telephone book and/or directory enquiries and then arrange for a near neighbour, clergyman or social worker to attend. Or if the prospect comes from the board, ask him to wait while your friend can pop round. No prospective viewer will object to waiting a few moments – not if his intentions are honourable.

Even if you got an agency that promised to accompany viewers, that would not mean to say that, having given a false name and address, the conperson, whose face you now know, would not come back to wreak villainy upon you. In any case, estate agents have not been able to protect themselves or property against violence.

Selling a vacant house that is at a distance from your home is really a simple job. Don't fall for being the cat and allowing the mice to play. What you require is someone to hold the particulars and the keys, who was a friend and neighbour of the previous occupant. Get your board up with your own telephone number on and you are in business. Such a keyholder will have a friendly and true interest in getting you good money because he will wish to protect the value of his own greatest asset, which lies nearby.

CHAPTER 7

Selling

Fixtures and fittings: what is included?

More trouble and anguish is caused by the failure of people to decide what they are selling than by any other single cause. Get it clear right at the start.

When you do move, leave more than you said you would. It doesn't need to be much to make the purchasers feel they have done better than they really expected.

As a matter of courtesy, curtain rails and all but the most expensive light fittings should be left. Don't mention them all in the particulars, or some smart alec will say he doesn't want them, so 'how much off the price' for putting you to the trouble of taking them down.

What constitutes a fixture and a fitting, nobody seems to know. So try appealing to common sense; it's quicker and cheaper than consulting a professional.

Custom seems to say that fixtures are permanencies and semi-permanencies that one can't simply pick up and walk away with. Basically it includes things which are attached to the property. One way of looking at it is whether removal of the thing in question would damage the property. Television aerials, for example, are fixtures. You can put the lamp shade under your arm and walk away with it but the light switch is a different matter. It is the bits and pieces other than what are obvious parts of the house (such as the doors) and what are obviously not part of the house (such as a heavy plant pot in the garden that's too heavy to lift) which cause the trouble. Situations where it's not strictly breach of contract to remove an item but would be a breach of good faith to do so should be avoided. All this is not to say that you simply cannot take the doors. Of course you can – but you must make it clear to the purchaser that you so intend because anyone can reasonably assume that a door is a fixture and part of a house. So have a slow walk round every room and look at everything in it. Look, and think about things like the cooker or fixed washing machine that someone else might assume should count as a fitting and be included in the price without being detailed or argued about. In each of the rooms make a decision. Is it to be left or not?

Make a list of the things which someone might assume you are including in the price. Decide which you would sell and at what price. Mark the prices on a separate list from your list of particulars, the drawing up and printing of which will form the content of a later section. This early appraisal of what you are selling is your first step towards your valuation. Most buyers now expect to receive the Fixtures, Fittings and Contents Form published by the Law Society and available through legal stationers.

Valuations are easy: use comparisons

If you go to a rent or land valuation tribunal or arbitration, you will see and hear the professionals at it: people who can hardly squeeze through the door for the spread of letters behind their names.

'It's far too much. One on the east side of it went for much less', says the one in the natty blue suit. 'Ah, but one on the north and another on the west side brought substantially more', drawls the fat one.

The arbitrator listens to their comparisons and decides on something near the middle. In the end, comparisons and compromise are the only sensible way.

You can compare your own house with similar ones, and do it as well as anyone else. As a matter of fact, you have started already. Since the day you bought the house you, like other proud owners, have taken an interest in the property for sale in your district. You will, of course, have marked and remembered the ones that were offered for sale at more money than you browbeat the previous owners down to, and ignored the ones sold at a lower figure. You did right at the time; it made you feel much better and more successful. You must also remember that estate agents often don't actually have any formal qualifications in property valuation. Some, but not all, have experience of the market. There is no reason why you can't carry out a comparison yourself.

But it's down to brass tacks now; how accurate your valuation is will determine how long it will take you to sell, and whether you get what you ask, or what someone else is prepared to give.

You need to collect information on two points: how much similar properties have *actually* fetched, and what opposition there is in the market on this very day.

Forget what you were asked to pay when you bought. If you actually paid less than the original asking price for your house, that price was the best that the vendor could get for it. If the vendor could have got more he would have. If you were left thinking you had been done a favour, try to remember how it was done and use that bargaining skill when your prospects arrive, and do them a favour. It's only fair.

You will sell quicker than the opposition if they have decided their price by adding up such things as: so much to pay off the mortgage, deposit for new house, new car, new washing machine and a good holiday – what the vendor wants as opposed to what his property is worth.

Do not let anyone flatter you into wishing for the moon. There are plenty of agencies who, to get a job, will raise your hopes unduly. They know the market. They also know that vendors will always come to their muttons later. In the meantime it swells the number of houses they have on their books. It makes them look big now at the expense of making you look small later on when you have to reduce your price.

After 1 April 2000 it has become easier to find out what properties actually fetched in the neighbourhood, because it became compulsory to provide this information to the Land Registry. You don't need to do lots of searches at the Land Registry to find this information out. You can go onto www.ourproperty.co.uk and sign up for free. This site allows you to search particular streets so that you can find out what properties actually sold for – invaluable ammunition in the armoury of the private vendor, particularly if the house next door sold in the past few months.

You should then start comparing your property with properties that are currently on the market by collecting details of properties of a similar age and type from your local paper's property column. If an agent to whom you apply for particulars asks for your name and address, give it. Don't play about with the 'It's for a friend' routine. The thing here, as in all house buying, selling and conveyancing procedures, is: be bold. And that is what we will call the users of this book: 'Mr & Mrs Bold'.

When you have found some properties which you think will make useful comparisons, go and do the viewing bit. Ask the vendors how they decided on their price. If the way they shape the reply is persuasive, note it for future use; if not, make a note not to say such silly things yourself when the time comes.

I know it is extremely hard, but do not look for the faults, and therefore justifications for why your house is better and consequently worth more than theirs. Try to see those elements that are better than yours and could justify the vendor's price. For instance, if the house you are viewing is set well into the middle of a large development, give it points for not having to suffer as much early morning traffic noise as a house at the entrance and exit of the same estate. But if yours is at an entrance, do not continue comforting yourself with the vain thought, 'Oh, we soon got used to it, after a while you don't hear them. In any case, we might get someone whose job takes them out before anyone else.' Such musings, when you first moved in and discovered the disadvantage, might have made you feel better about the bargain you had made, but it's for real now.

Don't be shy about viewing other properties just for your own valuation purposes. No doubt others will do the same to you later. In any case, when you have read the section on 'Showing them round', you will realise that no viewer is an absolute waste of time.

Tradition says that purchasers always want something knocked off, so when you have worked out the going rate for a house such as yours, add about two per cent on to that figure to arrive at your asking price, thus leaving yourself a little room for negotiation. We will look at what, when, where and how to bargain later.

When you are fixing your opening price do not let anyone flatter you into asking way over the odds, with the hare-brained notion that you might catch an out-of-town buyer (more about them later too!) or someone who is desperate or doesn't know what he is doing. 'You can always come down later' is a prescription for an idiot. Of course you can always come down … and down … and down again. Making a deal when time has run out and it is you who is desperate is no time to decide on a price. So do so before you announce the sale. Make up your mind what you will take and not what you will be given.

It is silly to miss a perfectly good buyer who won't even come to view during the period you are trying for top price. By the time you come down to a realistic figure your buyer could be happily settled into another house. Your best buyers are those who come first. Don't miss them. Give them credit for having researched the market and done their comparisons too.

If you ask too much, your house will become a drag on the market even after being reduced below its real value. Don't let greed make you miss a buyer. You only need one!

Buyers know that private vendors do not have to pay agents' fees and therefore expect that fact to be reflected in the price asked. So take that into account when you decide what is the lowest price you will take. Vendors of property advertised by agents do not get the asking price. What they do get is what is left after the traditional two per cent put on to knock off has been negotiated away; less the professional creaming off; less the dreaded VAT and advertising costs. Because private vendors' houses sell quicker than agency houses, your advertising costs should be lower than theirs; you pay no VAT or the rest of the list. So you can keep your price down and still make more money than if you let an agent mess about with it.

Now set about making the house itself look attractive.

Window dressing

This is the acquisitive society. We are all at it. But last year's luxuries give way to this year's pressing desires. And we need somewhere to store what, to us, are former favourites to which we are sentimentally attached, but to viewers will look like junk.

As soon as you decide to sell and have given notice of intention to your lender, get rid of the junk as quickly as the dustbin men will take it away. Bottles, jars, containers of all sorts that you never had time to fill with home-made preserves. Magazines and newspapers you intended to read again and never did. Offcuts of material from cotton to chipboard that you were sure would come in useful, together with the bent nails and screws which never did either. The clothes you hoped would come back into fashion. Let the lot go. Make it look as if there is bags of cupboard room. The fewer things there are on the wall-to-wall carpeting, the larger the room looks.

We all imagine that a house or garden that is neat, tidy and well kept will easily remain so. Viewers seem to think so, too. A mucky house in a tatty garden has to be sold muck cheap. So, tidy it up. It makes the happy home look more spacious and valuable immediately you have done so.

Modernisation

If, after looking at other properties, you feel that you have been left behind in the race to fit new kitchen units, central heating, bathroom suites and the like, think long and hard before, in a bid to compete, you decide to make such improvements yourself. You will have to add the cost to your asking price. And what if the first person to answer your advertisement would have bought, except that the style of your new bathroom suite brought out an instant attack of the dry heaves? As a matter of fact, you can, in your advertisement, use an unmodernised state to mark yours out from the rest.

'Built 40 years ago and now due for a face-lift, will suit handyman' – there's a disadvantage turned into an advantage for you!

If you have not already been tempted to become a do-it-yourself home improver, the present is not the time to experiment. A pressed-for-time reluctant handyman's botching shows.

There are plenty of enthusiastic improvers who are never so happy as when the house is in the process of transmogrification. Who are you to deny them the pleasure – at a price? Let them do it at their leisure. What is more, there are always one or two hopefuls looking for just such houses as yours, and to hear that the house has 'every modern refinement' is an immediate turn-off for them, even though in the long run such a house will cost them more than a fully modernised one.

If you have made changes to your home, do make sure that you have copies of all the necessary documentation consenting to the works of modernisation or alteration in your possession when you sell.

Decorations

Viewers are a suspicious lot. Is there any wonder? So, although you are not covering up any cracks and damp patches, a full paint-and-dec job is not recommended. It would be unlikely to deceive anyone, anyway. It's a simple device and people know about it. No matter how old the decorations and fittings, the essential thing is for the house to be clean and give the impression that it could be lived in until such time as a buyer can cover up your 'vile interior decorations'. There is no harm in a bit of judicious touching-up. Odd spots where paint has been chipped off over the years can be improved with a deft stroke of coloured chalk.

Give the whole house a spring-clean. In particular:

- Clean and polish the windows.

- Shine up the furniture.

- Burnish the brasses.

- Replace or cut shorter the dirty ends of dropcords.

If you are selling an empty house where someone has died, or moved out into an institution, make sure you remove all remaining day-to-day personal effects such as engagement calendars, part-used tubes of toothpaste, and bottles of pills and potions which evidently failed.

The hall

Decide where the negotiations are to take place after viewers have looked round the rest of the house (the hall is a good choice), and give it the full treatment, knowing the viewer will get the first, and final impressions there. If you have the nerve for it, during the negotiations, you can say modestly, 'Sorry about the state of the hall. It's the only place we haven't got round to.'

Central heating

Let air out of the radiators. You don't want the diabolical bangings to start in the middle of a viewing session.

Gates, fences and paths

Take an objective look at the outsides. If the gate is hanging off, take it down to the rubbish tip or put it well out of sight so that your purchaser can discover it later, and smarty that he is, put it back securely. It won't matter what kind of lazy so-and-so he calls you then – you won't be within earshot. If a fence is dilapidated, tidy it up. A viewer might wonder if you are in dispute with a neighbour about whose responsibility it is. And if there is a sacked estate agent's board hanging around – get rid!

Tidy up the verge, sweep the pavement and gutters. As a matter of fact, you should do this whether you are selling or not. Look after the area and it will look after you. If you have some white paint left over from doing the outside walls, or failing that some white emulsion, add plenty of thinners and give a concrete drive, path or steps the treatment. If you are not sure it will 'take' on your particular brand of concrete, experiment on a small section first. A parked caravan or boat should be moved to some other friendly haven for a while and any oil stains cleaned off. Buyers don't always have sufficient imagination to conjure up a vision of how expansive your uncluttered drive would be. But if they start eyeing it up because they too own a caravan you can come clean and inform them, going on to say, if it is true, that you have never had any complaints from council and neighbours.

Gardens

Tidy up. If the job would be too much, get some weedkiller for the beds and then give it a light forking. 'Lovely colourful garden this can be, just haven't had time this year, except to make it ready for planting.' If you can't even do that much, wait until just after Christmas; there is not much to choose between one snow covered garden and another, but in any case, get cracking with the weedkiller on the paths; it is neither time-consuming nor costly. Lop any overhanging shrubs, which, after a shower of rain, would drench a viewer's coat sleeves as he pushes by.

The front door

If necessary, replace the front door handle, letterbox and any other adornments. In summer or autumn a colourful hanging basket can work wonders. If there happens to be a hook to hang one on, it would be cheap at the price. If the door sticks, for goodness sake have it adjusted, even if it means your family having to put up with a few draughts for a week or two. It is the first impression that counts, and your viewer's first is formed while standing staring at your front door.

Ventilation

No matter what the season and what the cost in extra heating, open doors and windows every day, making sure the house gets a complete blow-through, particularly if some chain-smoker has just been in to view.

Delightful as the roly-poly dachshund draught excluder might look at the foot of a door, send it walkies. You don't want viewers to think that you live on windy ridge.

House names

If your house has both a number and a name, take the name down. Names are a matter of taste and we all know there is no accounting for that. A Yorkshire person might find 'Beck Side' pleasantly inoffensive – but a southerner …!

What if your house is only identified by the name? It isn't everybody who knows that the name can be changed by telling the local authority (usually buildings department) of one's intention, so you are allowed to drop that into the conversation. However, if the name includes, more or less truthfully, the words 'old' or 'cottage', that is more than all right. They are sure winners at attracting viewers.

The message that you should be getting so far is: spend only what you must on making your house and its environs look attractive and free from problems. You should do the same even if you decide to use a property shop. Having done what you can, you are now ready to put a For Sale board in your neat garden, or For Sale bills in your sparkling windows.

For Sale boards

From first to last you need viewers. It is said that one picture is worth a thousand words and one demonstration is worth a thousand pictures. So, unless you have the most compelling reasons against it (they are sometimes prohibited in Conservation Areas – check with your local authority), you must put out a For Sale board. If not a board, then a bill in the window. You will be surprised how many people will see it, even if you live in a cul-de-sac. Postmen, milkmen, newsagents, canvassers and neighbours can all spread the word if you only let them know.

Estate agents admit that they get 30 per cent of their buyers from For Sale boards and went barmy at the government's proposals for only one small board in any garden and no 'sold' boards anywhere. But now that the law has been changed, they are having to settle for spending more of their clients' money on newspaper advertising.

If estate agents are sending hopefuls to other houses in your vicinity, they are bound to see your board or window bill, and if your outsides look OK they won't want to buy the one the agent has for sale without first hearing about and seeing yours. In fact, they might only cruise by the agent's; they know all about that one already from the particulars they collected. Curiosity killed the cat, and your board will attract the curious.

It is worth the expense of getting a professional-looking board. Window bills or For Sale boards can be hired and put up by firms found under 'signs' in the Yellow Pages.

How to put up your own For Sale board

You need:

- about eight feet of 3 x 1 inch wood for a post, if it is to be sunk into the ground, less if you screw it to the gate post;

- four bricks;

- a screwdriver;

- a garden spade.

Do not have anything more on your board than 'FOR SALE Apply within' and your telephone number. 'By appointment only' is rejecting, and wise birds think: 'Hello, you can only go when the bagpipe teacher next door isn't giving lessons.' 'View weekends only' tells the burglar when to call. Let them get out of their cars and ask you for the details or, if you are not indoors, they can have a quiet look around the outside. Why not? You've nothing to be ashamed of, have you? If you have, get it attended to, now!

If you are putting the board in soil, dig a hole about eighteen inches square and about eighteen inches deep. Stand the board in the hole. Place two bricks at the bottom of the hole, one on either side of the post and parallel with one another, cover with about six inches of soil, then place a further two on top of and at right angles to the first two. Fill in and tamp down. You will be surprised at how firm your home-made board will be.

If you have a wooden gatepost, have the post for your board a little shorter, drill a couple of holes about eighteen inches apart in it, and screw the post to the gatepost.

If people come in from a board or a window bill you are halfway there. You haven't wasted an afternoon waiting in, when you could have been watching your favourite football team making a mess of it again. Indeed, you could have been doing something useful like drafting an advertisement to open up the market even further.

Advertising

This is a case of following the crowd. If it works for them it will for you;

hopefully, your board in the garden will have done the trick and, if not, your very first advertisement might.

Not all advertising has to be paid for; if you can come up with a story about why you are moving that looks like a news item, you could keep all the money in your pocket.

Anyone changing job, emigrating or doing anything adventurous or unusual should certainly contact the local newspaper and radio station to tell them about it. If you have children at school, is there a school magazine? Other parents might want to buy your house, believing that it is the atmosphere seeping out of your walls that makes your children so well behaved and brilliant. Do you have a parish magazine? Do you belong to any organisation to which you can give advance information of your move by sending an apology for absence, so that it goes into the minutes? You are not supposed to advertise in a radio interview, but what is more natural than, to the presenter's question 'when', you should reply 'when the house is sold, and that will be the biggest wrench because I doubt whether we'll get another with a spring of real ale gushing from the rockery and an open view over the nudist camp' … Keep the list going until you are stopped.

If you are moving away to be near your daughter, who everyone will be glad to hear has just had a baby, tell them. You've met some of the people in the area to which you are moving, and though they can't compare (who could?) with your locals, they seem a splendid bunch.

All these little strokes can be pulled for the sake of a short letter and a postage stamp or a telephone call. At the newspapers, ask for the news desk. At radio stations, ask for a presenter by name if you know one. They all need something to fill their columns and programmes and you really ought to help – where's your public spirit? Another 'free' advertisement is someone else's, so answer private 'wanted' advertisements.

Still another way of keeping your money where it rightly belongs is by putting postcards in local shop windows. At least it lets the talkative shopkeeper know.

Advertisers who spend millions on media space know that only a proportion of it works; the trouble is they don't know which! Estate agents have a better idea because their advertising is specific and so it is easy to monitor the source of each response. They know where and when is best; follow their example and use the same papers on the same days as they do.

Do not be tempted by reductions for a series of advertisements. If your first attempt does not work, you might want to alter the 'copy' in some way.

The copy: composing your advertisement

There are three formats to choose from:

1. **Display:** One which will be placed among other 'boxed' adverts. The trouble with display is that it can get lost among the others, so ask if you can have a choice of borders. Borders to display adverts can be varied. Look through the paper at the different styles and choose. If you do not see anything outstanding, ask if they will accept a border drawn by you. If they will, get a sheet of Letraset transfers from an artists' shop and make your own. White print on black background, if you fancy it, is called 'reversing out'.

   It won't cost anything to ask if you can have your advert placed in one of the better positions. Although we read from left to right we only do so when we have time. Right-hand pages and top-and-bottom right-hand corners are said to be best.

   If there is a property section, the first page is best and failing that, the last. Ask: if you don't ask, you don't get.

2. **Semi-display (classified):** Your advert appears in the column to which the class of thing you are offering refers – hence classified advertising – in your case the class is property. You will have noticed that a semi-displayed advertisement has lines (rules) separating it from other advertisements and you can choose where you want capital letters and where smalls, and how many spaces between the lines.

3. **Classified:** What you get for your money varies a little between newspapers, but generally it is a capital letter for the first word and the rest in smalls, apart from proper names where good grammar demands a capital. Do not spurn the classified. Anyone who is actively in the market will be searching the whole paper. They won't miss you; neither will the nosy parkers who are usually gossips and will spread the word for you.

Advertising in national newspapers is costly. The first thing to consider is this: research shows that nine out of ten buyers move less than 10 miles, and only one in a hundred moves more than 100 miles.

For every reader of one of the nationals, there are ten for the local paper and the cost of advertising in a national is ten times that of a local, added to which, buyers don't expect to see local properties advertised nationally, unless there is something very special about them.

So stick to the locals, unless your house is special because:

- it is in the upper bracket and has loose boxes, paddocks, fishing rights, private golf course, sound and video recording studio or other necessities for the rich;

- it is in the area to which a large company is relocating staff from all over the globe; or

- houses in the area are being sold as weekend homes.

In any case, a local buyer is much easier to deal with than the man from Timbuktu.

The wording: what to put on; what to leave out

You need a headline. As we know that people don't move very far and their choice is governed by district and price, these are two essential elements of your advertisement. If nothing else is read, those two items are, so make them your beginning and end. Least said, soonest mended.

Say what is for sale; give the asking price and arrangements for contacting you. Best to give the enquirers an invitation to view over the weekend. If they all come at once, so much the better; it proves what a good house it is, otherwise why are so many people interested? People always want what they think others want.

If you have an answerphone, assume that every call is a response to your advertisement, and put a message on giving viewing particulars. Just because callers are ringing about some totally unrelated subject, it does not mean to say that they or their friends wouldn't be delighted to buy your house now that they know it is for sale.

Don't bother unduly about the name and address of an interested party. The wicked give fake ones anyway. Estate agents dress it up as part of the confidential professional service that they are giving you, when they insist on names and addresses from enquirers. But the real reason is far more mundane: their own need to prove that they introduced the buyer – their commission claim rests on it.

From escorting a lady to view once or twice, I knew that she was insisting on a walk-in pantry. I also knew she adored wisteria; she thought it the epitome of elegance and class. I got a house for sale in exactly the right location for her and not only was there a wisteria but it was in full bloom. I telephoned and said we were giving her the first chance, even before full particulars were ready. One of our representatives was going to view in an hour's time. Could he pick her up on the way? Yes, it was a bungalow; yes, it had a garage. But for the moment that was all we knew, apart from the fact that, in an aside, the owner had said the wisteria was a picture. The lady viewed, found for herself that there was no walk-in pantry, and went on to convince herself that walk-in pantries weren't the be-all and end-all of life. But to get a wisteria like that going from scratch could take at least seven years. SOLD, to the lady who liked wisteria.

However, if you have a fine wisteria or fine anything else, do not put it into your advertisement. There are people who can't stand the sight nor smell of things creeping up the walls, but if they view and are impressed by your electronically operated garage doors, they will make light work of digging the offending plant out. On the other hand, the one buyer you want might not come if he knows about those doors; his cat might have lost a life in one.

Photographs

Sometimes, there is a case for using a photo of a detached house if it is individually styled, but as builders have, in recent years, built thousands of detached houses having only minimal variations in their elevations there are few compelling reasons for using one.

As for semi-detached or terraced (mews, town, etc.) houses, I don't know how anyone interested in buying a house in this country can have avoided learning what they look like. Indeed, the mere mention of a development is sufficient to bring to mind the type of houses there. So why our eyeballs have to be rattled week after week, with page after page of silly little photos of semis and terraced houses I'll never know, and as for a tiny picture of a block of flats ... who wants to go viewing a barracks? Because that is what many agency photos make them look like.

Instructions to printers

Always make your instructions to printers as clear as you can. Compositors work at speed and they are not mind-readers. Instructions should always be circled and preferably in a different colour.

Words that will conjure up a picture in the reader's mind must be carefully chosen:

- **backing onto woodland:** burglars lurking
- **oak beams:** charm, cosiness
- **exceptional opportunity:** why hasn't somebody taken it, then?
- **great potential:** work
- **sea view:** peace or bank holiday chaos on the roads
- **overlooking river or lake:** damp for the old, too deep for the young
- **near golf course:** can nip over the fence for a few quick swings or collect other people's lost golf balls
- **old:** immortal, tried and trusted
- **Victorian:** solid, spacious
- **prestigious:** schoolteachers and many others know the words come from prestidigitation – which means trickery!
- **cottage or cottage style:** if you can use it, do so. It's the biggest crowd-puller there is. But the picture some people conjure up at the thought is so chocolate-boxy that you are in grave danger of disappointing them, should they come and you have no white palings, no roses round the door and it's simply an old house in a street.

So, don't overdescribe: people will drive by instead of coming in to keep an appointment. You are buying disappointment and will lose confidence.

There is a buyer for everything

If your For Sale board and your first advertisement don't work, immediately remember that the hallmark of true entrepreneurs is that they are never 'counted out'. They try and try again. So alter your advertising copy a little. Go from one section of the paper to another; if you didn't succeed in the classified, try display and so on.

Tomorrow is another day. New buyers come into the market every single day.

Don't advertise more than twice in the same paper in the same week. Be ready to change the wording.

Your predecessor sold the house to you, your old neighbours sold to your new ones. The area isn't littered with empty houses that no one will live in. Of course you will sell your house and you will sell it yourself, keeping your money where it belongs.

Particulars

People have come to expect a set of particulars. If for no other reason, that is why you should have some, but you must not allow interested parties to use them as a substitute for viewing. At the risk of boring you, curiosity killed the cat.

Salesmen believe that one demonstration is worth a million words. It is certainly true of houses. Differences can be so subtle, only inspection can prove which is the best buy. Yet people are basically idle, it does not take a lot to put them off. They sit in their armchairs, leafing through a fistful of agents' particulars, and no matter how well a house has been proposed and worthily recommended, they will blackball it without actually seeing it for themselves. If they got everything they thought they needed to know from the particulars, what need is there to view? How can a house get sold if it is left to buyers to decide, on a whim, which is best for them? They need our encouragement to work at it, which translated into a few words means: view and buy ours.

Try to restrict the distribution of your particulars to those who have been shown round. Give a copy to help them remember you and yours better than all the other run-of-the-mill properties they have seen.

Example particulars

PARTICULARS OF PROPERTY FOR SALE

Mr & Mrs R Bold

offer

FOR SALE PRIVATELY
(no agents)

14 Plevna Place, Blossomton

£155,000 Freehold

Registered at Her Majesty's Land Registry Title No. EDN999707

* Entrance Hall
* Lounge
* Separate Dining Room
* Kitchen
* Utility Room
* Cloaks with WC
* Good decorations
* Central Heating
* Large Bedroom with en suite shower

* Second Bedroom
* Good third Bedroom
* 2nd and 3rd Bedrooms have washbasins
* Bathroom with WC
* Well insulated loft
* Quality fittings throughout
* Manageable gardens
* Garage and car port off wide street

Gas, electricity and mains water are connected. The Council Tax paid last year amounted to £790.

Vacant possession by arrangement.

There are nursery and playschools within walking distance. A sitter-in club operates in the district. The Orchard shopping centre is just around the corner, as is the regular bus service to town. Ten minutes' car journey to mainline and inter-city trains.

Plevna Place is off Orchard Road which is directly off the A444 at Bericote Cross Roads close to the local park.

Viewing at any reasonable time.

If you wish to confirm, please telephone (01234) 28370

This house is in a very pleasant and respectable neighbourhood and has been very reasonably priced at £155,000 for an EARLY SALE.

No agents   Mr & Mrs Bold, 14 Plevna Place

These particulars are believed to be correct but do not constitute an offer or any part of a contract.

Estate agents can get away with the most appalling rubbish and the silliest descriptions, because people don't take a lot of notice of their 'bijou residence of great charm and delight', knowing it means 'a poky hole with old-fashioned fittings', although agents can now be prosecuted if they do misrepresent key information.

Private vendors can stick to plain language. Describe but don't overdo it. Big is as good as six-and-three-quarter metres – or is it kilowatts? Who knows? Who cares, apart from surveyors, who have to make a great performance with their tape measures in an effort to impress the gullible. If your rooms are the wrong size for other people's carpets and you have given the game away in your particulars, they won't view. If they only find out when they come, they'll be delighted to hear that one of their neighbours-to-be is a carpet fitter, who needs a bit of weekend work: he's good and he's cheap!

Photographs

If you think a picture stuck onto your particulars will help prospects to remember your house, get some self-adhesive mini-prints made. All you need to do is send the developed 35mm negative to one of the specialist printers who advertise their services, and for very little you will get 50 prints almost by return of post.

When taking the photograph, stand on a stepladder; it helps to keep the walls in proper perspective. Wait until fog, cars, vans, police, cats and dogs and canvassers are out of the way. Shut the garage doors, draw all but decorative curtains well back and take all of the washing in.

Drafting

If you can type the particulars so well and good, but if your handwriting is clear, that's something different. Failing your being a typist or a handwritist, your local duplicating agency or photocopier will do both the typing and printing on A4 size paper for you. Choose a copier who has a standard border that your particulars can be laid on for copying. Just because it's cheaper for quantities, don't buy more than you need. Twenty should be plenty. In any case, you might want to make some adjustments later.

On our specimen particulars shown on page 58, we have tried to give the prospects plenty of reading. Not as much as would make them feel they knew it all without viewing, but more information than they are likely to get from an agent.

If your house is registered, this is obviously a good thing to show. Estate agents don't show it, and one can only speculate on the reason. It can't possibly be the cost – it's free! Perhaps they don't understand the matter, or if they do they want to keep the knowledge to themselves believing that a little knowledge is a dangerous thing for clients to have.

But as Huxley says, if a little knowledge is a dangerous thing, where is the man who has enough to be safe? Or as I would have it: a little knowledge in the hands of house buyers is a dangerous thing for the professionals in their search for easy pickings. But no matter who is right, estate agents and solicitors don't seem unduly disturbed at the moment. They know that no matter how many For Sale boards rot away, how many sold-subject-to-contract slips dance on and off the boards, how many mortgage applications fail, how many bridging loans have to be paid or chains collapse, most people get moved, jobs get cobbled together somehow, and if sleep is to be lost, it won't be theirs. They have seen it all before.

If, because you have a mortgage or for any other reason, you haven't got the deeds to flash under a prospect's nose, put your name and address on a Form OC1 and send it to the Land Registry with a fee of £4. In reply you will receive an official Land Registry certificate of search, proving the registration and the title number. You can then show it to a prospect, who might be one of the growing band of buyers who know they can buy without the aid of a solicitor. Knowing so early on in the proceedings whether the house is registered or not is valuable. In any case it is something new and different, and gives a stamp of approval to the proceedings: they'll remember *your* house all right.

Although you would not wish to print it on the particulars, another thing you could usefully do would be to call at the local council office and ask if there is anything special about to happen round your way, such as a new building, a sewage farm or road widening. It is as well to know about it now. Knowledge is power, and sometimes very profitable. Some kinds of development enhance a house's value. If so, you don't want to sell to some speculator; keep the profit for yourself.

Disclaimers

All estate agents write one at the foot of their particulars, some briefly and some at great length, such as:

Allwind & Waters state for themselves and the vendors of the property described herein that the acceptance of a copy of these particulars is made on the understanding that the applicant has read and understood the content and meaning hereof and that these particulars are intended as a general guide only and do not constitute any sort of contract or offer or part thereof and that no person of either sex in the employ full or part time of Messrs Allwind & Waters has any authority to make any representation warranty or give any guarantee whatever in relation to this property.

Why any honest, hard working qualified and competent persons should subject people with whom they are trying to do business to such an eyesight test I don't know. If staff are incompetent, they should be moved on, and certainly not be let near the tens of thousands of pounds of 'what is most probably our most important and valuable possession'.

Private vendor's disclaimer

Having been rigorously honest and above all painstaking about the things you do put in, you can use the delightfully simple: These particulars are believed to be correct but do not constitute an offer or any part of a contract.

Showing them round

Lonely, elderly and single people fear lest having a board in the garden will attract all sorts of villains. That fear is no reason for paying a thousand pounds or more to an agency.

Though an agent might get the name and address of every enquirer, do you really expect any villain whose dearest wish is to rape, plunder, pillage and set fire to you to give a correct address? Even if an agent accompanies every enquirer, having once seen the house and ingratiated himself, the enquirer can call back unaccompanied and wreak villainy upon you.

If you don't use, or haven't yet got, a chain on your door, you must. If you don't, sooner or later you will be done over, selling a house or not, agents or no agents. You can always keep an enquirer on the other side of the door and make an appointment for a time when a friend can come round, or even when you have arranged for other viewers to come.

Ask yourself, could anyone sell me a house I didn't really want? Even if he had graduated from a top business salesmanship school, got a gold medal from the professor for it, had all the patter and ready-thought-out glib answers to all the searching questions, had manoeuvred you into saying 'yes' at every twist and turn in the conversation, including the final yes, so that you could get home in time to watch The Party Political Broadcast – would you really feel bound? Wouldn't you find some reason for, at least, forgetting it?

Buyers have plenty of time to forget it. The cooling-off period allowed in consumer protection legislation is but a fleeting moment compared with the time solicitors take to get contracts signed and exchanged – the point at which, and not before, neither party can back out except at the risk of severe penalties.

No matter how many books you have read on selling, no matter how many seminars, courses or lectures you have attended to be talked at, or successful role-plays you have accomplished about selling, the message with regard to selling houses is that if they have been properly prepared, they don't need super-salesmen: **they sell themselves.**

Your task is to allow someone who wants your house to know that it is for sale, and then to let them have it (the house). Put no obstacle in their path. Smooth that path. Prepare yourself, and any other members of your household who might come in contact with viewers to do just this:

1.   Let them in.

2.   Show them round.

3.   Let them know that others are interested.

4.   Bargain if you must.

5.   Carry out the instructions on what to do when a buyer says 'I will'.

If people knock on the door in response to seeing the board in your garden, and you are not alone in the house, let them in. Only if the most embarrassing scene is being enacted within should you ask them to come back later. From first to last, remember that doubtless this is your most prized possession that you are trying to sell. You must be prepared to work at it and accept some inconvenience.

You only need one buyer and he may well be standing before your very eyes. It might cost you another £50 in advertising before you get another viewer, so a bird on the doorstep can be worth two in the bush.

If people ring up for an appointment to view, remember the walk-in pantry lady, and say as little as possible over the phone.

Do not worry too much about the problem of time-wasters. They might arrive at the same time as a genuine prospect, and the so-called time-waster might just jerk the prospect into action.

When the viewers come in daylight make sure the curtains are drawn well back. Have doors onto landings and passages open to let light in. It all makes a house look more airy and spacious.

For evening viewers, use only the softest of lighting and try to have lamps already switched on. Don't switch lights off as you vacate rooms.

They might think you extravagant, but if they ask to see the electricity bills, they will be convinced that they, being more careful than you, will have less to pay.

Decide beforehand who is to lead the conducted tour if there should be more than one of you at home when the viewers arrive. Leave the others seated comfortably in the lounge. They must not be smoking, arguing or drinking anything because you don't want to look unfriendly by not offering a portion to the visitors. The television, radio or CD player should only be playing if your neighbour is giving a bagpipe lesson. Otherwise, all that the loungers have to do is politely acknowledge (they must not ignore) the presence of the viewers. Children should be introduced properly.

Those who are light-fingered work to the four As: they will steal anything from anybody, anywhere, any time. So don't leave pocketable things around. Don't actually search viewers as they leave, but just have it at the back of your mind that everybody is not as honest as you are.

You should enter each room first, and then invite viewers to follow you. If the view is worth seeing, ask them to step to the window. Open cupboard and wardrobe doors to show how spacious they are. Draw attention to thermostats on radiators and situations of power plugs. Do not draw attention to things that are big enough to see such as fireplaces and tiled walls. Demonstrate water pressure at sinks, baths and WCs. Similarly, an electronically controlled garage door needs to be demonstrated, because it too is not immediately obvious to the unassisted eye.

When you've shown them round, invite their questions and answer as honestly as you can. If you don't know the answer, say so.

If a viewer says, 'Oh dear, I thought there might be a bidet', keep your witty remarks to yourself until after he's gone. And don't let it cast you down. It could be you've got a buyer here and such carping is a tactic in the strategy of bargaining, about which more later.

You can't put anyone off buying their dream home but do avoid any unintended insult. They'll only get their own back later if you give one.

Safety lies in getting as many clues about them as soon as possible. Ask the Royal question, 'Have you come far?' The answer to that or subsequent get-to-know-right-by-guessing-wrong statements will help you get the picture and determine your future chat.

If you are asked how long your house has been up for sale and the truthful answer is: just this week, say so. If it is a while longer say, 'Oh, not long, houses along here never are'. If the viewer is a smarty and bowls you a guess-wrong-to-get-to-know right, such as 'A week?' it's own-up time folks, because such a questioner will treat you with the utmost suspicion from then on if you don't.

Don't introduce negative thoughts by bragging about the money you have spent on eradicating woodworm and the guarantee against its recurrence that you got.

Owner-occupiers are inordinately proud of their houses and when they are conducting prospective purchasers round, it shows, so the sensitive viewer will often say anything to avoid giving offence when trying to bring the visit to a comfortable close. Team viewers, such as husband and wife, will naturally wish to discuss together the merits of the house, not in front of the vendor, but after leaving, and the real purchaser can quite easily turn out to be the one who walks round without saying a word, and succeeds in leaving you with the feeling that you have been wasting your time.

Prospects who have made appointments will turn up to view. At the gate, they may realise that yours is not for them, but for courtesy's sake will come to the door.

However, as soon as a viewer steps over the threshold, most of us get a feeling of whether what we have to offer is what he is looking for. If you sense it is not, show him round and show him out. In the cases where you feel that there is a glimmer of hope, keep him there and take your time in showing him as much as possible, with such little tricks as asking him to admire the view. But do not let the conversation stray, for long, from points about the house; keep to such things as the local shops and the price.

Nevertheless, the safest plan is to treat every viewer as a buyer, but ignore what they say, or fail to say, initially about their intentions. Prefer to wait for further action to develop and until it does, keep on showing viewers round.

How to negotiate

You will have already calculated what is the very best deal you can hope for and what is barely acceptable to you: what are the optional extras you will sell and what are the extras you intend to include in your price. You can then bargain on these points if required to. Being prepared, you won't have to rely on the other party to make up your mind for you.

Do not bargain at all unless you have to. Put it off as long as possible. As you are showing the nicest part of your nature, the more time viewers have to get to know you, the less they will want to offend by offering too little. In any case, there are still a few around who find it embarrassing and ill-mannered to bargain and that is still another reason why your price must be realistic in the first place.

If, initially, you are asked, 'Will you take an offer?' answer 'Of course, come in and have a look round and we'll have a talk about it'. Then get off the subject with, 'Have you come far?'

The opening from a serious prospect

It usually goes something like: 'Will you take an offer?' Well, you are open to an offer; it all depends what he has in mind. When you are given a figure, no matter what it is, look shocked. If no figure is forthcoming, keep fencing, saying that you have stated your price and hope to get it, but for a quick decision from a good buyer you will talk. By the way, has he sold his house? Will it be cash, or will he require a mortgage; how quickly could he complete?

There is a lot of guesswork in bargaining. He who has the most facts wins, so get to know as much as you can about the other party as soon as possible. In a bargaining situation, delay is a most useful weapon so use it if you can. If he won't talk, you must ask questions; the other side then has to reveal some of his hand.

Reluctant bargainers

If you really don't feel up to all the argy-bargy, you could advertise 'no offers'. But as your first task is to draw as many viewers as possible and 'no offers' could stop some coming, prefer to wait and reply to offers with, 'I know that people expect to bargain for houses, but I have never been accustomed to it and have therefore made sure that my asking price is the most reasonable that anyone could expect to get it for'. Then hand them a copy of your particulars on which you have already written that little lot, or words to that effect.

Never accept the first offer. The deal will collapse if you do, because the prospect thinks he could have got it for less. Never say no, say maybe. Hide this book from the gaze of prospects. Because you are selling for yourself, they think you are an amateur and they will be relaxed, an ideal bargaining atmosphere – don't lose it.

Give satisfaction. People get more satisfaction from the things they have to work for.

Bargaining points

Use things you intended to include in the purchase price as bargaining points; for example, if you had included the carpet and curtains, you can counter with 'all right, but I couldn't possibly include the carpets and curtains at that price'.

Half a loaf is better than none, particularly if your half has the butter on.

Making a benchmark

When some people receive their first offer, they are known to say, even though it is hardly true, that they have got as good an offer already, so if, just for the look of the thing, the new man will add £2,500 to his offer, that could tie things up and leave things comfortable all round.

Anglers need patience

If people don't bite first time, don't worry, they might have taken the bait.

The harder you fight in the beginning, the less you give away in the long run.

Keep reminding the bargainer of the bargain he is getting, compared with what is being offered elsewhere.

Use Stamp Duty Land Tax bands. Stamp Duty Land Tax is payable at one per cent on properties over £120,000; three per cent on properties over £250,000 and five per cent on properties over £500,000. If you really want somewhere around, but less than the figure which happens to be the point at which Stamp Duty Land Tax becomes payable, or at which the rate of Stamp Duty Land Tax changes, make your asking figure a little above it. You can then, with a long face, agree to bring your price down to save him tax. The purchaser has won, honour is satisfied, big deal!

Never show triumph. Always let them appear to win.

If they send an expert

He is on their side. About the dry rot, lay off the tommy rot; don't try to influence him. If you can overcome your generous instincts, don't even offer a cup of tea. Let him report – 'Hard people, they won't give anything away, don't seem to care whether they sell to you or not, maybe got a queue'.

The manipulators

This is the one who, when you think it is all agreed and you are waiting for contracts to be signed, comes back time and again for more. Remedy: ask for a final set of demands in writing. Another good reason for knowing about contracts and how solicitors work. Read on – all will be revealed.

Box yourself in

Cut off your retreat. Burn down your bridges: tell the bargainer that you are anxious to move quickly and, to get a quick sale, you set your price where you did, in spite of being told that you could get far more. As a matter of fact, agents have never stopped ringing, offering to do just that, but you know what they are – anything to get people signed up. But you have pitched your price with just the odd bit added on, to allow a modest bargain and you can't possibly go lower, what with the mortgage and all that.

Do not leave the bargaining to an agency or a solicitor but if you find he has got involved don't tell him your rock bottom deal. He wants the job out of the way; he has not got the time for lengthy bargaining sessions.

If in doubt

Say nowt.

Forget pride

Derogatory remarks about your pride and joy are intended to cost you money.

Free option

If you agree to let someone know, if and when you decide to reduce your price, make sure that you have got an offer out of them first so that when you do go back, you go with a new price that allows you some elbow room.

Problems

They do not go away – they go into corners and breed. Our ruin is often caused by not what we say, but what we fail to say and/or get into writing.

Closing an interview

'We are expecting someone else soon. Will you let me know by next Wednesday as I have half-made promises elsewhere.'

To sum up

Cups of tea, a guided tour of your holiday snaps, or a privileged look into the eggcup containing your gallstones will not sell your house. Nor will playing the super-salesman. Your job is to get the viewers. Houses sell themselves if you will only:

- Let viewers look round.

- Let them bargain if they must.

- Let them agree to buy.

- Let them pay a deposit.

- Let them go home.

- Be natural – be yourself.

- Be a listener as well as a talker.

- Be modest about the house.

- Don't show off; it's the house that is on view, not you.

What to say when a buyer says 'I will'

'Who is your solicitor?' 'I am acting for myself and you can tell your people to get in touch with me. Will you please pay me a deposit now as a sign of good faith?'

Of course, people have to get mortgages. Of course, many have to get their own houses sold and, of course, if they are really serious they will have done as much as they can towards sorting these problems out before they meet you. Ask them where they are at in the process and if possible check their answers. Acting for yourself you can then so easily be honest and fair to everybody – but chiefly yourself.

For instance, you can keep a buyer keened up while you are looking for reserves by being ready to say, 'I do hope you will be able to buy it, but as you know, there's many a slip twixt cup and lip, so I will have to keep the board out. But I promise you that you are top of my list. I won't sell to anyone else without getting in touch with you. That's fair, isn't it?'

Even if there are a dozen, they are all top of the list, because you don't really fancy the chances of the previous ones if someone turns up an hour later with the folding money, ready to sign a contract then and there. It can happen and it can be done – see later.

For expedition, the seller should prepare a complete set of papers ready for the buyer including the following:

- Property Information Forms
- Fixtures, Fittings and Contents Form
- Office Copy entries and a filed plan
- Copy of lease (if leasehold)
- Copy of any relevant Consents (to modernisation, etc.)

It is also advisable to get local water and environmental searches completed.

Never say die

If your home is clean, neat, tidy and properly priced, your buyer will come. See the bargain-hunter off. Keep on showing viewers round right up to the minute you get a contract signed.

CHAPTER 8

Home Information Packs

There has been a lot of talk for some time now about Home Information Packs ('HIPs'). HIPs are designed to make the process of house buying simpler and prevent buyers from wasting time and money carrying out searches and having surveys done if the vendor then decides to pull out. This is the big problem with house buying in England and Wales – until contracts have been exchanged, either party can simply pull out. The Labour government decided to introduce HIPs to limit wasted expenditure.

The idea behind HIPs is very simple and straightforward. The vendor gets together information that the buyer will want to know before he purchases the house – documents to prove title, a 'Home Condition Report', local land charge search and a drainage and water search. This takes this aspect of expenditure out of the hands of the buyer and imposes it on the seller, so the cost of selling houses is likely to increase. However, it does mean that if the vendor pulls out, the buyer hasn't wasted a lot of money (or so the theory goes).

At the time of writing (July 2006) the requirement that every vendor have a HIP is not yet in force. This is due to come into force on 1 June 2007. However, there has recently been a lot of speculation in the media that HIPs are not all that they are cracked up to be and, in particular, the Home Condition Report will not be acceptable to many lenders, who will still require a formal valuation which the borrower will need to pay for, leading to duplication of work and potentially wasted expenditure. This will remain to be seen.

So when the requirements do come into force, what will a vendor be required to do?

Basically, you will not be able to put your house on the market until you have prepared a HIP. It is to be anticipated that these will be available from legal stationers. There is certain information which is mandatory, such as an Office Copy of the register and an official copy of the title plan to a property if registered; if unregistered, an Index Map search and deeds showing title (as to which see chapters 13 and 14 on registered and unregistered conveyancing). In addition, you will need a 'sale statement', local Land Charges Search, drainage and water search and, of course, the Home Condition Report. There is certain other information which can be included voluntarily, such as guarantees for recent building work. It is best to include this if it is available. If such information isn't included and it is obvious that work has recently been done, buyers might start to wonder why the information has not been provided. If copy documents are included in the pack, they must be certified copies of originals.

From a buyer's point of view, he is entitled to request a copy of the pack or of particular documents in the pack. Any copy documents should be certified copies of the original (i.e. certified by a solicitor or commissioner for oaths). The buyer will have to pay for the reasonable copying charges and probably the fee of the solicitor certifying that these are true copies of the original. However, this is likely to be cheaper and quicker than obtaining the local land charge search from the local authority and so reduce delay. If a vendor does not provide a copy document within 14 days of it being requested, he will be liable in damages to the purchaser and will have to pay the costs of the purchaser having to carry out his own search to obtain the relevant document. Marketing your house without an HIP may also subject you to criminal penalties.

It remains to be seen how this all pans out. However, HIPs will probably be available from legal stationers. In addition, vendors can simply follow the instructions for purchasers as to doing the searches to get the thing up and running. But after 1 June 2007 be sure that your 'For Sale' board does not go into your garden until you have got the documents together or you could find yourself in trouble.

CHAPTER 9

Contracts

A contract is a legally binding agreement to do something. Contracts for the sale and purchase of land must be in writing, contain all the important terms agreed by the parties and, importantly, must be signed by the parties. Either both parties may sign one document or there can be an exchange of identical documents, one signed by each party which are literally 'swapped'. This is the usual position when selling houses. Parties must be identifiable and over 18 years of age. Lunatics and some drunkards are debarred. What transforms a simple agreement into a contract is that the contract is made for 'consideration'. Consideration is a matter of inducement for something promised, so it has to be valuable, for example, money.

A vendor's contract says in effect: you, Mr Rashley, have induced me to promise you vacant possession of my house by offering to pay me £75,000. And if Mr Rashley puts his signature to this agreement (upon that valuable consideration of £75,000) called a contract (that the vendor, too, has signed), and fails to keep his bargain, then he is bound and can be sued if he does not complete the bargain contracted for.

The Law Society and Oyez publish a property contract called an 'Agreement (incorporating the Standard Conditions of Sale (Fourth Edition))'. All the main headings required for a contract for the sale of a freehold or leasehold house situated in England and Wales are there – see example at the end of this chapter. If you are selling, have three copies ready as soon as you put the house on the market.

Solicitors will choose from either the Law Society's contract or draft their own. The conditions are set out in full on the inside of the Agreement. These conditions occupy line after line of fine print (literally as long as an arm). So stand well back and if any of it has been altered, have a closer look, and if you still do not know what is going on, ask for an explanation. Often, the standard conditions will be altered by means of 'Special Conditions' which form a page at the front of the contract.

Just remember:

Vendor: You want the money.

Purchaser: You want the house.

That's all there is to it!

Contracts for the sale of land (in our case with buildings on) usually include the following:

1. **Description of the parties:** Names and addresses of both vendor and purchaser.

2. **Description of what is being sold:** Only where only part of a registered title or unregistered land is included in the sale should a plan of the area accompany the draft contract. In all other cases, the inclusion of a plan is unnecessary.

    If the property is unregistered, there should be, if the conveyances say so, a plan among the deeds. If there isn't a mention of such a plan, then there will be a description. Often there are both. Plans are easier to understand than descriptions, but just because a plan is included does not mean that this takes precedence over the description on the deed . If registered, you will receive a copy of the plan with the Office Copies (something else which you will learn about in chapter 11).

    There may be included in the description of what is being sold, a recital of any rights that are sold with the land, such as light, water, way and drainage. Usually the contract just refers to the Office Copies, where this is all noted or in the case of unregistered land, to an earlier document containing these rights. However, these rights can be mentioned here in general terms at this stage, and answered in a little more detail when requisitions (questions) on (about the) title (ownership) are received after exchange of contracts. The fourth edition of the Standard Conditions of Sale provide that the buyer is not allowed to ask questions regarding title after exchange of contracts if the vendor proves his title before exchange of contracts. He is only allowed to ask questions about things if he learned about them for the first time after contracts were exchanged. If the vendor doesn't adduce title before contracts are exchanged, the purchaser has six working days after he adduces title to ask any questions about the title that he may have.

3. **The price.**

4. **The amount of deposit (customarily ten per cent of the price, but often less)**, and how it is to be paid and by whom it will be held acting as stakeholder (agent/bank manager/solicitor or vendor and purchaser who open a joint bank account for this purpose only). If the other side has a solicitor who will agree to be stakeholder, you can agree. Otherwise, the deposit is relatively unprotected as it can be released to the seller before completion. If completion did not happen for any reason, the deposit monies may not be very easy to recover. However, if completion fails to occur due to the fault of the buyer, the deposit will be forfeit.

It is quite normal for a seller to borrow his buyer's deposit for use as his deposit and so on up the buying chain, if there is one. This applies only by agreement, as set out in Standard Condition 2.2.2. This often means it is the poorest person at the bottom of the chain who has to stump up the deposit, then used by each person up the line.

The fourth edition of the Standard Conditions contains restrictions on how the deposit can be paid. A banker's draft is no longer acceptable. Unless the Standard Conditions are altered, the deposit must be paid either by cheque drawn on the client account of a solicitor or licensed conveyancer or by 'direct credit', i.e. CHAPS transfer.

5. **The date for completion:** This is a matter for agreement between the parties. The purchaser should make up the difference between the deposit paid and the purchase price on the completion date, and in exchange the vendor should give full vacant possession. What, you may ask, if either side finds that they can't complete to the exact date? Don't be frightened, and, furthermore, don't despair – it isn't a legal

problem yet. Whether you are doing the job for yourself or paying a Skinner, the hiccup would have occurred and it would have been yours to cure. However, it is advantageous to complete as soon as possible to prevent paying unnecessary interest. This will be prescribed by the contract and will be a few per cent over the base rate.

If your opposite number to the contract gives what sounds like a good reason for delay, then you must come to some new understanding, and if your vendor is being silly and says he wants more money, has changed his mind about the house he wanted to buy or move into, or simply changed his mind full stop, then you have to make some decisions. What are your options? If it is postponement, you can calmly accept his new date. But if you decide that the contract should be kept, then you must give the other party written notice to complete. The notice must be reasonable and take into account the circumstances of the particular case. If you are faced by this very unusual circumstance, have a look at the standard notice period in Condition 6.8 of the Standard Conditions of Sale, which gives ten working days with which completion must take place. But check the 'Special Conditions' first to see whether this has been altered in any way.

If you had a problem with your washing machine, you would first look at the instructions and if you were stumped, you would not be afraid to consult a service engineer. So if after giving notice you have not got a sensible new arrangement, then consider going to a solicitor for advice only.

The only (very rare) circumstance in which either or both of the parties to the contract can insist that the contract be completed or come to an end on the very date contracted for is where a clause has been inserted in the contract saying that 'time is the essence' of the contract. If time is not of the essence of the contract, service of a notice to complete has the effect of making time of the essence. Therefore, the other party must complete on the date that the notice to complete expires, which is the number of days (after service of the notice) which is set out in the contract. If time is or has been made of the essence and, say, a purchaser says, 'but I can't complete until the day after the date specified for completion or the expiry of the notice', the vendor is at liberty to put the contract at an end and confiscate the deposit. If it is the vendor who cannot or will not complete, and time is the essence, the purchaser can put an end to the contract, demand the deposit back, and, if he has suffered any loss, possibly sue for damages.

6. **The capacity in which the vendor sells:** You must choose between 'full' and 'limited' guarantee in the contract. Full title guarantee is for both freehold and leasehold. It implies that vendors:

   (a) have the right to dispose of the property as they are purporting they have;

   (b) will at their own cost do all that they can reasonably to give the purchaser the title that they purport to give, which includes doing what they reasonably can to ensure that the purchaser is entitled to be registered with at least the class of title registered before the disposition;

   (c) assert that the property is free from all financial charges (e.g. mortgage) and incumbrances and all other rights exercisable by third parties that the vendor knows about and could reasonably be expected to know about, but you do not have to refer to items already on the register or 'overriding interests' of which the purchaser has notice.

   The circumstances whereby a vendor could not give full title guarantee include:

   (a) where a trustee disposes of property under a will, then he would not sell with full title guarantee;

   (b) a mortgagee in possession, which would also not sell with full title guarantee;

   (c) executors selling following the death of the former owner.

7. **Extras (or 'chattels'):** Items that are not fixtures and fittings, which can pass by delivery, and have been bargained for separately are sometimes included by reference to a separate inventory. If included in the purchase price (stated in the contract) and a separate value has been agreed for them, that price is stated in this clause, particularly if doing so will reduce the Stamp Duty Land Tax payable on the transfer or conveyance (more about this later).

8. **Covenants:** These are usually included in the contract by reference to the Office Copies for registered land. However, they may be noted in the contract and a full copy may be attached to the draft contract. This is usually only appropriate on sales of part of land where the vendor wishes to take covenants from the purchaser to restrict the use of land in the future or of unregistered land.

   The seller should always mention those covenants he knows of, even if he has no idea who can enforce them, or whether they can be enforced. The buyer must decide what relevance they have. The clause in the contract will say that the purchaser, having been supplied with a copy, is deemed to have full knowledge of them and no requisitions (questions) or objections shall be raised in respect thereof. Normally this means that the vendor will answer questions about the covenants having been kept, but that he is not getting himself involved in trying to get any of them changed and the purchaser cannot back out just because something turns out to be worse than he first thought.

9. **Freehold or leasehold:** In the latter case the lease should be referred to. Put the lease through the copier and attach to the draft contract. Again provide in the draft contract that there are to be no requisitions or objections, but be prepared to answer sensible questions if you know the answer for sure. If you are buying freehold and Skinner offers limited title guarantee or puts any fancy work on the contract that you do not easily understand, the Registrar will always give limited guarantee in cases of doubt. Do remember though that limited guarantee is insufficient for those purchasers with a mortgage. Full title guarantee will usually be required as this is a higher assurance as to the title.

10. **The rate of interest to be paid or contract rate** for the period between the completion date in the contract, and the date on which completion actually happens. Fix the rate at a little above your bank's minimum lending rate, or the prevailing building society rate, or just write 'Law Society rate', which is usually a rate above the base rate, currently four per cent above the base rate of Barclays Bank.

11. **Title:** A statement about how the vendor intends to prove that he is the owner. This is done by:

    (a) registered property: saying that the Office Copies will be supplied; or

(b) unregistered property: quoting a conveyance or some other good root of title of the property which is at least 15 years old. More about (a) and (b) later.

12. **Risk:** What happens if the house is destroyed or seriously damaged between the date you exchange contracts and the date you were to complete? If the Law Society's contract is being used, the answer is simple. The buyer can withdraw from the contract and ask for his deposit back.

Under the Standard Conditions of Sale, the risk remains with the seller until completion but solicitors do usually vary this in the contract depending on the circumstances.

Be very wary of buying under a contract that places the risk on the buyer from date of exchange. In the absence of any contract clause to the contrary, when the parties exchange contracts, in a sense the property becomes the buyer's. It is his property subject only to paying the price and taking a transfer or conveyance. So at common law, if it is destroyed, it is his problem. It may also be the seller's if the buyer cannot raise funds to complete – which may well be the position if money is being borrowed.

Historically, the buyer is insured from exchange but insurance is not the whole answer. The reinstatement monies are not really likely to equal the purchase price and a bridging loan to complete may not be readily available given the buyer needs the purchase price but the land and the smouldering ruins are likely to be worth considerably less. If you draft your contract using the Law Society's contract, you are unlikely to change the position, but if you are the buyer reading this to see what the vendor is up to, note that if the written contract says 'Condition 5.1 does not apply', it means the risk is yours!

So that's what a basic contract is all about. Further clauses can be added, and in the crusade against the gazumper on the one hand and the gazoffer on the other, suggestions follow in the next chapter for some additional clauses that have already saved thousands from nervous breakdown.

Completed example of Standard Conditions of Sale

CONTRACT
Incorporating the Standard Conditions of Sale (Fourth Edition)

Date	:	*12 July 2006*
Seller	:	*Mr & Mrs R Bold*
		14 Plevna Place, Blossomton ED2 8JD
Buyer	:	*Mr John Smith*
		12 Quain Road, London SW10 7XX
Property (freehold/leasehold)	:	*14 Plevna Place, Blossomton BX10 1AB*
Title number/root of title	:	*EDN999707*
Specified incumbrances	:	*N/A*
Title guarantee (full/limited)	:	*Full*
Completion date	:	*21 August 2006*
Contract rate	:	
Purchase price	:	*£155,000*
Deposit	:	*£15,500*
Chattels price (if separate)	:	
Balance	:	

The seller will sell and the buyer will buy the property for the purchase price.

WARNING	Signed
This is a formal document, designed to create legal rights and legal obligations. Take advice before using it.	*Clint Smart* *Constance Smart* *Thomas Bold* *Prudence Bold* <div align="right">Seller/Buyer</div>

Completed example of Standard Conditions of Sale (continued)

STANDARD CONDITIONS OF SALE (FOURTH EDITION)
(NATIONAL CONDITIONS OF SALE 24th EDITION, LAW SOCIETY'S CONDITIONS OF SALE 2003)

1. **GENERAL**

1.1 **Definitions**

1.1.1 In these conditions:
- (a) "accrued interest" means:
  - (i) if money has been placed on deposit or in a building society share account, the interest actually earned
  - (ii) otherwise, the interest which might reasonably have been earned by depositing the money at interest on seven days' notice of withdrawal with a clearing bank

  less, in either case, any proper charges for handling the money
- (b) "chattels price" means any separate amount payable for chattels included in the contract
- (c) "clearing bank" means a bank which is a shareholder in CHAPS Clearing Co. Limited.
- (d) "completion date" has the meaning given in condition 6.1.1
- (e) "contract rate" means the Law Society's interest rate from time to time in force
- (f) "conveyancer" means a solicitor, barrister, duly certified notary public, licensed conveyancer or recognised body under sections 9 or 23 of the Administration of Justice Act 1985
- (g) "direct credit" means a direct transfer of cleared funds to an account nominated by the seller's conveyancer and maintained by a clearing bank
- (h) "lease" includes sub-lease, tenancy and agreement for a lease or sub-lease
- (i) "notice to complete" means a notice requiring completion of the contract in accordance with condition 6
- (j) "public requirement" means any notice, order or proposal given or made (whether before or after the date of the contract) by a body acting on statutory authority
- (k) "requisition" includes objection
- (l) "transfer" includes conveyance and assignment
- (m) "working day" means any day from Monday to Friday (inclusive) which is not Christmas Day, Good Friday or a statutory Bank Holiday.

1.1.2 In these conditions the terms "absolute title" and "official copies" have the special meanings given to them by the Land Registration Act 2002.

1.1.3 A party is ready, able and willing to complete:
- (a) if he could be, but for the default of the other party, and
- (b) in the case of the seller, even though the property remains subject to a mortgage, if the amount to be paid on completion enables the property to be transferred freed of all mortgages (except any to which the sale is expressly subject).

1.1.4 These conditions apply except as varied or excluded by the contract.

1.2 **Joint parties**
If there is more than one seller or more than one buyer, the obligations which they undertake can be enforced against them all jointly or against each individually.

1.3 **Notices and documents**

1.3.1 A notice required or authorised by the contract must be in writing.

1.3.2 Giving a notice or delivering a document to a party's conveyancer has the same effect as giving or delivering it to that party.

1.3.3 Where delivery of the original document is not essential, a notice or document is validly given or sent if it is sent:
- (a) by fax, or
- (b) by e-mail to an e-mail address for the intended recipient given in the contract.

1.3.4 Subject to conditions 1.3.5 to1.3.7, a notice is given and a document is delivered when it is received.

1.3.5
- (a) A notice or document sent through a document exchange is received when it is available for collection
- (b) A notice or document which is received after 4.00pm on a working day, or on a day which is not a working day, is to be treated as having been received on the next working day
- (c) An automated response to a notice or document sent by e-mail that the intended recipient is out of the office is to be treated as proof that the notice or document was not received.

1.3.6 Condition 1.3.7 applies unless there is proof:
- (a) that a notice or document has not been received, or
- (b) of when it was received.

1.3.7 A notice or document sent by the following means is treated as having been received as follows:

(a) by first-class post:	before 4.00pm on the second working day after posting
(b) by second-class post:	before 4.00pm on the third working day after posting
(c) through a document exchange:	before 4.00pm on the first working day after the day on which it would normally be available for collection by the addressee
(d) by fax:	one hour after despatch
(e) by e-mail:	before 4.00pm on the first working day after despatch.

1.4 **VAT**

1.4.1 An obligation to pay money includes an obligation to pay any value added tax chargeable in respect of that payment.

1.4.2 All sums made payable by the contract are exclusive of value added tax.

1.5 **Assignment**
The buyer is not entitled to transfer the benefit of the contract.

2. **FORMATION**

2.1 **Date**

2.1.1 If the parties intend to make a contract by exchanging duplicate copies by post or through a document exchange, the contract is made when the last copy is posted or deposited at the document exchange.

2.1.2 If the parties' conveyancers agree to treat exchange as taking place before duplicate copies are actually exchanged, the contract is made as so agreed.

2.2 **Deposit**

2.2.1 The buyer is to pay or send a deposit of 10 per cent of the total of the purchase price and the chattels price no later than the date of the contract.

2.2.2 If a cheque tendered in payment of all or part of the deposit is dishonoured when first presented, the seller may, within seven working days of being notified that the cheque has been dishonoured, give notice to the buyer that the contract is discharged by the buyer's breach.

2.2.3 Conditions 2.2.4 to 2.2.6 do not apply on a sale by auction.

2.2.4 The deposit is to be paid by direct credit or to the seller's conveyancer by a cheque drawn on a solicitor's or licensed conveyancer's client account.

2.2.5 If before completion date the seller agrees to buy another property in England and Wales for his residence, he may use all or any part of the deposit as a deposit in that transaction to be held on terms to the same effect as this condition and condition 2.2.6.

2.2.6 Any deposit or part of a deposit not being used in accordance with condition 2.2.5 is to be held by the seller's conveyancer as stakeholder on terms that on completion it is paid to the seller with accrued interest.

2.3 **Auctions**

2.3.1 On a sale by auction the following conditions apply to the property and, if it is sold in lots, to each lot.

2.3.2 The sale is subject to a reserve price.

2.3.3 The seller, or a person on his behalf, may bid up to the reserve price.

2.3.4 The auctioneer may refuse any bid.

2.3.5 If there is a dispute about a bid, the auctioneer may resolve the dispute or restart the auction at the last undisputed bid.

2.3.6 The deposit is to be paid to the auctioneer as agent for the seller.

3. **MATTERS AFFECTING THE PROPERTY**

3.1 **Freedom from incumbrances**

3.1.1 The seller is selling the property free from incumbrances, other than those mentioned in condition 3.1.2.

3.1.2 The incumbrances subject to which the property is sold are:
- (a) those specified in the contract
- (b) those discoverable by inspection of the property before the contract
- (c) those the seller does not and could not reasonably know about
- (d) entries made before the date of the contract in any public register except those maintained by the Land Registry or its Land Charges Department or by Companies House
- (e) public requirements.

3.1.3 After the contract is made, the seller is to give the buyer written details without delay of any new public requirement and of anything in writing which he learns about concerning a matter covered by condition 3.1.2.

3.1.4 The buyer is to bear the cost of complying with any outstanding public requirement and is to indemnify the seller against any liability resulting from a public requirement.

3.2 **Physical state**

3.2.1 The buyer accepts the property in the physical state it is in at the date of the contract unless the seller is building or converting it.

3.2.2 A leasehold property is sold subject to any subsisting breach of a condition or tenant's obligation relating to the physical state of the property which renders the lease liable to forfeiture.

3.2.3 A sub-lease is granted subject to any subsisting breach of a condition or tenant's obligation relating to the physical state of the property which renders the seller's own lease liable to forfeiture.

3.3 **Leases affecting the property**

3.3.1 The following provisions apply if any part of the property is sold subject to a lease.

3.3.2
- (a) The seller having provided the buyer with full details of each lease or copies of the documents embodying the lease terms, the buyer is treated as entering into the contract knowing and fully accepting those terms.
- (b) The seller is to inform the buyer without delay if the lease ends or if the seller learns of any application by the tenant in connection with the lease; the seller is then to act as the buyer reasonably directs, and the buyer is to indemnify him against all consequent loss and expense.
- (c) Except with the buyer's consent, the seller is not to agree to any proposal to change the lease terms nor to take any step to end the lease.
- (d) The seller is to inform the buyer without delay of any change to the lease terms which may be proposed or agreed.
- (e) The buyer is to indemnify the seller against all claims arising from the lease after actual completion; this includes claims which are unenforceable against a buyer for want of registration.
- (f) The seller takes no responsibility for what rent is lawfully recoverable, nor for whether or how any legislation affects the lease.
- (g) If the let land is not wholly within the property, the seller may apportion the rent.

3.4 **Retained land**
Where after the transfer the seller will be retaining land near the property:
- (a) the buyer will have no right of light or air over the retained land, but
- (b) in other respects the seller and the buyer will each have the rights over the land of the other which they would have had if they were two separate buyers to whom the seller had made simultaneous transfers of the property and the retained land.

The transfer is to contain appropriate express terms.

4. **TITLE AND TRANSFER**

4.1 **Proof of title**

4.1.1 Without cost to the buyer, the seller is to provide the buyer with proof of the title to the property and of his ability to transfer it, or to procure its transfer.

4.1.2 Where the property has a registered title the proof is to include official copies of the items referred to in rules 134(1)(a) and (b) and 135(1)(a) of the Land Registration Rules 2003, so far as they are not to be discharged or overridden at or before completion.

4.1.3 Where the property has an unregistered title, the proof is to include:
- (a) an abstract of title or an epitome of title with photocopies of the documents, and
- (b) production of every document or an abstract, epitome or copy of it with an original marking by a conveyancer either against the original or an examined abstract or an examined copy.

4.2 **Requisitions**

4.2.1 The buyer may not raise requisitions:
- (a) on the title shown by the seller taking the steps described in condition 4.1.1 before the contract was made
- (b) in relation to the matters covered by condition 3.1.2.

4.2.2 Notwithstanding condition 4.2.1, the buyer may, within six working days of a matter coming to his attention after the contract was made, raise written requisitions on that matter. In that event, steps 3 and 4 in condition 4.3.1 apply.

4.2.3 On the expiry of the relevant time limit under condition 4.2.2 or condition 4.3.1, the buyer loses his right to raise requisitions or to make observations.

4.3 **Timetable**

4.3.1 Subject to condition 4.2 and to the extent that the seller did not take the steps described in condition 4.1.1 before the contract was made, the following are the steps for deducing and investigating the title to the property to be taken within the following time limits:

Step	Time Limit
1. The seller is to comply with condition 4.1.1	Immediately after making the contract
2. The buyer may raise written requisitions	Six working days after either the date of the contract or the date of delivery of the seller's proof of title on which the requisitions are raised, whichever is the later
3. The seller is to reply in writing to any requisitions raised	Four working days after receiving the requisitions
4. The buyer may make written observations on the seller's replies	Three working days after receiving the replies

The time limit on the buyer's right to raise requisitions applies even where the seller supplies incomplete evidence of his title, but the buyer may, within six working days from delivery of any further evidence, raise further requisitions resulting from that evidence.

4.3.2 The parties are to take the following steps to prepare and agree the transfer of the property within the following time limits:

Step	Time Limit
A. The buyer is to send the seller a draft transfer	At least twelve working days before completion date
B. The seller is to approve or revise that draft and either return it or retain it for use as the actual transfer	Four working days after delivery of the draft transfer
C. If the draft is returned the buyer is to send an engrossment to the seller	At least five working days before completion date

4.3.3 Periods of time under conditions 4.3.1 and 4.3.2 may run concurrently.

4.3.4 If the period between the date of the contract and completion date is less than 15 working days, the time limits in conditions 4.2.2, 4.3.1 and 4.3.2 are to be reduced by the same proportion as that period bears to the period of 15 working days. Fractions of a working day are to be rounded down except that the time limit to perform any step is not to be less than one working day.

4.4 **Defining the property**

4.4.1 The seller need not:
- (a) prove the exact boundaries of the property
- (b) prove who owns fences, ditches, hedges or walls
- (c) separately identify parts of the property with different titles

further than he may be able to do from information in his possession.

4.4.2 The buyer may, if it is reasonable, require the seller to make or obtain, pay for and hand over a statutory declaration about facts relevant to the matters mentioned in condition 4.4.1. The form of the declaration is to be agreed by the buyer, who must not unreasonably withhold his agreement.

4.5 **Rents and rentcharges**
The fact that a rent or rentcharge, whether payable or receivable by the owner of the property, has been, or will on completion be, informally apportioned is not to be regarded as a defect in title.

Completed example of Standard Conditions of Sale (continued)

4.6 **Transfer**

4.6.1 The buyer does not prejudice his right to raise requisitions, or to require replies to any raised, by taking any steps in relation to preparing or agreeing the transfer.

4.6.2 Subject to condition 4.6.3, the seller is to transfer the property with full title guarantee.

4.6.3 The transfer is to have effect as if the disposition is expressly made subject to all matters covered by condition 3.1.2.

4.6.4 If after completion the seller will remain bound by any obligation affecting the property which was disclosed to the buyer before the contract was made, but the law does not imply any covenant by the buyer to indemnify the seller against liability for future breaches of it:
(a) the buyer is to covenant in the transfer to indemnify the seller against liability for any future breach of the obligation and to perform it from then on, and
(b) if required by the seller, the buyer is to execute and deliver to the seller on completion a duplicate transfer prepared by the buyer.

4.6.5 The seller is to arrange at his expense that, in relation to every document of title which the buyer does not receive on completion, the buyer is to have the benefit of:
(a) a written acknowledgement of his right to its production, and
(b) a written undertaking for its safe custody (except while it is held by a mortgagee or by someone in a fiduciary capacity).

5. **PENDING COMPLETION**

5.1 **Responsibility for property**

5.1.1 The seller will transfer the property in the same physical state as it was at the date of the contract (except for fair wear and tear), which means that the seller retains the risk until completion.

5.1.2 If at any time before completion the physical state of the property makes it unusable for its purpose at the date of the contract:
(a) the buyer may rescind the contract
(b) the seller may rescind the contract where the property has become unusable for that purpose as a result of damage against which the seller could not reasonably have insured, or which it is not legally possible for the seller to make good.

5.1.3 The seller is under no obligation to the buyer to insure the property.

5.1.4 Section 47 of the Law of Property Act 1925 does not apply.

5.2 **Occupation by buyer**

5.2.1 If the buyer is not already lawfully in the property, and the seller agrees to let him into occupation, the buyer occupies on the following terms.

5.2.2 The buyer is a licensee and not a tenant. The terms of the licence are that the buyer:
(a) cannot transfer it
(b) may permit members of his household to occupy the property
(c) is to pay or indemnify the seller against all outgoings and other expenses in respect of the property
(d) is to pay the seller a fee calculated at the contract rate on a sum equal to the purchase price and the chattels price (less any deposit paid) for the period of the licence
(e) is entitled to any rents and profits from any part of the property which he does not occupy
(f) is to keep the property in as good a state of repair as it was in when he went into occupation (except for fair wear and tear) and is not to alter it
(g) is to insure the property in a sum which is not less than the purchase price against all risks in respect of which comparable premises are normally insured
(h) is to quit the property when the licence ends.

5.2.3 On the creation of the buyer's licence, condition 5.1 ceases to apply, which means that the buyer then assumes the risk until completion.

5.2.4 The buyer is not in occupation for the purposes of this condition if he merely exercises rights of access given solely to do work agreed by the seller.

5.2.5 The buyer's licence ends on the earliest of: completion date, rescission of the contract or when five working days' notice given by one party to the other takes effect.

5.2.6 If the buyer is in occupation of the property after his licence has come to an end and the contract is subsequently completed he is to pay the seller compensation for his continued occupation calculated at the same rate as the fee mentioned in condition 5.2.2(d).

5.2.7 The buyer's right to raise requisitions is unaffected.

6. **COMPLETION**

6.1 **Date**

6.1.1 Completion date is twenty working days after the date of the contract but time is not of the essence of the contract unless a notice to complete has been served.

6.1.2 If the money due on completion is received after 2.00pm, completion is to be treated, for the purposes only of conditions 6.3 and 7.3, as taking place on the next working day as a result of the buyer's default.

6.1.3 Condition 6.1.2 does not apply and the seller is treated as in default if:
(i) the sale is with vacant possession of the property or any part of it, and
(ii) the buyer is ready, able and willing to complete but does not pay the money due on completion until after 2.00pm because the seller has not vacated the property or that part by that time.

6.2 **Arrangements and place**

6.2.1 The buyer's conveyancer and the seller's conveyancer are to co-operate in agreeing arrangements for completing the contract.

6.2.2 Completion is to take place in England and Wales, either at the seller's conveyancer's office or at some other place which the seller reasonably specifies.

6.3 **Apportionments**

6.3.1 Income and outgoings of the property are to be apportioned between the parties so far as the change of ownership on completion will affect entitlement to receive or liability to pay them.

6.3.2 If the whole property is sold with vacant possession or the seller exercises his option in condition 7.3.4, apportionment is to be made with effect from the date of actual completion; otherwise, it is to be made from completion date.

6.3.3 In apportioning any sum, it is to be assumed that the seller owns the property until the end of the day from which apportionment is made and that the sum accrues from day to day at the rate at which it is payable on that day.

6.3.4 For the purpose of apportioning income and outgoings, it is to be assumed that they accrue at an equal daily rate throughout the year.

6.3.5 When a sum to be apportioned is not known or easily ascertainable at completion, a provisional apportionment is to be made according to the best estimate available. As soon as the amount is known, a final apportionment is to be made and notified to the other party. Any resulting balance is to be paid no more than ten working days later, and if not then paid the balance is to bear interest at the contract rate from then until payment.

6.3.6 Compensation payable under condition 5.2.6 is not to be apportioned.

6.4 **Amount payable**

The amount payable by the buyer on completion is the purchase price and the chattels price (less any deposit already paid to the seller or his agent) adjusted to take account of:
(a) apportionments made under condition 6.3
(b) any compensation to be paid or allowed under condition 7.3.

6.5 **Title deeds**

6.5.1 As soon as the buyer has complied with all his obligations on completion the seller must hand over the documents of title.

6.5.2 Condition 6.5.1 does not apply to any documents of title relating to land being retained by the seller after completion.

6.6 **Rent receipts**

The buyer is to assume that whoever gave any receipt for a payment of rent or service charge which the seller produces was the person or the agent of the person then entitled to that rent or service charge.

6.7 **Means of payment**

The buyer is to pay the money due on completion by direct credit and, if appropriate, an unconditional release of a deposit held by a stakeholder.

6.8 **Notice to complete**

6.8.1 At any time on or after completion date, a party who is ready, able and willing to complete may give the other a notice to complete.

6.8.2 The parties are to complete the contract within ten working days of giving a notice to complete, excluding the day on which the notice is given. For this purpose, time is of the essence of the contract.

6.8.3 On receipt of a notice to complete:
(a) if the buyer paid no deposit, he is forthwith to pay a deposit of 10 per cent
(b) if the buyer paid a deposit of less than 10 per cent, he is forthwith to pay a further deposit equal to the balance of that 10 per cent.

7. **REMEDIES**

7.1 **Errors and omissions**

7.1.1 If any plan or statement in the contract, or in the negotiations leading to it, is or was misleading or inaccurate due to an error or omission, the remedies available are as follows.

7.1.2 When there is a material difference between the description or value of the property, or of any of the chattels included in the contract, as represented and as it is, the buyer is entitled to damages.

7.1.3 An error or omission only entitles the buyer to rescind the contract:
(a) where it results from fraud or recklessness, or
(b) where he would be obliged, to his prejudice, to accept property differing substantially (in quantity, quality or tenure) from what the error or omission had led him to expect.

7.2 **Rescission**

If either party rescinds the contract:
(a) unless the rescission is a result of the buyer's breach of contract the deposit is to be repaid to the buyer with accrued interest
(b) the buyer is to return any documents he received from the seller and is to cancel any registration of the contract.

7.3 **Late completion**

7.3.1 If there is default by either or both of the parties in performing their obligations under the contract and completion is delayed, the party whose total period of default is the greater is to pay compensation to the other party.

7.3.2 Compensation is calculated at the contract rate on an amount equal to the purchase price and the chattels price, less (where the buyer is the paying party) any deposit paid, for the period by which the paying party's default exceeds that of the receiving party, or, if shorter, the period between completion date and actual completion.

7.3.3 Any claim for loss resulting from delayed completion is to be reduced by any compensation paid under this contract.

7.3.4 Where the buyer holds the property as tenant of the seller and completion is delayed, the seller may give notice to the buyer, before the date of actual completion, that he intends to take the net income from the property until completion. If he does so, he cannot claim compensation under condition 7.3.1 as well.

7.4 **After completion**

Completion does not cancel liability to perform any outstanding obligation under this contract.

7.5 **Buyer's failure to comply with notice to complete**

7.5.1 If the buyer fails to complete in accordance with a notice to complete, the following terms apply.

7.5.2 The seller may rescind the contract, and if he does so:
(a) he may
(i) forfeit and keep any deposit and accrued interest
(ii) resell the property and any chattels included in the contract
(iii) claim damages
(b) the buyer is to return any documents he received from the seller and is to cancel any registration of the contract.

7.5.3 The seller retains his other rights and remedies.

7.6 **Seller's failure to comply with notice to complete**

7.6.1 If the seller fails to complete in accordance with a notice to complete, the following terms apply.

7.6.2 The buyer may rescind the contract, and if he does so:
(a) the deposit is to be repaid to the buyer with accrued interest
(b) the buyer is to return any documents he received from the seller and is, at the seller's expense, to cancel any registration of the contract.

7.6.3 The buyer retains his other rights and remedies.

8. **LEASEHOLD PROPERTY**

8.1 **Existing leases**

8.1.1 The following provisions apply to a sale of leasehold land.

8.1.2 The seller having provided the buyer with copies of the documents embodying the lease terms, the buyer is treated as entering into the contract knowing and fully accepting those terms.

8.1.3 The seller is to comply with any lease obligations requiring the tenant to insure the property.

8.2 **New leases**

8.2.1 The following provisions apply to a contract to grant a new lease.

8.2.2 The conditions apply so that:
"seller" means the proposed landlord
"buyer" means the proposed tenant
"purchase price" means the premium to be paid on the grant of a lease.

8.2.3 The lease is to be in the form of the draft attached to the contract.

8.2.4 If the term of the new lease will exceed seven years, the seller is to deduce a title which will enable the buyer to register the lease at the Land Registry with an absolute title.

8.2.5 The seller is to engross the lease and a counterpart of it and is to send the counterpart to the buyer at least five working days before completion date.

8.2.6 The buyer is to execute the counterpart and deliver it to the seller on completion.

8.3 **Consent**

8.3.1 (a) The following provisions apply if a consent to let, assign or sub-let is required to complete the contract
(b) In this condition "consent" means consent in the form which satisfies the requirement to obtain it.

8.3.2 (a) The seller is to apply for the consent at his expense, and to use all reasonable efforts to obtain it
(b) The buyer is to provide all information and references reasonably required.

8.3.3 Unless he is in breach of his obligation under condition 8.3.2, either party may rescind the contract by notice to the other party if three working days before completion date (or before a later date on which the parties have agreed to complete the contract):
(a) the consent has not been given, or
(b) the consent has been given subject to a condition to which a party reasonably objects.
In that case, neither party is to be treated as in breach of contract and condition 7.2 applies.

9. **COMMONHOLD LAND**

9.1 Terms used in this condition have the special meanings given to them in Part 1 of the Commonhold and Leasehold Reform Act 2002.

9.2 This condition applies to a disposition of commonhold land.

9.3 The seller having provided the buyer with copies of the current versions of the memorandum and articles of the commonhold association and of the commonhold community statement, the buyer is treated as entering into the contract knowing and fully accepting their terms.

9.4 If the contract is for the sale of property which is or includes part only of a commonhold unit:
(a) the seller is to apply for the written consent of the commonhold association at his expense and is to use all reasonable efforts to obtain it
(b) either the seller, unless he is in breach of his obligation under paragraph (a), or the buyer may rescind the contract by notice to the other party if three working days before completion date (or before a later date on which the parties have agreed to complete the contract) the consent has not been given. In that case, neither party is to be treated as in breach of contract and condition 7.2 applies.

10. **CHATTELS**

10.1 The following provisions apply to any chattels which are included in the contract, whether or not a separate price is to be paid for them.

10.2 The contract takes effect as a contract for sale of goods.

10.3 The buyer takes the chattels in the physical state they are in at the date of the contract.

10.4 Ownership of the chattels passes to the buyer on actual completion.

Completed example of Standard Conditions of Sale (continued)

SPECIAL CONDITIONS

1. (a) This contract incorporates the Standard Conditions of Sale (Fourth Edition).

   (b) The terms used in this contract have the same meaning when used in the Conditions.

2. Subject to the terms of this contract and to the Standard Conditions of Sale, the seller is to transfer the property with either full title guarantee or limited title guarantee, as specified on the front page.

3. The chattels which are on the property and are set out on any attached list are included in the sale and the buyer is to pay the chattels price for them.

4. The property is sold with vacant possession.

(or) 4. The property is sold subject to the following leases or tenancies:

Seller's conveyancers*:

Buyer's conveyancers*:

*Adding an e-mail address authorises service by e-mail: see condition 1.3.3(b)

©2003 Oyez The Solicitors' Law Stationery Society Ltd,
7 Spa Road, London SE16 3QQ

© 2003 The Law Society

11.2003 F41896
5065046
★ ★ ★ ★
4th Edition

Standard Conditions of Sale
Copyright in this Form and its contents rests jointly in SLSS Limited and the Law Society

CHAPTER 10

Gazumping and gazoffing

No buyer wants to be gazumped.

Most vendors think they should get more than they have already been offered (and accepted verbally), and fancy a bit of gazumping for themselves.

Vendors hate it when their subject to contract buyer goes off – they are *gazoffed*.

So this will be an even-handed chapter. In business, few people do their opposite numbers any favours. Why should you expect the housing business to be any different?

You must keep control of events and keep your wits about you, as you do when buying a car or a cardigan. You can't possibly win if you 'leave it all' to solicitors and agents. The lazy and shy buy themselves a lot of worry and aggravation by allowing themselves to be tied up with an unsatisfactory buyer or seller, about whom they do not know enough. They bring in too many cooks, who before spoiling the broth consume a lot of it.

Weak chains that leave you wide open to a gazumper or a gazoffer are created because people who wouldn't dream of going out to buy anything else without cash or credit card gaily go viewing houses and 'promising' to buy tens of thousands of pounds' worth of bricks and mortar, without a round'un in their pockets. Vendors have already promised 'to buy something from someone who has already promised' – and so on and so forth. The pressure is on from day one of the promise. Mortgages being sought; solicitors making mountains out of molehill 'searches'; buyers have to be found to close one end of the chain and vendors the other. The weeks tick by with everybody making excuses to everybody.

Agencies prefer purchasers who have houses for sale, as they are a fruitful source of business. Failing that, someone who will enrich them by over £600 by buying a mortgage endowment scheme from their agency. But the slightest hiccup or attack of greed has only to rear its ugly head and it's trouble for all. Big trouble.

It is time for some novel ideas. They won't come from solicitors, estate agents or moneylenders, with whom the market is crowded, all trying to get a slice of your cake. Any time they have for inventive thinking is devoted to that one objective.

The government's conveyancing committee found that over the last 10–15 years, the period of time a sale remains subject to contract has gradually lengthened.

One would have predicted that the time taken would have become shorter. Mortgages are easier to get than they have ever been; a prime reason why purchasers can't sign up is, always was and always will be that they need to be satisfied that the vendor has good title to the property. In those last 15 years, the areas of the country covered by the Land Registry have increased by nearly 50 per cent. Not much remains unregistered. Everybody in the business knows that anything to do with contracts and conveyancing is simpler, easier and swifter once property is registered than it was before.

Everybody also knows that the longer the time between a buyer saying 'I will' and a contract being signed, the greater the opportunity for gazumping, gazoffing and corruption.

So why don't the parties get signed up? What has happened to cause the delay in getting on contract?

The only coherent reasons that come from the professionals are that some local authorities take weeks and months to return the searches, and: 'We are still pursuing our enquiries on the title'.

Less coherent to the layperson, but equally daft, is: 'We are waiting for engrossments'. 'Engross' means 'write', and engrossing a contract means entering a few lines into the blanks on a printed form.

By the time you have read a little more, you will recognise these for the threadbare excuses that they are, for not having done little jobs that could have been done in their own offices. For instance, you can see in the Appendices a copy of an actual search form; judge for yourself how long it would take to fill that in and despatch.

What is new is the proliferation and size of chains in which so-called purchasers haven't yet signed up with their own purchasers, who haven't yet signed up with theirs, even unto the third and fourth 'purchaser'. There are more and longer chains. This is what is new. Why?

How many estate agents per 100,000 houses were there in your town 15 years ago? How many are there today? Four times, five times, six times? And they are all fighting for a share of what remains of the saleable houses, after nearly a third of the vendors have chosen the best purchasers for themselves and given the agencies the cold shoulder. So when an agency gets a house that is really saleable and can choose among potential buyers, it would be daft to choose someone who had nothing to sell! Ergo, a chain is born.

Agents can be very persuasive when they are forging another link in the paper chain. They seem to have a good argument when they say it saves a lot of time and prevents breakdowns in communication if you take their total package, thus keeping the whole thing under one roof. The promise is false; it can't be kept, because, as we have seen, the people who attempt to hold chains together are solicitors, and it is a rigid rule of the Law Society (their union) that a solicitor must not act for both parties to a transaction unless both clients are previously established as such. So if there is to be a master mariner at the tiller to navigate seas littered with the twin icebergs of gazumpers and gazoffers, it can only be yourself.

The cure

Flitsville no longer suits you, and you will be a winner if you can decide to sell first. So be business-like, sit down quietly with everybody who lives in your house and whose life will be affected, and decide what you will do, where you will go, how much you can afford, how you will buy, and how you will go about selling.

If you want to move to within a few miles of where you are now, join the 90 per cent all of house buyers who move less than 15 miles. Look at the local property-for-sale columns. How many houses are advertised in the price bracket you will be able to afford? How many more are skulking in agents' files? If, at the time of your family conference, there are half-a-dozen houses for sale that would suit you (if the vendors knocked a couple of thousand off), be sure that if, when you have sold yours, all those six have been sold or withdrawn, another five or six will have taken their place. Why get yourself into chains, gazumping, gazoffing and generally wasting your time, survey and other fees and everybody else's? You can avoid all this if you sell first. And be sure that when you turn up able to produce an official contract for sale of your own house, and mortgage offer, you will be a sight for sore eyes to any vendor. If they say they can't move out in time, put it to them, 'You could move in with relatives, friends, bed and breakfast, or pay for us to go in an hotel for the interim.'

A vendor needs to find out the strength of an interested viewer's capacity to buy. In order of preference they are:

1. first-time buyers who have a note from a lender saying that, subject to valuation, more than sufficient monies to buy your house will be on offer (even try to see their bank book showing that they have the difference between the loan and the purchase price on deposit);

2. an 'own house sold' buyer (see their contract);

3. a 'must sell my own house' buyer.

The excuse 'We have not completed the searches' sounds awful, doesn't it? In reality, searching at this stage consists in sending off two forms with ready-printed questions on them to the local authority, which fills in the answers and returns them.

Think! Surely any vendor's Skinner should know how long the local authority is taking to return search forms in that area, so why didn't the agency which brags that it liaises with solicitors get the process started with the new property when it put Flitsville on the market? What are these searches?

How to prepare the 'legal' side of your sale

Not only purchasers need replies to the local authority searches before putting pen to contract. If there is a skeleton or a potential crock of gold in the council's cupboard, don't you think, as a vendor, that it would be a good thing if you knew these things before putting your house on the market? You can easily search to find out if your house is registered. If you don't know whether or not your house is registered, you find out by applying for an 'Index Map Search'. You fill in Form SIM including a description of the property, enclose the relevant fee and the Land Registry will tell you whether your house is registered, and the title number. If it is registered, all the nonsense about investigating title is a cover-up for delay and an attempt to justify high fees. So you can prove your title before you start to sell, because once anyone's ownership has been registered at HM Land Registry that title of ownership is guaranteed by the state. If the house is paid for, you should be in possession of your Land Certificate. However, since the Land Registration Act 2002 came into force in October 2003 the Land Registry considers that a Land Certificate no longer has any legal significance. The vendor proves title by obtaining an official copy of the register. This is done by sending off Form OC1 (with current £4 fee) and get a photocopy from the Registry. You can show this copy to serious prospects; that's the investigation of title seen off.

The last place on earth to have left deeds or Land Certificates is a solicitor's office. I have seen piles of deeds on open wooden shelves, stuffed into old sideboards and, at best, 'fire resistant' metal cupboards. A solicitor likes you to leave valuable documents with him. It is his way of trying to make sure that you will go to him again and again. So well and good if this arrangement suits both parties, but it is nice to be able to change. There is power in holding the deeds – so have that power for yourself. Get them into the old homestead – safely filed under the piano lid as did the old gent, to whom I will introduce you later.

At this stage it is worth checking the Council of Mortgage Lenders' *Handbook* referred to in chapter 1 just to see if you have some problems that need to be addressed. Do you have deeds that refer to covenants but details on which are not available? Did you get married a second time and think it was a wonderful idea to transfer your houses to you and your new husband or wife? These and other situations are problem areas and although you might ignore them, your buyer is unlikely to do so. See what the *Handbook* says about indemnity insurance.

Not STC, but CST (subject to contract, contract subject to)

There will be occasions where the vendor and his purchaser very much want to secure the sale but cannot, because something is missing, for example uncertainty on a completion date, absence of a local authority search certificate, some problem in obtaining a satisfactory survey or perhaps a mortgage offer.

These are all problems that can be covered by an adequately drafted contract clause, or at least they can be if neither party has a problem with someone else they are dealing with in a chain. Perhaps the first rule to follow is do not contract to buy a new house if you have not sold your existing house. That can cause an expensive headache. Selling before buying is normally less of a gamble. You can at least park your belongings in store and yourself and your family with relatives. Perhaps this is not to be advised if property prices are moving up by the day! So if you wish to sell or buy and you can live with the uncertainty on the completion date and both sides are in this happy position, perhaps a completion date three to six months hence would give all concerned a chance to settle their affairs.

The other problems can be dealt with by making the 'contract subject to' or 'CST' to a satisfactory solution to the problem, in hand. This is usually unappealing to a buyer due to the great uncertainty of the matter. The buyer cannot ensure when or if the problem will be resolved. There could be a dispute as to whether it had been and this can make life difficult, particularly if there is a sale to tie in. However, should you agree to such a condition, the cardinal rule is to define what you need to know before you can safely go ahead; make sure the contract can be terminated if an answer is not forthcoming after two to three months (say) and decide how to link this to a completion date.

Suppose, for example, you want to exchange before you have a satisfactory search. You can make the contract subject to that, but questions need to be addressed. Satisfactory to whom and what would not be satisfactory? Suppose it shows the local authority is taking enforcement proceedings for the removal of an extension erected without planning permission? Would that be satisfactory? Probably not. Suppose it says they are widening a road

150 metres away? Would that be satisfactory? Think what questions are being asked, what the answers might be and what would not be acceptable. Generally, where these clauses are used, the parties agree a search is satisfactory if nothing is revealed that would have a material impact on the value of the house. This still leaves room for uncertainty and so if the buyer has a few bottom lines, cover them as well.

Suppose the buyer is willing to exchange if a satisfactory mortgage offer is available? Here too, what is satisfactory? Tie this down. If you are the buyer, perhaps any offer would be satisfactory, so if the seller has a relative who is a loan shark, perhaps the seller could engineer an offer 'you cannot refuse', to quote the movies.

Final comment: when drafting, you may know what you want and may be able to express it, but half the trick with any drafting is asking what you do not want. Make sure you cover it and if in doubt take the advice of a solicitor.

CHAPTER 11

The Registers

There are two systems of land conveyancing in England and Wales: the registered system, in which case title to the land is registered at the Land Registry, and the unregistered system, where the title is not registered at all. The unregistered is the older, but not many years will pass before all land is registered and thus conveyancing of property made much simpler for all. By the way, all references to land include everything built on it.

So, it helps if the layperson conveyancer gets an early grasp of the point that all conveyances are of *land* whether built on or not. Whether it sells for a million or one pound, the recipe is the same.

Official records of the property with which you are about to deal may be found in the three main categories of registry:

1. **The local council**, which are required to keep a register of notices affecting dangerous structures, public notices about infringements of building regulations, compulsory purchase orders, smoke control zones and other things they want to make sure do or do not happen to the property. When we come to it, you will see that you quite easily find out about that little lot by the simple expedient of sending off a couple of forms (LLC1 and CON 29) which have printed on them the questions you need to ask.

    When buying, you must always carry out a local search. In addition, an environmental search and a separate water drainage search are now required by lenders. It is important to realise that searches relate to the land you searched and no other. If the neighbours have planning permission to build something you will be offended by, the search will not tell you this, so if you are concerned, go to the council. Ask to see some staff in the planning department and ask what they have on the area that you think might be of importance.

2. **The Land Charges Department** at Plymouth, which keeps a register of various charges (mortgages), interests (e.g. rights of way or restrictive covenants) and notices such as second mortgages and Class F charges (right of spouse to occupy the matrimonial home) which relate to unregistered land so cannot be registered at the Land Registry. Pending writs or orders (bankruptcy) and pending actions (bankruptcy) are also kept at Plymouth, and you will need to send off a Form K16 to find out about any bankruptcy orders, writs, etc., whether you are buying on registered land or not.

3. **The Land Registry** is the third place where official records of land transactions are kept. This is the one that did the trick of simplifying the act of transferring the ownership of a house from one owner to another. Where a house is on registered land, all the tiresome business of proving title and tracing back the covenants and conditions through a series of conveyances is dispensed with, because it was done once and for all when the title was registered. And not only that; when the Land Registry sends you a copy of the register which shows that Feather owns the property, a state guarantee is incorporated in it. If the Register shows you as the owner, that ownership is guaranteed by the state.

Initially, the Land Registry Act 1862 covered only London and made registration of title compulsory for any sale which took place after 1898 in that area. No extension of the compulsory system of registration was made until 1925. Since 1925, the system of registration has been gradually extended to cover the whole country. However, though what you are buying is in a compulsory registration area, it doesn't mean to say that the owner's title is already registered. If the owner bought before compulsory registration came in for the area, it will only be registered if it is on a biggish, newish development, or if it was voluntarily registered (pre-1966).

The piecemeal extension of the registration system means that if you are buying in Lambeth, you can be certain that the title will be registered, unless it has been in the same ownership, or constantly transferred by way of gift, since February 1900 (or before); on the other hand, not many properties in Plymouth will be registered because registration only became compulsory in January 1974.

Until 1966, any owner could voluntarily apply to have his ownership registered. But in 1966, registration became limited to compulsory areas, plus those cases where the Registrar can make an exception, for example where the title deeds were lost or destroyed during the War, or where there are complex building developments taking place.

If you went to the Land Registry and looked at the actual register, what is produced on the following pages is what you would see. It is also what would be reproduced on the Land Certificate in Mr and Mrs Smart's possession, if they had no mortgage. In view of Charge No. 3 in the Charges Register, the Land Certificate would have been held at the Land Registry, and a Charge Certificate issued to and held by the Building Society as proof of their interest. Following the coming into force of the Land Registration Act 2002, Charge Certificates are no longer issued and the Land Registry will simply supply the lender with a copy of the register. Registered owners and mortgage lenders will also be able to obtain a title information document, but this is for information only. As you will by now appreciate, what matters is the official copy of the register.

Though we refer to the Land Registry (singular) it contains a number of registers (plural). These are: The Property Register, Proprietorship Register and Charges Register. The references made to your property in these registers constitute what used to be known as the 'deeds' to your property and can consist of as few as four pieces of paper having as little as two dozen lines of typing on them.

The Registrar will, at a cost of just a few pounds, supply copies ('Office Copies') of these entries. You are still the registered proprietor (i.e. shown as being the owner of the property at the Land Registry, albeit subject to the existence of the charge), even though your lender may own a significant part of the property by nature of the mortgage. The registers at the Land Registry are no longer confidential and anyone may inspect and obtain copies of the entries. Since 1 April 2000, registered titles disclose the price the registered proprietor paid for his interest in the property. A word of warning: a Land Registry photocopy of the title and of any deeds noted on the title can be produced in court as if they were original deeds; ordinary photocopies do not enjoy this statutory blessing and although this may seem a waste of time and money, a purchaser should always insist on an official Office Copy.

Specimen of Land Registry entry

HM Land Registry

Title Number : EDN999707

Edition Date : 16 March 1995

A: Property Register

containing the description of the registered land and the estate comprised in the Title.

EDENSHIRE : BLOSSOMTON

1. (16 March 1967) The **Freehold** land shown edged with red on the plan of the above Title filed at the Registry and being 14 Plevna Place, Blossomton, (ED2 8JD).

2. (16 March 1967) The land in this title has the benefit of the rights granted by but is subject to the rights reserved by the Transfer dated 6 January 1972 referred to in the Charges Register.

B: Proprietorship Register

stating nature of the Title, name and address of the proprietor of the land and any entries affecting the right of disposal

Title Absolute

1. (16 November 1977) **PROPRIETOR:** CLINT SMART and CONSTANCE SMART both of 14 Plevna Place, Blossomton, Edenshire, ED2 8JD.

C: Charges Register

containing charges, incumbrances etc. adversely affecting the land

1. (16 March 1967) A Conveyance of the land in this title dated 27 January 1967 made between (1) Thomas Dick (Vendor) and (2) Charles Harry (Purchaser) contains the following covenants:-

   "The purchaser for the benefit of the remainder of the vendors land hereby covenants with the Vendor to the intent that the burden of this covenant may run with and bind the land hereby conveyed to observe and perform the stipulations and restrictions set out in the schedule hereto.

   THE SCHEDULE before referred to:

   1. No further building shall be erected on the said land without the consent of the Vendor.

   2. Not at any time to carry on or suffer to be carried on the said land any trade or business for the sale of intoxicating liquors and no building erected on the said land shall be used except as a private dwelling house.

Specimen of Land Registry entry (continued)

Title Number : EDN999707

C: Charges Register continued

2. (14 February 1972) A Transfer dated 31 January 1972 made between (1) Sunshine Investments Ltd and (2) Brian Feather and Pauline Feather contains restrictive covenants.

   NOTE:- *Copy in certificate.*

3. (16 November 1977) **REGISTERED CHARGE** dated 1 November 1977 to secure the moneys including the further advances therein mentioned.

4. (16 November 1977) **PROPRIETOR:** HEART OF ENGLAND BUILDING SOCIETY of Jury Street, Warwick.

END OF REGISTER

NOTE A: A date at the beginning of an entry is the date on which the entry was made in the Register.
*NOTE B: This certificate was officially examined with the register on **16 March 1995.***

Specimen of Land Registry entry (continued)

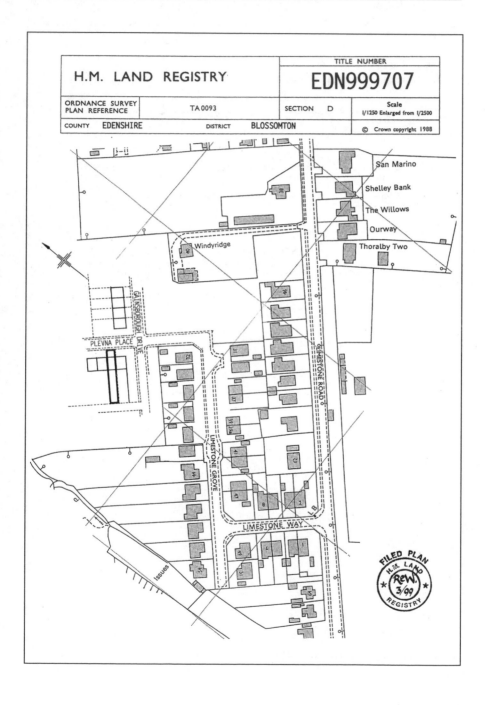

If the vendor contracts to supply an Office Copy or to deduce title in manner stated in section 110 of the Land Registration Act 1925, he is in breach of contract if he fails to do so. This Act used to set out what a seller is obliged to do to give satisfactory evidence of title to a buyer. It has been repealed as from 13 October 2003. The law now leaves it up to the parties to decide what evidence of title they require, but condition 4.1 of the Standard Conditions of Sale provides for proof of title by Office Copy entries, and you need to watch out in case this has been altered. One consequence of not complying with the requirements of the contract is that if the purchaser does not complete on time, no interest can be demanded for late payment and the powers available to the vendor to rescind cannot be exercised till after the breach is remedied.

The key to unlocking the files at the Land Registry is the title number, which is a reference number. Every registered property has one. The title number appears at the top of each page of the Office Copies. So that you can see how the Land Registration system works in practice (and what a pleasant surprise awaits you when the simplicity of it all is proved to you on the arrival of the Office Copies), let us take a look at a set that shows the various types of entry which could appear on Mr and Mrs Smart's title to No. 14 Plevna Place, Blossomton, Edenshire, title number EDN999707.

A swift look through our example will convince you that it is mostly self-explanatory; where it is not immediately clear, hold tight, just a little detective work and clarity is at hand. However, first of all note the number of pages and check you've got them all. Just for fun, the old-style manual register of your property may consist of say five pages and you only get three. Don't panic; it turns out that two are blank, and somewhere on your Office Copy it will be noted 'pages 4 and 5 are blank. Not photographed'.

Section A: Property Register: Describes the land by reference to the title plan and the postal address, because that is sufficient to identify it. In the case of leasehold property, details of the lease (date, parties, term and ground rent) are given. This section may also mention any rights of way which benefit the line, such as rights to pass over a private road. In this section there is also mention of an entry in the Charges Register – its bark is worse than its bite, more about it later.

Section B: Proprietorship Register: Here we see that in our example the proprietor has Title Absolute and this is the one that you will usually come across and want the property to have if you are a buyer. It is the best class of title and applies to 99 per cent of freeholds. The Registrar only gives the description Title Absolute where he is entirely satisfied about the owner's ownership of the property. Title Absolute means that the ownership is guaranteed by the state.

A leasehold property can have Title Absolute. This is only so in cases where the Registrar can guarantee that the lease was validly granted, because the lessor (grantor of lease) had proved that he owned the freehold or a longer lease of the land. Good leasehold title is shown in those cases where the superior title has not been investigated by the Registrar and is acceptable now to lenders only if it satisfies the CML *Handbook* (paragraph 5.4.2). Banks, building societies, etc. therefore require proof before the funds are released to the buyer.

Possessory title

This is very rare indeed. It is the weakest form of title and exists where full evidence is not supplied, perhaps because deeds were lost or because it is based on adverse possession, for example so called 'squatter's title'. Possessory title is acceptable now to lenders only if the CML *Handbook* is satisfied (paragraph 5.4.3).

The Proprietorship Register shows the present owners. Until recently, Land and Charge Certificates also showed the names of previous owners. Office Copies now issued do not show previous owners, as in our example. Likewise, the price paid was shown in some old-style manual registers; all registrations since 1 April 2000 show the price paid.

Look closely at the Office Copy. Look if a price appears on the Office Copy. If not, this is not actually anything to be alarmed about if the date next to the vendor's name in section B, the proprietorship register, is before 1 April 2000. There was no requirement to record a price before this date. If the date of registration is after 1 April, however, ask why no price is shown. If the property was the subject of a gift, even a partial gift where an owner transfers the house into his name jointly with that of spouse or partner, you must appreciate that if the person making the gift is later bankrupted, that gift can be annulled if it took place within five years from the date of the presentation of the bankruptcy petition.

Purchasers in good faith are protected, unless they were aware of the surrounding circumstances and 'the relevant proceedings'; and unless they can prove to the contrary, they will not be regarded as having purchased their home in good faith! They will know of the gift, of course, from the Land Registry entry and they will be at risk.

For this reason, where the buyer can tell the property was the subject of a gift within the preceding five years, it may well be unmarketable unless the seller can satisfy the buyer and his lender that no problems can arise. The purchaser can do this by applying for solvency and bankruptcy searches (see page 128) against the donor of the gift to check that he was solvent at the time of making the gift to ensure it cannot be set aside. However, it can be set aside if it was made within the last two years even if the donor was solvent at the time of making the gift. There is a further problem if the gift is between husband and wife: the husband is presumed to be insolvent at the time of the gift unless the contrary can be shown. If these assurances cannot be given – and it is difficult to see how they can be conclusively given – the seller should organise and pay for adequate indemnity insurance.

If you are borrowing to fund the purchase, you cannot ignore this. No solicitor who knows of this will sign off a certificate of title for one of the CML lenders, unless insurance is taken out. For those of you with access to the internet, have a look at section 5.12 of the CML *Lenders' Handbook for England and Wales* at www.cml.org.uk.

Section C: Charges Register: This is where the elementary detective work comes in. So gather round, while I tell you the story behind the sample produced here.

On 16 March 1967, a teetotal farmer called Thomas Dick sold his smallholding together with his house and rhubarb shed to Charles Harry, on condition that Mr C. Harry wouldn't do any further building and wouldn't convert the house to a pub, or the shed to a disco. The years went by and Mr C. Harry got it into his head that he would like to build a few houses on the land, so on his accountant's advice he and his Mrs formed Sunshine Investments and tried to look up Mr T. Dick, but he couldn't even be dug up, for he had been cremated. They therefore searched out his kith and kin, and found, as is sadly the case in such matters, that kith and kin, reacting against the strong strictures of husband and father, had turned to the bottle with a vengeance once he was out of the way, and, now being on the hard times he had predicted for those who took to the drink, were easily persuaded to remove the restriction on building – for a consideration.

Sunshine Investments, alias Mr C. Harry, built the houses and sold one to Mr Feather, who subsequently sold to Mr Smart, from whom you now wish to purchase. However, before Sunshine Investments were able to do their bit towards solving Mr Feather's housing problem (their own too) the Blossomton Council planning committee had to be pacified, and they made it a condition that no one actually went to live in the new houses until the new main sewer being built from Here to There had been completed. As the condition has obviously been complied with, the entry is now of no interest to anyone.

Sunshine Investments also got themselves a solicitor, Mr Newman. He was a young solicitor, and being rather inexperienced in the business, thought that creating the legal framework was all art and no science. Like all young artists, he did not know where to stop. He got out the volumes of Forms and Precedents, got every reference on restrictions, covenants, exceptions and reservations, and tacked them on to every transfer to every purchaser. It mattered not that there were no cesspits; he put in the rules governing cesspits, and preceded the rule with the words: 'if ever there be …'

The Registrar couldn't put all Mr Newman's blatherings into the Charge Certificate, but they existed, so 'copy in certificate' was inserted as a 'Note'. You will be sent a copy. Sometimes the copy will consist of the last conveyance which was drawn before the land became registered. In any case, it will list the restrictions on the property. And that is the copy that the vendor must attach to or refer to in the draft contract at 'Incumbrances'.

There is not a lot you can do about restrictive covenants. You either accept them or try doing what Sunshine Investments did and buy out the covenantee or once you've bought the land, apply to the Land Tribunal to have them discharged/modified, which is both difficult and potentially costly. Anyway, have a look through them, and if you had intended putting up kennels for dog breeding purposes and find that there is a restriction on using the land for any business purpose, put your thinking cap on. If there is no other property around, you'll be pretty safe, but if the house is on an estate, no doubt all the other houses have similar restrictions entered on their titles. You would only need one neighbour, one light sleeper who never seemed able to go shopping without stepping into a pile of ordure, for your life to be made a misery and your doormat fouled with summonses. That said, there is unlikely to be anything really onerous in the covenants, if indeed there are any at all. But for the general run of people, what are the covenants most likely to turn up? They fall into a pattern and the commonest are:

1. not to use the house for any trade or business;

2. to keep the fence or fences in repair either by yourself or with the assistance of your neighbour;

3. not to build another house on the plot or extend the present one without permission from the previous owner;

4. if you build a house on the plot it must be of at least £x in value;

5. not to do anything to cause a nuisance;

6. the dos and don'ts applicable to all owners on the estate.

So, if you find any or all of 1–6 above in either the Charge Certificate or in the copy of covenants, etc. which comes with the Charge Certificate, how do you interpret them for your own purposes? If you are sufficiently irreverent you have no doubt cracked the code for yourself. Irreverence is the key to the door to doing your own conveyance, and a sure shield against being showered with a load of bovinus excrementus which might result in a loss of confidence, which would never do. However:

1. So what? You are buying the house to live in.

2. Probably nothing could be done, as money would have to be spent to enforce it.

3. Put it this way: if the house has a double garden and you were buying with the idea of putting a little bungalow on for your granny, you would ask the vendor to put you in touch with the person whose consent is required. Ten to one it can't be done, because he will have changed his name to Wraith, and there is but the ghost of a chance of finding his kith and kin who either know or care about the covenant. So you could go ahead and be pretty certain that you were safe. There are, of course, insurance companies who will indemnify you against the risk of someone turning up and trying to make trouble. Covenants are taken for the benefit of land so you may have to take advice as to whether any of your neighbours could enforce the restriction. You can take out an insurance policy for a one-off premium against such problems which protects you and future owners of the property.

4. As at 3 above. You might ask Skinner to produce evidence that the house you are buying actually cost that amount to build, but you are unlikely to receive much of a reply unless it is something in the nature of 'there is no builder's receipt in the deeds but the vendor has received no notice of breach of covenant'. In any case, inflation will no doubt have dealt with this little problem.

5. Other people might think that we cause nuisance, but we know that it is they who cause it. They are wrong and we are right, but perverse as always, they think they know best. So we can accept this covenant because first, we never cause nuisance and second, we have an ordinary common law obligation, like everybody else, not to cause nuisance anyway.

6. If we didn't like the results achieved already by this covenant, we would not want to live here anyway. There is an added bonus for the layperson conveyancer because you will know, and have a copy of, this little lot and if any of them start upsetting any of us we will know that as usual they are in the wrong.

Covenants are promises, and the only difference between a covenant and any other kind of promise is that it is contained in a deed. At some point in the history of the buying and selling of the land in question, some owner has said in effect to a buyer, 'I will only sell to you if you will promise this, that and the other, and also promise that when you sell, you will have your buyer make the same promises to you and so on ad infinitum'. Do remember, however, that lenders will require indemnity insurance to cover breach of covenants.

There are one or two important things to be said about this ruling-from-the-grave covenanting. It may be difficult to say who could enforce it anyway. One thing to remember is that covenants are taken to protect land and will only be enforceable against a 'successor in title' (that's you) if they do confer some benefit on the land. In general, it is difficult, if not impossible, to enforce any covenant expressed to be in favour of a person, without reference to land he owns or owned which is affected by the covenant. It must also be remembered, however, that it is not only the original covenantee (i.e. the party who managed to extract the promise in the first place) who can enforce a restrictive covenant – if the covenant benefited land then owned by the covenantee, the present owner of that land will probably be able to enforce the covenant. You would have to read the deed creating the covenant to find out which of your future neighbours have that power. If the house is on an estate, chances are all of the houses are subject to the same restrictions so all your neighbours will be able to enforce the covenants. If you come across a 'no building or extension' covenant in the Charges Register of a property you are thinking of buying, and your inspection has shown the covenant to have been broken, what do you do about it? The first thing is to ascertain how long the extension or building has stood there. In addition to the owner's say-so, ask for some independent evidence to be produced. Although not conclusive, if reliable evidence shows the breach occurred more than 12 years earlier, the covenant is generally no longer enforceable. But the breach is still a blot on the landscape, as the CML *Handbook* (paragraph 5.7) requires indemnity insurance to be obtained if the breach is less than 20 years old. Any person who retains a solicitor to act for him whether as a purchaser or as a bank or building society will or at least should know of this requirement and should demand that the vendor fund insurance against risk; not necessarily the risk that the covenant is enforceable, but the risk that any owner who tries to sell or mortgage within the 20-year period will be faced with a demand that he meet the cost of such an insurance policy. These CML rules have to be complied with by the buyer or the funds will not be released. The questions of enforceability of covenants are notoriously tricky and it is best to take legal advice if you do plan to do something that would infringe a covenant.

If you are the vendor, you can put the potential buyer's mind at rest by offering to insure him against risk for the next ten years. If you are the buyer, you can pull a long face and say that but for your partner's silly emotional feeling for the place, you would have cried off immediately and you will now do so unless a few pounds are knocked off the price agreed before you knew about this diabolical covenant.

Vendor: Having read earlier about bargaining, you will know that emotion will overpower reason every time so if you can catch the eye of his partner for a few seconds, test the strength of the emotion – if it is genuine you are home and dry at your original price.

However, for purchasers who can manage to pull off the reduction-for-covenant gambit, the next step is to get the insurance and that is the dead hand of the past dealt with.

Entries 3 and 4 refer to the present owner's mortgage. 'Charge' is an abbreviation of 'Legal Charge' and that is the fancy term for mortgage.

In our example, we have not been able to cover all the things that might be entered on a Charges Register. For instance, one of Smart's lenders might not like further mortgages to be entered unless they know about it, so you get 'no disposition of the property may be made without the prior consent of the proprietor of Charge No. ....'. Don't worry, the lenders will not let go without their money, so their charge (mortgage in this case) will be deleted when you come to register your new ownership.

Another really irritating one is where there is an entry that the land is subject to covenants set out in a deed dated the umpteenth of Nerth. In the remarks you then read 'deed not lodged with the Registry'. These people might never turn up to bother you. But like it or not, because of the CML *Handbook* (paragraph 5.7), the prudent purchaser will now insist that his vendor fund indemnity insurance for the reasons stated above.

You're not really reading a whodunnit, so you are allowed to see how Mr Newman's story ends when you come across the real mother and father of Rigmarole in, and referred to in, the Property Register, and it starts off about sewers and unmade roads and rights across them. Ten to one you will find that the rigmarole was inserted as a condition of planning permission being granted for the estate to be built. Once the house was completed and its drains connected to the main sewer in the road, and the council had taken over responsibility for the maintenance of the road (it had become a public highway) and the sewer, the rigmarole became of academic interest only, except in so far as all subsequent inspectors of Office Copies have, at least, to give it a quick glance. It is worth checking though to see whether the road has been adopted by the council – if not your right to access of the property over it becomes important.

It is unlikely that you will come up against a caution. Cautions are a dying breed. No more cautions can be entered on the register after 13 October 2003 but 'old' cautions still remain. Like many other terms and phrases in the lawyers' armoury, 'caution' has an ominous ring to it, so let us cut it down to size before the few readers to whom it might apply are faced with it. Cautions were, almost without exception, hostile. That is because a caution was used where the owner of the property would not co-operate with a person who requires protection of his interests. Now a person would enter a 'unilateral notice'. If you come up against a caution, the vendor should already know about it, and as he wants his sale to you to go through, should already have made arrangements for the caution to be removed. The difference between a notice and a caution is that if the sale goes through despite the caution, the purchaser is not bound by the right unless it is an 'overriding interest'. However, if the right is protected by a notice, it will have priority over the purchaser's interest.

The most common caution you are likely to see entered nowadays is one by a wife or partner who wishes to let all who are interested in purchasing know that, though the house was not bought in joint names, it is, in fact, the matrimonial home. Registering the caution makes sure that if the person whose name the house is in tries to sell or mortgage the house, the cautioner will get to know if anything is stirring, and can then take appropriate action.

A prospective purchaser who finds a caution on the register will quite rightly ask the vendor to have it removed by clearing up whatever problem exists between himself and the cautioner. A caution against dealing can be withdrawn at any time without fee, using Form WCT. The vendor will persuade or induce the cautioner to write to the Registrar asking for the removal of the caution (Form WCT) from the Register and the caution will be removed promptly and without involvement of fuss or feathers.

However, if the vendor knows the caution to be simply silly and vexatious, he himself can apply for its removal using Form CCD. He must do one or the other or both, and purchasers need proof that he has done so before completion. The Registrar then gives the cautioner notice of the proposed dealing, and informs him that he intends to remove the caution. The onus is then on the cautioner to take action, and if he doesn't make a serious objection within 15 business days after notification, the caution is cancelled. The caution has been 'warned off'. When he hears from the Registrar, the cautioner may, if he wishes, put his case to him. If the Registrar thinks that cause has been shown, he must order that the caution is to continue until withdrawn or otherwise disposed of under Land Registration Rules 2003. If it is not possible to dispose of the objection by agreement, the Chief Land Registrar must refer it to the Adjudicator of

HM Land Registry. The Adjudicator can either deal with the matter himself or require that one party start proceedings in the High Court or the County court within a particular time. There is an appeal from the decision of the Adjudicator to the High Court.

Note B at the end of the Register tells you when the copy, in our example 16 March 1995, was taken from the actual Register. Office Copies come to you from the Registry by first-class post, but even so they are obviously out of date by the time you are proving to yourself how simple it all is by glancing through the entries. On 17 March the Smarts could have sold the house to Mr GA Zump, and he could have registered the transfer to himself on 18 March 1995 before you have time to do anything about it. Here you are with a copy of the register which clearly shows Smarts as the owners on 16 March; how could one possibly stop the ubiquitous Mr Zump? There is a way, and again, it is a form, OS1 by number. You will meet it again later and be properly introduced.

CHAPTER 12

Introducing conveyancing for laypeople

This chapter is an introduction to conveyancing. Liken it to the picture on the lid of a jigsaw puzzle box. Having studied it, you can then start interlocking the pieces contained in the rest of this Guide.

Having read so far, you are ready to do your own conveyance. While reading what follows, if you have a flow diagram-cum-checklist, keep it by your side.

There is, of course, a lot that is slightly technical which you might have to read twice before you think that you have grasped the point. You will certainly, as with any technical instruction, find that understanding comes the quicker when, instead of just the printed page, you have the actual nuts and bolts of the job in front of you. Every time you wire an electric plug it becomes easier – it's the same with conveyancing.

In the days when a solicitor could act for both parties, even if he had never acted for them before, I met an aged gentleman who was selling a house he had lived in for over thirty years. When he was asked who his solicitor was, he said, quite simply, 'I don't need a solicitor. I own the house, the deeds are under the piano lid, and when I get my money, the buyer can have keys, house and deeds, and I'm off into a Home with the proceeds.' I gave him a receipt for the deeds and took them to Donald Turnbull, solicitor for the purchaser, who, being the wise old bird he was, made no fuss and got on with it. After all, what had he to do? He looked at the last conveyance in the pile, made sure that the purchaser therein named was the aged gentleman, and bingo, aged gent had proved title (it is even simpler and safer nowadays where we have registered title). A month later the old boy was ensconced in the Home, terrorising the Matron with his merciless logic.

So if you have got your house paid for, follow the example of the aged gent, by getting your title deeds to the property which prove you are the owner. Whether your house is paid for or not, *get the whole file of your purchase transaction* from the solicitor who acted for you years ago and pop the papers under your piano lid to be ready. However, if the property is subject to a mortgage, the deeds will be with the lender.

As you take your first, confident step, keep firmly in mind that you are out to achieve three things:

1. Save yourself a lot of money, particularly if you are buying as well.

2. Get the purchase price safely out of the buyer's pocket and into yours.

3. Make certain you are completely shot of the house and have no continuing liabilities, which you do by virtue of Clause 3 in the 'Special Conditions of Sale'.

No. 1): to save all that lovely money, read on. No. 2) only requires that you are numerate and can count the money in banknotes or recognise a telegraphic transfer for the same sum. You may have jibbed just a tiny bit at No. 3). Don't. Just think of the hassle, worry and money you're about to save yourself. In any case, even if you pay Skinner & Deskbound, you will no doubt have to do most of the running about for yourself, and also fill in the kind of forms that solicitors send to their clients nowadays.

Selling a registered house

Whether you intend to travel 50 yards or 50 miles, your journey begins with a single step. You may not know whether you can walk 50 yards let alone 50 miles, but you have not much to lose by risking one stride, and emboldened by the success of that one stride, you will not lack confidence for the next two. So let me give you, the layperson conveyancer, the confidence to take that first stride by explaining step-by-step how to complete the simplest of all housing transactions, that of selling a second-hand, freehold, registered house in England or Wales, which is free of mortgage.

Step No. 1 is to get out your Land Certificate and copy the title number on to Land Registry Form OC1, Application for Office Copies and add your name and address. Look in Appendix 2 at the back of this Guide for details. If you don't know your title number, don't panic. You can deal with this in two ways: either write on the top of the form 'TITLE NUMBER REQUIRED' and fill in the rest of the details, or you can find out the title number for free by inserting the postal address in the property enquiry form at www.landregisteronline.gov.uk. A few days later, you will then receive a set of copies of everything carried by the Land Register about your house. This does not extend, however, to individual documents noted on the register, such as a transfer where the title says 'Copy in certificate' or where the copy is filed with another certificate. Your buyer will ask for these and they can be ordered using Form OC2.

While waiting for the Office Copies to come from the Land Registry, spend a few minutes making up three copies of the contract. Keep one copy for your file and put the other two, with the Office Copies, when you receive them, into an envelope, addressed to the purchaser or his Skinner, with a covering letter saying that you are acting for yourself in the sale of your house. Stund, of Skinner & Stund, will probably shudder with horror, but will write back acknowledging receipt, and, as though such a thing had never been heard of before, will ask you to confirm that you are indeed acting for yourself. In return for your confirmation, he will send you a letter giving the game away that he knew all the time that people are doing their own conveyancing nowadays. He will then say he must make it clear that he will 'take no responsibility for you in law or otherwise'.

There is no kind of business in the land that isn't regulated by general and particular laws which protect those with whom they deal. All that is being made clear is that he owes you no duty of care and that you won't have any redress if you rely on his advice as to how you should conduct your transaction. Nobody can write themselves out of the law, and nobody should know that better than Stund. What 'or otherwise' means I just don't know – you try asking. I've never managed to get a sensible excuse, let alone an explanation. Though you might feel like writing in retaliation, don't bother; it is best to take no notice. You have already landed a left and a right where it hurts most, in the pride and in the pocket.

You may now receive from Skinner printed 'Enquiries before Contract' or 'Pre-contract Enquiries' or even his own endless list of typed questions; they are all known colloquially in the trade as 'preliminary enquiries' and they may be referred to as such by Skinner, whatever they are actually called. They comprise questions for you to answer! Or you may be asked for the 'Seller's Property Information Form'; the idea is the same: to supply routine information to the buyer, but here the seller has to obtain the form and volunteer the answers. I recommend that the seller should complete the Standard Property Information Forms as they are simpler and easier to fill in. These can be obtained online from legal stationers. Part I is to be completed by the seller and Part II by the seller's solicitor if one is being used.

It is up to each solicitor to decide whether to send you enquiries or ask for you to volunteer answers by means of the 'Seller's Property Information Form'. However, these are different from an examination paper, because you only have to answer the questions to which you are absolutely certain you know the answers. If you don't know the answers, or are not certain about them, you calmly ask the examiner to check up for himself by replying 'not as far as I am aware, but please make own enquiries', or simply put 'I don't know'. At first reading, the form may appear quite fearsome. But really it is quite straightforward, if you keep it firmly fixed in your head that you don't intend giving any hostages to fortune, and you intend cleaving to the old established precept of *caveat emptor*, which is Latin for let the buyer beware. Buyers please take note. This does not mean you can write 'I don't know' for every question; if you do know the answer you must say so.

In the parcel under the piano lid, you might find the form your solicitor received from your vendor's solicitor when you bought. From that, you will see how little a solicitor is satisfied with, when he is protecting his paying customers in the parlous procedures entailed in the biggest business operation of his client's life. 'To the best of my knowledge, no, but please rely on your own searches.' 'I don't know.' 'There may be, but never brought to my attention.' These are the kind of woolly replies to give and expect to woolly questions. Remember also that if you answer any question 'to the best of my knowledge' or, more cryptically, 'not to my knowledge', the law expects you to have made reasonable stab at finding out the answer. If you cannot be bothered and use these phrases to avoid the trouble of checking out the answer, do not be surprised if you get a writ (now called a claim form) for any loss your buyer thinks he suffered because of your insouciant indifference to his question.

Remember, conveyancing is an administrative business transaction, and only becomes contentious when such things as fraud raise their ugly heads, i.e. if someone had recently given the property to you as seller to remove it from the clutches of his creditors.

However, Skinner could pick on some answer you have given and ask you to be more specific. If so, and you honestly don't know the answer, just stick at it, saying you have nothing to add. If he seems to be giving you the run-around, consider the possibility that he knows the proposed purchaser has gone off. If you do suspect this, check up with the purchaser direct. **Though solicitors consider it unethical for one solicitor to speak with another solicitor's client, there is no law, rule or ethic on earth that prevents the two principals (in this case vendor and purchaser) discussing matters between themselves.**

When your replies to the 'Enquiries before Contract' or 'Seller's Property Information Form' have been accepted and your contract approved, it will be signed by Feather and sent back to you. You now collect the deposit and in exchange, hand over your copy of the contract which you now sign. Do not be surprised if the solicitor tells his client you should not be paid the deposit, in case you pinch it. The solicitor may suggest he be allowed to act as 'stakeholder' rather than you. All this expression means is that whoever has the money must hand it to the seller if the sale completes. If it does not, it stays in limbo unless the contract is repudiated. In this case the seller gets it if the buyer is in default, but it is returned to the buyer if the seller is in default. If you have this problem, you will have to deal with it as best you can, but remember if you are buying a house at the same time and are using the Standard Conditions of Sale, you can still require your buyer to allow the money to be released to the solicitor who is acting for the person selling your new property to you. Remind your buyer's solicitor of this; that might persuade him to review the position. He, after all, will know that if you are paid money without quibble and do pinch it his insurers will probably have to refund it.

If you have arranged for someone else to act as stakeholder, repair to his office and exchange the contract you have signed for the one signed by the purchaser, and see to it that the balance of the deposit is handed to the stakeholder. Contracts have now been exchanged. Your sale is now tied up.

If the buyer backs out, you have to decide whether to be merciful or merciless. That is to say, you give him back all, part or none of his deposit, depending on the circumstances.

After exchange of contracts, Skinner may send a questionnaire entitled 'Requisitions on Title'. Treat it with Olympian calm. Requisition means question. Title means ownership. So, he is asking you questions to find out if you are the owner, when all the time you know and he knows you are the owner, because it says so on the Land Registry Proprietorship Register, and your title (ownership) is thus guaranteed by the state. In reality it is very unlikely you will be asked much about the title. If you have proved title before contract under the fourth edition of the Standard Conditions of Sale, there can be no further questions. They keep changing the form, so you may get questions raising problems which have already been solved, like 'where completion will take place', and 'have you got receipts for rates and suchlike bills paid?'. In the main, the questions are to do with practicalities: what's the position on rates, do you have the deeds, how do we get the keys, where do we send the money and so on. I know it's difficult, but try to be courteous, remembering all the while that even if you were paying a solicitor, all these problems would still be yours to solve, because he would only be acting as a postbox.

Skinner, on behalf of your purchaser Feather, now sends you a Land Registry Form TR1, in draft state, for your approval. This is the form which authorises the Land Registry to transfer the house out of your ownership into Feather's. The draft only calls for names and addresses to be filled in, the money, the property and the class of title, i.e. full or limited. If the draft is in order, accept it and write acknowledging the fact. Sign the Form TR1 at the first signed 'as a deed line' in the presence of a witness, who also signs, and then hold on to it (see Appendix 7 for details). There is nothing to do now, but while away the time before completion date by dreaming about what you will spend the money on.

If your buyer is supposed to sign it because it contains an indemnity covenant, make sure the buyer signs it before you do. Indemnity covenants? Go back to chapter 11, 'Section C: Charges register' for a refresher. The law on covenants is a bit of a tangle. If you sign a transfer that contains them, the person who sold you the house (or others depending on the circumstances) can sue you if your buyer breaks any of the covenants. Covenants on land are an area (law not geography) where lawyers in Victorian days got themselves into a bit of a tangle. First, they decided positive covenants involve spending money: to keep a fence in good order or to contribute to maintaining a fence, drains or a road. They decided negative or 'restrictive' covenants do not involve spending money: covenants not to run a bawdy house, for example. Then they decided that if X makes covenants with Y to do something (i.e. only to use the property for residential purposes) that do not involve spending money, anyone who can prove they have or acquired the right to enforce restrictive covenants can sue Y's successors.

This is not the case with positive covenants. So you need your buyer to promise to indemnify you if he breaks them and you are sued. The only remedy your vendor may have in these cases is to sue you, if he can find you. If you can get the money back from your buyer, fine. If not, tough! The Standard Conditions of Sale require your buyer to add an indemnity clause to the transfer, but do not be surprised if the point is overlooked and it never appears in your transfer. As the person at risk, it is for you to make sure it is not left out when you are sent the draft transfer for approval.

If your house has a leasehold title, the landlord can continue to pester you for the rent and service charge if your buyer does not pay it, unless the lease was granted after 1 January 1996. You do not need an indemnity covenant in this instance since the law implies one.

Remember also the covenants you give in the transfer. Your promise to sell with full title guarantee, for example, places certain duties on you. If the house has a leasehold title you promise that you have complied with all the covenants (referred to in section 4 of the Law of Property (Miscellaneous Provisions) Act 1994 – see www.opsi.gov.uk). The sales of leasehold property are deemed to include this covenant unless expressly excluded. Solicitors normally make a point of adding a clause to the effect that these covenants should not be construed as your promise that the premises have been repaired and decorated in strict conformity with the lease.

Sometimes purchasers will ask you to let them have the keys before completion. If Feather needs to get the money from the sale of his own house to Dither, in order to buy yours, it can be difficult for him. But if Dither gets knocked down by a bus on his way to complete, and you have let Feather into possession of your house, it will be a great deal more difficult for you.

Sellers of a vacant property will no doubt be asked to accept an undertaking from Feather that if you let him have the key solely for the purpose of decorating and repair, he will not go into possession. Now it might seem a bit dog-in-the-manger to refuse, and Skinner might try to assure you that it is the usual thing, and the undertaking he has drafted for Feather to sign gives you ample protection. If you feel under pressure, write to Skinner and ask for his personal indemnity underwriting the Feathers' undertaking. You never know, he might give it. But if he can't trust his own client, how can you?

Letting a purchaser into possession before completion can also have implications for Stamp Duty Land Tax. This is the tax which has replaced Stamp Duty on sale of land. Stamp Duty is a charge on documents – so the tax wasn't payable until the transaction completed and the transfer signed. Stamp Duty Land Tax is a charge on transactions and is payable within 30 days of the 'effective date'. In general the 'effective date' is completion – so all well and good unless the transaction is 'substantially performed' before this date. Allowing a purchaser into possession before completion amounts to 'substantial performance'. This won't make too much difference if you allow the purchaser in one or two days before, but it might cause problems if you let him in two or three weeks before completion is due to take place.

A CHAPS payment is the layperson conveyancer's best friend, but a solicitor is unlikely to make such a payment and trust you to hand over the deeds. A personal completion utilising a bank draft is more likely, but note that the fourth edition of the Standard Conditions of Sale excludes the possibility of paying the money due on completion by banker's draft, so unless this has been altered, payment must be made by 'direct credit', i.e. CHAPS transfer.

If the buyer is all tied up at his end and cannot attend the completion personally, leave the keys with a neighbour you can trust. A further qualification to being trustworthy that the neighbour requires is to be on the telephone, because the keys must not be handed over until you have rung up saying all is well. On completion day toddle along to the appointed venue. You will have with you your Land Certificate, the completed Form TR1, the lease if a leasehold property, any other title documents you hold and the keys (if not with the neighbour). If the deposit is being held by a stakeholder, Skinner will, in addition to handing you the balance of the purchase price, give you a letter authorising the release of the deposit. You give Skinner the Land Certificate, Form TR1 and the keys. And that is your sale completed. That is conveyancing in a nutshell. Now to the detail.

CHAPTER 13

Conveyancing: the sale and purchase of a registered house

The previous chapter on selling a registered house confined itself to the work a vendor of such a house is faced with. The reason for limiting its scope was so that you could judge for yourself the simplicity of the operation. Indeed, anyone who is good at making a précis will have already noted that a very simple transaction indeed could be carried out, and it goes like this:

A purchaser goes to a house that is for sale and says, 'I will give you £175,000 for it if you can prove to me that you are the owner'. The vendor says, 'Come back in a couple of hours with the money'. The purchaser returns with the money and confirms that the vendor is ready to leave and the house is vacant. The vendor has his Land Certificate and a signed Form of Transfer in one hand and the keys in the other. The purchaser swaps his £175,000, for those three items. The deal is done.

The purchaser sends the Land Certificate and the Transfer to the Land Registry along with Form AP1 – Application to change the register, the Land Transaction Return SDLT1 – see page 153), Form DI, in which you should insert any 'disclosable overriding interests' such as legal rights of way or leases of which you are aware and the registration fee. He is now the registered proprietor.

Because people tend not to take other people's word for things nowadays, it takes a bit longer than this, but basically what appears above is the beginning and end of a sale and purchase of registered land. It contains everything that has to be done to transfer ownership.

The instructions that follow are for the purchase and sale of a freehold dwelling in England or Wales which is already registered.

The procedures for buying from a council are completely different; leases and gifts are special cases.

The instructions should also be read with reference to chapter 9, regarding contracts. For the purpose of illustration, we will assume that you are a first-time buyer and need to take a mortgage, or that you are the vendor of a £175,000 house. There is some repetition of what has gone earlier – unfortunately, it cannot be avoided so please look on it as part of the teaching and learning process.

Vendor: As soon as you seriously put your house up for sale, send off an Application for Office Copies Form OC1 (see Appendix 2) and Form OC2 if necessary. Fill in your name and address and title number, which you have got from your Land Certificate, your lender or the solicitor who acted for you when you bought (he cannot charge you for this service, by rights he should have performed it earlier), and – with a cheque for £4 for each copy required – send it to the appropriate Land Registry, the address of which you will find in Appendix 10 or online at www.landreg.gov.uk (it's not always obvious which is the appropriate Land Registry). Notify your lender/s that you will be redeeming your mortgage/s.

Purchaser: Until you are sure you can find the money for the purchase, sign nothing, apart from the lender's application form. Any letters you send to anyone must have written somewhere about them 'Subject to Contract' and it is safest to keep on doing that right up to the point where you do sign the contract.

I take it for granted that you will keep your wits about you, and have at some time completed a licence or passport application form, and have, therefore, clerical expertise. That little caution given, I will not labour the points that are usually made ad infinitum and ad nauseam elsewhere about how careful one must be. It would be all right if such labourings genuinely helped people either towards a better understanding, or to being able to cope for themselves and ease their worries, but when, after scaring the living daylights out of you, the only advice given is: go to a professional to deal with a contract for you, survey for you, buy for you, sell for you, it's just a waste of reading time. You can always leave things to others – at a price – and people had to when they were illiterate.

One cardinal rule, and it goes for all business transactions, is: never let go of both ends. Have the house, or have the money. The cynic would say, preferably have both, but never be in the position where you have neither.

Before committing yourself to anything, re-read the section on contracts because the vendor whose heart you warmed with those magic words, 'I would like to buy your house', has been on the phone to Skinner and gleefully said that he has found a buyer and Skinner says, 'Leave it all to me'. What, at this point, Feather has left to him is the sending of a draft contract and that is what in the fullness of time you can expect to receive, but he might also write to you as he did to our vendor in the previous chapter, saying that he won't be responsible for you in law or otherwise. If he does, join in the fun by ringing up Feather and ask what Skinner is covering up – what is wrong with the house, is it down for road widening, is there a deed missing, has he got the scrolls or hasn't he? – plus any further nonsense you can think up. Then forget about it.

Vendor: Send off to the purchaser's solicitor two copies of your draft contract, the Property Information Forms and the Office Copies, which you should have received by now. You should also include the Fixtures, Fittings and Contents Form, which should be completed on all residential sales. This should list those items which are to remain in the property and those which may be taken by the seller.

Purchaser: Receive draft contract and possibly Office Copies. If you do not get a Land Registry Office Copy and file plan, demand it. The Standard Conditions of Sale make it the duty of the seller to prove his title in this way, admittedly only after the contract, but it is customary for the seller to supply these before contracts are exchanged. Do not be fobbed off with a photocopy made in the office of your seller's solicitors. This may be useful as a starter, but do not leave the matter there. The Land Registry frequently update the format of these so why be fobbed off with something that might well be out of date?

Peruse the Office Copies in the light of the knowledge you gained from chapter 11, 'The Registers'.

Put the draft contract on one side for a while. Content yourself with asking the vendor's solicitors if they are sending you the Seller's Property Information Forms and if not, send them two copies of the Enquiries before Contract or preliminary enquiries. Before you do, have a quick look at these, and if the questions they contain don't cover everything you would like to ask about, and hopefully get a sensible answer to, put those extra questions in writing. For instance, buyers of new houses should ask: 'Is the design, construction and layout of the sewers such as will meet the criteria required for their adoption by the water and any other authority?'

Vendors now have to deal with preliminary enquiries (see page 112), if you have not sent the Seller's Property Information Forms already and purchasers can look over their shoulders. Indeed, anyone who has not coped with these enquiries before will do well to have his seconds ready in his corner, for this form will be the one that will (at first) make you wish you had never bothered, that is, until you have really started pencilling in some replies in the copy which is intended for you to keep. As you read on and pencil away, the colour will come back to your cheeks, and you will realise how childish it was to be frightened.

Most of the questions are easy, daft or both, but we will have a quick run down Enquiries before Contract, first noting that in some of the forms the column headed 'Replies' already has displayed in bold type at the beginning or end 'These replies on behalf of the vendor are believed to be correct but the accuracy is not guaranteed and they do not obviate the need to make appropriate searches, enquiries and inspections'.

The law assumes you have made all proper enquiries, so do not place too much reliance on this disclaimer. Also, the law on misrepresentation still applies, as should the good old British principle 'my word is my bond'. The following are common questions which appear in one form or another.

- One relating to boundaries and whether you know of any disputes about them. If you know the answers, give them; if you are not sure, use the formula 'I know of none' and give the same answer to the question on notices, particularly in so far as it refers to your predecessors in the house.

- One asking for copies of any Housebuilding Council guarantee, insurance policies covering defective title, or road maintenance agreements. If you have any, comply; if not, you can't, so just reply 'none in my possession'.

- Questions about whether services such as gas, electricity, water and drains are connected, and if any of them come to you through someone else's property: the first part is easy, the second is easier when you know how. Answer: 'Please rely on your own survey'. Deal with the question about access and roads in a similar fashion. About rights of way: if you know of any say so, if not, say 'I'm not aware'.

- There will normally be a question that could frighten you out of your wits and send you scurrying off for legal help. Don't let either happen. It asks: 'Please give full details of all overriding interests affecting the property as defined by the Land Registration Act 2002 Schedule 3'. This question refers to other people's rights over the property which are not recorded on the Register, such as the rights of people who live in the property who are not joint owners or have rights of way over the property. If you don't know of any, answer 'I am not aware of any, but the property is sold subject to any that there may be'. Having answered that question, you've broken its back.

It's downhill all the way now and you can answer the remaining questions with variations on our old friend 'I don't know of any, but please rely on your own survey'. Even with the question about Rateable Value, though you have the latest Council Tax bill sitting in front of you, it is safest and perfectly acceptable to reply 'I think £x, but please check with local authority'.

Even though you have specified the fitted wardrobes, shelving and such like in a final clause of your contract, this doesn't stop the question cropping up again. You will find this kind of duplicate questioning all the time. You just have to put up with it and give it the short shrift it deserves. You are asked how long will it be after the exchange of contracts, before the vendor (he means you) is able to give vacant possession. The usual period is one month, but of course you may make it longer, shorter or tag on to whatever date you give 'or before'. So give a date which you think is suitable to the purchaser and also make it clear where and how you insist on having the money: 'Vacant Possession will be given on completion which will take place at (state venue) on the umpteenth of Nerth. A CHAPS payment will be required for the balance of the purchase price'. A cheque or a banker's draft could bounce.

You will also be asked when possession of the property will be given. You answer, 'When I receive the balance of the money by CHAPS payment on completion'. No solicitor would agree to completion not taking place in his office; he would be negligent if he sent off his client to an alternative venue, money and the mortgage money by CHAPS, without having the deeds. If you are also buying a house, you may wish to add a suggested completion date to tie in with your purchase, but see later for more on this subject.

When the preliminary enquiries have been completed to your satisfaction, send them off. They may come back with supplementary questions, and some of them may appear to be intended to annoy you. Don't let annoyance creep in, just press on, courteously pointing out that you can only sell what you have got, but you are not a qualified surveyor, and if he wants to be absolutely certain where such things as the drains run, he is welcome to have a sniff around provided he does no damage.

It takes some believing, but this is the right way to deal with the Property Information Forms, and Skinner's acceptance of your answers will be your proof.

Purchaser: Receive the Property Information Forms form, duly completed and glean from them what you can. Though we made fun of the question about overriding interests on behalf of our vendor, do be careful that as a purchaser the laugh is not on you, because one of the overriding interests protected by Schedule 3 of the Land Registration Act 2002 is the rights of a person in 'actual occupation' of the land. This means that it is possible for someone, apart from the registered proprietor, to claim rights of occupation (and the courts will not shift them), even though they have not registered that right anywhere. It is wise to ask if there is anyone over the age of 17 living with the seller who is not also an owner of the house. If the answer is yes, it is wise to get them to sign the contract to provide a written assurance on their part that they claim no interest in the house and will vacate on or before the date the sale is to be completed. If you do not do this, they may still be there when you move in and with a better claim to the house than you! Another way to protect yourself is to make sure that the property is registered in two names and that you get a receipt signed by both registered owners. In matrimonial situations, the spouse's right of occupation is registerable for both registered and unregistered titles and does not take effect without registration. Overriding interests are not confined to rights to occupy or the rights (whatever they may be) of the persons in occupation; they include third party rights such as legal easements (like rights of way, rights of light), so someone may have a right of way over the property although you could not see it on the register.

So at the risk of repetition: throughout this Guide you will find endless warnings about making sure, before you sign a contract, that the vendor can give you vacant possession on completion, and *never ever* complete the purchase of a house before you have seen with your own eyes that the house is completely vacated, and that if there has been any kind of dispute about ownership and/or occupation, that the locks have been changed. If you think you may gain further enlightenment by asking supplementary questions, ask them, but remember they were stock questions, so you can't expect better than stock answers. Best of all is to make a trip to the property and, using the form as a checklist, go through the items with the vendor.

And it is at points like this that layperson conveyancers like us come out on top because we leave our desks and look at the problems – not the papers about them!

Have a look at boundaries, walls and fences with your own eyes. The general run of houses in town and suburban areas have clearly defined garden walls, hedges and fences, but in rural areas it isn't always so. However, first check what is within the boundaries against the plan in the Office Copies. A 'T' mark against a boundary indicates that the owner of the land on which the 'T' is situated is responsible for the upkeep of that boundary, wall or fence. Otherwise, strong (but not conclusive) evidence is that the owner of the land on which the fence posts are situated (which hold up the fence) is responsible for that fence. If there is more within the fences than the plan shows, it is possible that your vendor has pinched it. Ask him about it. Ask the neighbour. If there is a problem, it isn't much trouble to move a fence, but what about a garage? Always check that a garage is within the boundary shown on your plan. Indications that there may be a dispute about boundaries, or whose responsibility it is to maintain a particular fence, could be evidenced by its broken-down appearance. If you have any reason to suspect that there is any kind of dispute, go hotfoot to the neighbour and ask his point of view on the matter particularly if it is about a shared drive.

Disputes between owner-occupiers of suburban properties about who owns what and who can go where are the most frustrating, intractable, time-consuming and above all ruinously costly to resolve at law. If you come across a hint of such a dispute, my advice is, run a mile. Hard lines on the vendor who hasn't had the courage or foresight to come to terms with his neighbour; his best hope is that his prospective purchaser has not read this book and the business is being conducted at arm's length by Skinner, Write & Reams, so that Feather is blocked from the knowledge by a heap of paper and only finds the pig after moving into the poke.

If, in order to get to the house or garage, you have to traverse an unmade road, or anything which looks as if it may not be a public right of way (the council will tell you if it is, in reply to your enquiry form – see later), there should be a note on the Office Copy, saying you have a right of way over the track or common drive or whatever. On the other hand, does anyone else have a right of way over the land which is shown, on the plan, to be that which you are contemplating buying, and if so, who will be responsible for the shared access way's upkeep? If you have seen other people walking over the land, ask how long they have been doing this for and whether they have permission to do so.

If the copy of the deed plan which came as part of the Register has produced no satisfactory answer about the approach to the property, ask the vendor or the solicitor what is proposed. Usually, it will be that the vendor makes a statutory declaration that he has used the way for 20 years or more and this is usually thought to be acceptable. It is evidence that the access has been in use for so long and the law will adopt a convenient fiction to the effect that a right of way does actually exist. This also applies if the land is common land or a right can be acquired over common land under the Countryside and Rights of Way Act 2002. If the vendor has driven over the common land for 20 years, it is likely that a right of way by prescription has arisen, but get the vendor's solicitor to confirm this. If he cannot, insist on insurance. However, if it really is the house of your dreams, you really should consider taking legal advice.

It would be a surprise if you found a house that had electricity which was not connected to the mains. The owner would probably be so proud of his generator and his independence of 'those wicked power workers' that he would show it off without being asked. If the gas supply was bottled you could hardly miss the evidence. Nevertheless, check both.

If you have any doubt about the water supply, see the replies to your water drainage search, i.e. to discover if it is metered and connected to the mains. Do have a swift look for the lid of the cast-iron box which houses the stop-tap and is usually to be found just outside the boundary to the front garden. If you are buying out in the sticks and think that the water supply may be coming to you across someone else's land, write to the local water authority and ask them. If the answer you receive is in the affirmative, then you have a further point to investigate, 'what will happen if the water supply is stopped, for any reason, by this neighbour?' If the vendor or his solicitor had anything about these matters, there should be such a letter in existence from a previous purchase. Even if there is, it will still be worth while writing and quoting the letter and asking if things remain the same.

Drains can be a bit of a stinker. All your life you have simply pulled the string or pushed the plug, and what has to go has gone, and you never had to give a second thought as to where it was going or how it could possibly get there. The thought that it would answer back and refuse to go was too awful to contemplate. Buyers in built-up areas can be pretty sure it goes into the main drain; where it goes after that we don't worry our heads.

A house which is not connected with the main sewer will almost certainly drain into a cesspit/cesspool or a septic tank. In the case of the latter, the owner will need to have it emptied every four or five years, depending on the size of the family (the former do not have to be emptied). This is no problem. Everything functions as if there were a mains drainage, but when the tank is cleared by hydraulics into a tanker, there is a bill to pay. When the water companies started to send their bills separately from the Council Tax accounts, they divided the bill between water and sewerage charges, at which the septic tank owners said, 'Oh, no!' to the sewerage charge, and won their point. All of which little excursion into recent history is to tip you off that the water company's bill, unless it shows a specific charge for sewerage, will tell you that you do not have connection to the main sewer.

More difficult to establish is whether you drain through anyone else's land, or vice versa. The cases where this is likely is where a house has been built in the garden of another house. It could become really important if you wanted to build an extension or garage.

So have a look round at the manholes; you might learn something, but as manholes have sometimes been covered over, this inspection may not be sufficient. If you intend spending a lot of money on your extension or garage, get your builder in to have a poke around – if there is bad news he will delight in giving it to you. If necessary, look in the Yellow Pages for a firm that specialises in sniffing around the drains and get a quote.

You are told that no building requiring planning permission has been carried out in the past four years. Does that square with what you find on inspection? For our purposes, just about everything needs planning permission, but often the permission comes from the law: The Town & Country Planning (General Permitted Development) Order 1995. Telephone the planning department where the house is located to see what they can send you regarding these provisions. It is worth the effort. Houses can be enlarged without permission subject to certain conditions. Roofs can be added or enlarged. Porches can be added. Sheds, garages and swimming pools can be added. Parking spaces can be laid. Satellite antennae can be installed. In all these cases, if the works come within the very detailed limitations laid down by the law, no further planning permission is required. Overstep the mark, and it is! But they still have to get, and be built in accordance with, building regulation approval, which is a different thing from planning approval. If your vendor gives a categorical answer no, or even (if he has lived in the house for less than four years) the time honoured 'not as far as I am aware', you may think that sufficient. A solicitor would, unless someone like his client, have alerted him otherwise.

Vendor: Receive any supplementary questions and answer them as best you can.

Purchaser: Receive answers to supplementary questions and decide whether to settle for what you are being offered. If you are satisfied, you can now involve yourself in the expense of sending off a few forms with their appropriate fees.

If you are borrowing money, carry out a Land Charges Department bankruptcy search using Form K16, which is sent to the Land Charges Department at Plymouth. The search is against you and your partner if buying in joint names. All you do is write in your names as required in the form and pay £2 per name. It is required by your lender, so first ask if they plan to do their own. If so, you will be charged, so save your money. Otherwise, do it about eight working days before the date for completion. Your lender will wish to see the answer.

Enquiries of Local Authority CON 29, together with Search of Local Land Charges LLC1, can be posted to the local council, just as Skinner & Deskbound would do. Ask about the fee; it varies.

However, I suggest that you take them to the council offices, and do a real search around for yourself while you are there. Ask if you can have a look at the development map and the planning applications approved and pending. Don't attempt to use the jargon. Keep it simple. You will get two surprises. First, how much help you get if you start the service by smiling, and saying to the official, 'I wonder if you can help me?' and second, the amount of information you can so easily pick up that you won't if you simply rely on the forms. Care is needed, though. Some local authorities give less information on a personal search than they would in reply to a professional one (in some cases, it is the really important information, such as planning records, that is withheld).

The town development map is divided up and each division is coloured. Some are even coloured and hatched. How a division is categorised tells you what the council intends for it. If the area is coloured, say a dirty brown with black dots, it could mean that the area is intended for obnoxious industries. If anyone owns a house in that area and he wants planning permission to convert it to a bone and bladder boiling factory, he might get it. A nicely coloured pink area might mean an area primarily intended for residential use, and if you send off your forms of local search, those are the kind of answers you will receive. That is to say, you would learn it is an area intended for, say, obnoxious industries, green belt, inner ring road or residential – and that is all.

If you want to know if anyone is even thinking about doing something nasty at the bottom of the garden, ask. Particularly if you are buying property bordered by a peaceful plot of land containing succulent fruit and veg; even better, where beyond the prospective patch there are open fields. What a lovely view! What a set-up for anger and frustration, if you simply send off the forms in the usual manner and wait for what the gods send.

In a few months you could be looking at a brick wall and someone else's line full of washing where you thought you had a view over the undulating countryside. As soon as you saw the builders coming, you would be off to your legal advisers asking what you could do about it and why you had not been told what to expect. You will now find that in addition to facing a brick wall, you are banging your head on one and paying legal fees for the privilege of doing it. That's when it will be borne in on you that in spite of all your GCSEs, 'A' levels, degrees and diplomas, you are a twit. You bought land (with a house on it) in an area designated residential and you are now surprised when a house builder gets busy with the bricks and mortar creating residences in the area. My dear reader, this isn't a question for a lawyer, it's plain common sense and a problem of understanding the English language!

What can you do to save yourself from twittery? When you go to the local council offices, ask to see the list of planning permissions granted in the area over the last ten years or so (the spread of years is important; people often sit on development permission for years, but councils give the permission subject to time limits which vary – ask). Then be really cute and ask for the list of planning applications pending! You may even be able to get this information online from the council's website.

When you leave the forms, the official will tell you when to expect the LLC1 and CON 29 to be returned to you, bearing the council's stamp, which gives a warranty against negligent replies on their part. When they do arrive, have a look through for anything unusual. So unusual is it for anything unusual to appear, the authorities have duplicated replies ready. Even so, duplicated or not, you want the job doing properly, otherwise you wouldn't be doing it yourself, so you will scrutinise each answer. If you find anything you don't understand, call the local official and ask.

If, in spite of all the form-filling and chatting up of the officials, you still suspect there might be something nasty in the pipeline, have a chat with the Citizens Advice Bureau and the local newspaper to see if they know anything to the area's advantage or disadvantage.

There is very little to fill in on the two forms you take to the council offices. CON 29 form is in two parts. You require Part I answering and it will cost you a fee to have that done for you. Local authority fees tend to vary from council to council and may change frequently, so you need to ring them.

You will learn from the replies you receive about such things as whether the road fronting the property is maintained at the public expense, whether the council are about to grab any land within 200 metres of your boundary in order to lay new roads, and whether they or the appropriate Secretary of State intends constructing a road, underpass, overpass, forward pass, flyover or elevated road within 200 metres of the property. The form does not ask about 201 metres plus; that is why layperson conveyancers come off best, because they have a chat with the officials.

They do not have sleepless nights every time they read in the newspapers about some poor soul waking up to find the council ready with some diabolical scheme that will either knock the house down or tens of thousands of pounds off its value.

Part II of CON 29 won't get answered by the council unless you specifically asked them to do so. Have a look down the Part II questions and see if you think any of them might have a bearing on the house you are interested in buying. It will cost you extra for each of the questions in Part II that you tick, as an indication to the officials that you require that particular question answering. The kind of things you can learn from ticking a question range from 'Has the council authorised the service of a building preservation notice' to 'Has the council or the Secretary of State authorised the making of an order for the compulsory acquisition of the property?'

The requisition for a search of the local land charges register Form LLC1 is even easier to complete. It has to be sent in duplicate and it comes to you with a copy; all you have to do is insert a carbon, tick that you require all the register searching, put the address of your intended purchase and your own name and address in, enclose the fee and that is it.

There are further searches you should carry out using a letter or appropriate forms. First, telephone the local water company, ask who to speak to about water and drainage enquiries and then talk to them to see what a search costs. Then write with a cheque. Until recently this information came from answers to CON 29 but no longer. The water company will answer the questions and send along a plan showing what is connected and what can be found in the area, so if your house is not connected to their sewers, you will be able to see if there are sewers in the area and you will be able to ask the cost of connection.

Environmental issues are now all the rage. The CON 29 may give meaningful answers to environmental questions, but many solicitors now carry out online environmental searches or 'envirosearches'. For a fee, these will tell you what is happening in your area – if it appears – in any of a wide variety of paper records. Is your house in a flood plane? Was it built on infill land? What is the risk of subsidence? Have there been environmentally unfriendly activities in the area, etc.?

Two specialist searches that may be necessary are coal mining searches and commons searches. You now get coal mining information on your envirosearch (so far as it exists) and commons searches should be made only where it seems relevant to do so. If you are buying a house in an inner London borough, there is probably no need for this, but if you are buying in the country there probably is. Even if the area seems to have been residential for some time, open land nearby could be common land and there have been cases of houses being registered (incorrectly) as common land so it can be worth checking. This is particularly so if you are buying an idyllic house with a private access across 'Greenfield Common', or similar.

You **the purchaser** can now turn your attention to the draft contract. It has to be read through and a decision made as to whether the terms are acceptable or not. It is not a take-it-or-leave-it situation; that is why it is a draft contract. If there is anything about which you are not clear, speak to the vendor, his solicitor or both, and get one or the other to explain (not explain away with excuses such as 'it's usual') until you understand. If there is anything with which you cannot agree, strike it out. Here are nine points you should watch out for when perusing the draft contract:

1. Compare the information given in the preliminary enquiries with what the solicitor has written concerning the items, referred to as 'chattels' in the Agreement, which the vendor said he was including in the price agreed.

2. Is the amount of deposit stated correctly? If you are using the Standard Conditions of Sale, you can use the deposit from your sale as the whole or part of a deposit for your purchase. If you aren't using the Standard Conditions of Sale, put a clause in the contract allowing you to use your purchase deposit.

3. Check to whom and under what conditions the deposit is to be paid. You should insist that whosoever receives the deposit does so as stakeholder, because a stakeholder cannot part with the money unless he has been satisfied that completion has taken place. You may have paid a holding deposit to an estate agent, or even the whole amount of the deposit; if so, the clause about the deposit should take care of that situation.

4. There should be a clause stating the capacity in which the vendor sells, called 'Title Guarantee Full/Limited'. If such a clause does not appear in the draft contract, ask for one to be inserted. If the vendor owns in his own right, insist he sells with full title guarantee. If he does not, as

executor of an estate, for example, he will wish to sell with limited title guarantee. Be especially careful if the vendor is not going to sign but has appointed an agent under a power of attorney to sign. If he sells by power of attorney, you are entitled to a copy of the power; if as executor or administrator, probate or letters of administration with Will annexed out of the Principal Registry or district Probate Registry is sufficient proof of a person's death and of the executors' title to the property. In the case of a lender selling after a borrower's default, you will be pleased to hear that you do not concern yourself with whether the 'mortgagee (one who lent) in possession' is properly exercising his rights under the mortgage. You just need to know whether the power of sale has arisen by looking at whether the redemption date has passed. Ninety-nine per cent of vendors are giving full title guarantee and if yours isn't, ask his solicitor to give you the real evidence that he might have the right to sell.

It is not unusual, however, for a vendor to place some limit on his responsibilities. His solicitor will generally name the bits he does not want his client to subscribe to. You will have no idea what this means unless you look at the legislation, which is The Law of Property (Miscellaneous Provisions) Act 1994. A decent local library should hold *Halsbury's Statutes of England* and you can look it up there. However, if you are on the internet or have a friend who is willing to do this for you, print off a copy from www.legislation.hmso.gov.uk/acts.htm.

5. Here is a nice easy one for you. Check that the address and/or description of the property to be sold is correct. If the property being sold is part of an existing registered title, then you should also be provided with a plan, for more detailed description.

6. If you were told that you are buying a freehold, check that it says so in the description.

7. If your vendor agreed to include items such as carpets in the sale price, they should be in the contract, but if the price you are paying is just over the level at which Stamp Duty becomes payable, fix a price for the item (£x) and ask that the clause has added to it 'and £x of the purchase price shall be apportioned to these items'. On the other hand, take account of how this will affect your mortgage. Building societies don't lend on furnishings. So, say their maximum advance is

90 per cent and you are buying at £50,000, your top mortgage is £45,000; so if there is £2,000 worth of carpets, etc. included in the purchase price, the highest the building society surveyor can value the house at is £48,000 and the maximum advance is £43,200, so your deposit now becomes £6,800 instead of the number you first thought of. Bear in mind, however, that it is highly unlikely that a solicitor, acting for a vendor, would allow unrealistic apportionments to be made, since this would be a fraud on the Revenue. The Stamp Duty Land Tax return requires you to fill in the amount which is paid for chattels. This return is signed by you. The Revenue will enquire as to whether the apportionment is reasonable and may investigate if they don't think that it is. Therefore, I leave to your honesty and ingenuity the rest of the sums on which your decision rests.

8. Look at the rate of interest (contract rate) in the contract. This is usually 4 per cent above bank base rate. If it specifies the Law Society's rate, that is 4 per cent over the base rate of Barclays Bank. You will be expected to pay interest at that rate if you delay completion beyond the date which eventually gets inserted in the contract. The most likely reason for you getting caught with having to pay this type of interest will be if your purchase money is dependent on the sale money from your present house, and you can't make your purchaser complete simultaneously. If the rate is the same as in your sale contract, and you have your purchaser tied to 4 per cent above bank base rate also, then you have a source from which to collect any penalty money. Unfortunately, the period for which this interest is payable is limited. After the time allowed in each contract, the deposit is forfeited by the seller.

9. Covenants Clause: with the draft contract, Skinner should send you a copy of all the covenants. There is not much you can do about them, but you certainly want to know everything there is to know, because you buy property warts and all, and once you are the owner, you will be responsible for seeing that the covenants (if any) are adhered to.

You can also ask to be assured that the previous owners have kept to the covenants. For instance, if there is a covenant that only a certain type of house should be built on the plot, and plans should have been approved and agreed by some previous owner, ask to see the approvals. If there is anything in the contract you feel should be amended, mark it in red ink and send it back to the vendor.

Remember, if there is a suspicion that there has been a breach of covenant within the last 20 years, no Council of Mortgage Lenders (CML) member will lend money on the house unless someone pays for restrictive covenant indemnity insurance and since it is your vendor's blemish, not yours, make sure it is a term of the agreement that he pays and get an offer before you contract.

Purchaser: When agreement has been reached on the draft contract, you can put it to one side and give your attention to the replies you will have received to your enquiries of the district council.

The Enquiries of Local Authority form usually comes back with a printed list of answers. In 999 cases out of 1,000, it will confirm that the road is made up, taken over and maintained at public expense: that there are no road widening proposals, and no proposals to build a new road within 200 metres of the property. If you had been afraid lest the council had an army of workmen at the ready, itching to get on with demolishing a garage or extension which had previously been built infringing building regulations and planning permission, the replies will either confirm your suspicions or put your mind at rest.

If it turns out that the road is about to be made up, you will want to know what the cost is likely to be and how much the vendor is prepared to knock off the price to meet it. If the property is about to be pulled down for slum clearance or the infringement of building regulations, your course of action is obvious.

Having called at the council office, you will have put flesh on the bones of the more-or-less standard answers on the form. You will have found out if there is to be a motorway within 201 metres or whether there is any development scheme in the offing that could affect the property, being either a whole shopping precinct, or an application to convert the quaint little antique shop on the corner to a fish and chip shop. In the unlikely event of you getting a reply that you do not understand, either call in on the council or give them a ring.

Form LLC1 will drop through your letterbox at the same time. The council will either certify that 'the search requested reveals no subsisting registrations' or 'the search reveals the registrations described in the schedules hereto …'. If there are any schedules attached, they are likely to refer to smoke control and planning controls that have long since been dealt with. The search might show that an improvement grant was agreed. That does not mean to say the grant was taken up, but you will want to know from the vendor if it was, and if so, whether any part of it has to be repaid on a sale taking place. If there is any verbiage that you don't understand in the replies to your searches and you think it could affect you, ring up the council and ask – council officials are invariably helpful to the learner conveyancer.

You are now almost in a position to send off your signed part of the contract, either in the form it was originally drafted or as amended by agreement.

It is about this time you should be thinking of insurance and so reread the information on 'risk' at page 79. The first question is should the insurance come into force when you exchange or when you complete? Then how much do you insure for? It should be for the reinstatement value of the house and all necessary expenses and it should be inflation-linked. This sum may well be less than the price you are paying, but then the land is not going anywhere, is it? Only the buildings are at risk. If you are borrowing, the lender's valuer will probably have stated the minimum level of required insurance. Otherwise you are on your own!

In its offer of a mortgage, the lender may nominate an insurance company. Unless you have some root and branch objections to the nominees, get your insurance with them then write and let the lender know. Check that the offer of a mortgage which you have received is a firm one. In addition, if your purchase is dependent on receiving the money from your own sale, you will realise that ideally the contracts should be signed simultaneously, but this is difficult to imagine because it entails getting all the parties together at the same time in the same place, and if everyone is taking the same precaution then all would need to be ambidextrous. The only sensible solution, therefore, if your purchase is dependent on your own sale, is to make absolutely certain that you have received your sale contract signed by your purchaser and that any conditional clauses can and will be met, before you sign up to buy, and that if necessary you can find overnight accommodation.

So here is your checklist on the eve of exchange of contracts:

- Draft contract has been agreed and one of your copies has been returned unsigned to vendor.

- Satisfactory replies have been received in the Seller's Property Information Forms or Enquiries before Contract.

- You are satisfied with the replies you received to the forms you sent to the council, what you learned on your fact-finding tour and to your water company and envirosearch.

- If the Office Copies revealed anything such as a caution or a Matrimonial Home charge, the vendor has obtained cancellation of the registration of such a charge or notice.

- You have got a firm offer of a mortgage.

- If it applies, you have your own sale tied up. If a deposit cheque bounces, the contract is automatically washed out.

- You have checked that everyone over the age of 18 who lives in the house is prepared to move, whether their names appear on the register or not, by getting them to sign a statement to this effect in the contract.

- There are no problems with the survey of the property.

So here goes! Insert the agreed date for completion into the contract. This is usually one month hence, so if you feel there is still a lot of reading left in this chapter also remember there is one month to do it in. There is no reason why it shouldn't be earlier than the usual month if it will save either party paying money on bridging loans. Sign the contract and send it off to Skinner, together with the balance of the agreed deposit, which will need to be sent early enough to clear – the usual period is four working days, although if you wish to pay by personal cheque a special condition to this effect will have had to have been inserted in the contract. Alternatively, you can send it in the form of a bank draft or electronic transfer. For money laundering purposes the solicitor would probably be happier with CHAPS transfer. Finally, don't forget to put the date of signing at the top of the contract.

Two words of warning. Skinner needs to know whether he can exchange with you or whether you have other plans; for example, you are waiting for something like a search certificate, amended mortgage offer, or for your own buyer to reach the stage where he can exchange with you, so unless Skinner has your carte blanche to exchange on receipt tell him to hold it to your order till you are ready to release contract – that is, allow him to exchange with you. Also, if there is a chain with you in the middle, you may well find you cannot exchange at all since no one will trust you to honour your word. You can show them your tattoo 'Death before Dishonour', but it will cut no ice. What happens, for example, is the buyer at the bottom of the chain tells the next one up that he is ready and that contracts can be exchanged before, say, 4.30 that day. If the recipient is ready, he tells the next person up the line and so on. The system works because the authority given is irrevocable and is backed by the professional ethics that solicitors adhere to, all of whom should also be insured against error. You do not enjoy this sainted status and will be seen as the 'Weakest Link'. The answer is get Skinner to act as your agent, so it is his word people act on, not yours. What he does for you is purely a private matter between the two of you.

Vendor: We have not forgotten you! The astute reader will have realised by now how little a vendor has to know or do in order to be his own conveyancer. However, you must rouse yourself, at this point, to receive the signed contract from the purchaser. Check that the contract he has signed is identical to the one you have signed, otherwise the contract will be void. At this point have a word with the stakeholder to make sure the deposit will be paid.

Even if your purchaser is getting a 100 per cent mortgage, I think you should still insist on a deposit. After all, if he is such a good risk that the lender doesn't require him to have a stake in the house, he should have no difficulty in raising a bank loan for five per cent of the purchase price. If you don't get a deposit, your contract is shaky. As pointed out before, there is a difference between having rights and asserting them. You cannot get blood out of a stone. It is much more costly to sue for damages than to simply hold onto the deposit if he backs out of the deal. Sign your copy of the contract and send it to the purchaser.

Contracts are now said to be exchanged. The deal is now binding and neither side can back out without penalty. If you have a mortgage on the property, write to your lender saying that contracts have been exchanged. Ask them how much will be required to pay off your mortgage on the completion date. Also ask for the daily rate that will be charged in the unlikely event of completion being delayed.

Purchaser: Receive vendor's part of the contract and check details. Pay particular attention that both parties have signed if the house is owned jointly or even if it is not owned jointly, that all people in occupation have signed or at least given a signed release of their rights. While all this has been going on, you have been dealing with the solicitor for the lender. Every mortgage lender has a list of solicitors who act for it in the completion of mortgage advances – no others will be used by the lender. If there is a mortgage, everything bar agreeing to the contract will be done by the lender's solicitors.

Most solicitors are on the rolls of most mortgage lenders, although CML members are suspicious of sole practitioners. So when a purchaser gets a mortgage, what do you know, the solicitor acting for him in his purchase may also get instructions to act for the lender. It makes sense by saving too many solicitors trailing round too many other solicitors' offices to complete a sale.

The solicitor acting for the lender will write, asking you to produce a number of documents. As the information contained in the papers he requests could in the future be quite useful to the layperson conveyancer, photocopy them, because lenders usually keep the lot.

This is what they require:

- Enquiries before Contract and vendor's solicitors' replies or completed Seller's Property Information Forms;
- local authority search forms and replies;
- vendor's part of the original contract;
- Land Registry Office Copies;
- copy of transfer;
- replies to Requisitions on Title;
- copies of any other documents of title, i.e. deeds of covenants, licences for alterations, licenses to assign, etc.

You will have noticed one new item in the above list. It need not cause you any trouble. It is the transfer, the very form which does the trick of getting your vendor's name off the Land Register and putting yours on. The transfer form is TR1, and you will remember meeting it on the very first page of this chapter, and now you come face to face with it, you will find that, though of supreme importance, it is the easiest of the lot (example provided in Appendices at the end of this Guide).

Buyers on new estates will require Form TP1. The draft is usually provided by the developer, because he wants to put in a swathe of conditions that were not in the conveyance of the land to him.

After exchange of contracts, you are expected to send a draft of the transfer form to the vendor's solicitor. At the time of writing the TR1 available from the Land Registry and online provides at '1. Stamp Duty' a space where HM Revenue & Customs can impress the stamps following payment of Stamp Duty prior to registration. As from 1 December 2003, Stamp Duty has been replaced for land transactions by Stamp Duty Land Tax. Under the stamp duty regime if no duty, or duty at a reduced rate, is payable, you had to complete one of the two certificates below '1.' This no longer applies and if a transaction is exempt from Stamp Duty it must be certified by a 'self certificate' lodged with the transfer, which can be obtained from the Stamp Office orderline. Rather unhelpfully the Land Registry has stated that it will reject any transaction that is certified under the old regulations. It is to be anticipated that the form will be updated soon. If you think that your transaction might be exempt, for example because it is a gift, you need to check the categories which are found in Schedule 3 Finance Act 2003. Put an 'x' in the second box if the price of the house is priced £120,000 or below. A change from the Stamp Duty regime is that even if the price of a house falls below the threshold of £120,000, the sale must still be notified to the Revenue so that there is a certificate to the effect that any duty due has been paid. Fill in the title number, which by now you will almost have memorised, the address of the property you are buying, leave a blank for the completion date, put in the price you have dragged the vendor down to, exclusive of cost of any extras, then put in the name and present address of the vendor and finish the labour by inserting your own name and new address. If you are married or buying jointly with someone else, decide what is to happen when one of you dies (no. 11). So if you are buying jointly, put both your names. Whether the two names are those of spouses or not, the house can still be owned so that when one of you dies, the survivor takes all (joint tenants), or so that the deceased partner's share goes into the deceased partner's estate (tenants in common). If the latter option is chosen, the share is normally a half but does not have to be. In either case, the Registrar has to be informed and we will deal with how later – for the moment if you want the ownership to be in joint names simply put the two names on the form.

Finally, complete the certificate of value, which the Revenue man requires – he doesn't trust the property owning classes. If you can manage to buy a house for £120,000 or less, you have no Stamp Duty to pay. Agree to pay the vendor an extra £1 if he will leave the cat-flap and with a purchase price of £120,001 you will have to pay one per cent stamp duty (£1,200). Being a freeborn Englishman the Revenue man expects you to get up to every trick in the book in order to side-skip paying your money over to him. Unless you sign otherwise, he suspects you of trying to buy the house in bits: £5,000 for the billiard room, £5,000 each for each of the bathrooms and £2,000 each for each of the bedrooms and so on, all done in separate transactions. So the Revenue insist that you certify that the 'transfer hereby effected does not form part of a larger transaction or series of transactions in respect of which the amount or value or aggregate amount or value of the consideration exceeds £…'. If the purchase price is £120,000 or less, that is the figure you put in. You enter the next higher figure, either at which tax starts to be payable (£120,001) or at which Stamp Duty increases – at £250,001 it increases to three per cent and over £500,001 it increases to four per cent. You will have to file a Land Transaction Return, which contains a similar certificate. The bands for Stamp Duty Land Tax are the same as those on Stamp Duty.

Vendor: Receive the draft transfer and check it. Also check the amount being paid and the spelling of all names.

Purchaser: Your conveyancing doesn't have to be done overnight. If, from reading the instructions so far it seems to you that there are a lot of fiddling little things to do, bear in mind three things.

In the first place they are mainly practical and not legal. Second, even after contracts are exchanged, you should have approximately one month to do it all in. Lastly, but fruitiest of the lot, a number of people's hopes are riding on your buying the house and it is surprising how helpful others can be when they need to be.

During the next few pages references to yourself, your lender's solicitor, the vendor's solicitor, his lender's solicitor and where you are selling at the same time, your purchaser's solicitor and his lender's solicitor, not to mention the lender's solicitor for your own sale if you are changing lenders, could lead you to think that for completion day you might have to put up a marquee (light refreshments to be served) in the garden or, if wet, book St. Pancras Town Hall. *Not so.* Solicitors are capable of wearing many hats at the same time and you'll no doubt finish up with only one if you're a first-time buyer without a mortgage, or two if you are involved in a chain.

Send off two Requisitions on Title forms. This form asks questions about the date for completion and what money will be required: a completion statement. It also asks the vendor to produce receipts for outgoings and is mainly referring to rates, i.e. payments due under the lease such as the service charge or ground rent.

If the Seller's Property Information Form or Enquiries before Contract were completed again now, it asks, would the replies be as they were hitherto. A question concerns mortgages. It starts strongly with 'all subsisting mortgages must be discharged on or before completion' but then weakens and goes on to ask what form of undertaking to hand over receipts is proposed. So if on the Charges Register of the Office Copies you received there was a charge (mortgage) to a finance company, write in the space provided for additional questions: 'Form DS1 to be provided by mortgagee with charge certificate duly sealed and signed'. However, the DS1 will not be signed until after completion.

The vendor or his solicitor must twiddle his thumbs till the mortgagee condescends to type sign and post it on. He will not issue a DS1 before completion to a solicitor and certainly not to someone representing himself. Plus, some do not do this, taking advantage of the recent Electronic Notification of Discharge scheme.

The best a purchaser will get is a solicitor's undertaking to pay off the mortgage and send DS1 on as soon as he has it. The undertaking from the person acting as the vendor will not be acceptable to the buyer's solicitor regarding the production of the DS1 and it has to be given by a solicitor redeeming the mortgage. If the vendor is acting for himself, no purchaser should accept such an undertaking since it is not backed by The Law Society, but probably in this case the lender has their own solicitor to act on the redemption of the mortgage, so the purchaser can simply ask for information on what is due and then pay it himself out of the purchase price asking the lender's solicitor to supply the undertaking.

He can even do this if the lender is not paying anyone to represent their interest, but trying to get anyone in their offices these days who can be relied on for anything more than reading out blurb on a computer over the telephone can be a bit difficult. The whole point about big money lending institutions is that ideally everyone else does the work for them and without charging; in recent years the dumbest kid on the block, who will still happily do this, and pay insurers to pick up the tab if anything goes wrong, is the less than streetwise solicitor. He rests secure in the vanity that he is a professional, and a person of note in the community, while everyone else gets on with reality.

A note of warning here to purchasers acting for themselves: most mortgage lenders are CML members and they invariably require their borrowers to get legal advice on their responsibilities and liabilities as a borrower. Before you contract to buy the house, make sure the people you are borrowing from are not going to insist you get advice or need to sign before a solicitor even as a mute witness. The trouble with borrowing other people's money is that they can lay down rules like this. After all, they do not lend money for your convenience, whatever their marketing department might say.

The vendor's solicitor should provide any information and documents you will require in order to register your ownership, but he might, just for fun, retain papers or information you are going to need. But not to worry, because in sending you the Standard Conditions of Sale, he has bound himself to provide all the documents you will need.

Also, use the space at the end of the form into which you can feed any additional questions that your lender may ask in response to the documents you will have sent them. Their response will also almost certainly include:

- The printed mortgage form for you to sign in front of a witness. Have a scan through the mortgage form (legal charge) but don't invite a headache. It is a take-it-or-leave-it situation – no variations are allowed. Nowadays, most lenders require that mortgage documents are executed in front of a solicitor. They will also insist on the solicitor registering their charge (i.e. solicitors' costs and the registration fee) at the Land Registry and will expect the buyer to pay for this. As you are not planning to use a solicitor, arrange one of two things with such a lender, either to sign on completion in front of their solicitor or for them to waive the point. It isn't a legal requirement, being neither oath nor statutory declaration.

- An account made up of the fees you have to pay their solicitor, Land Registry fees, pre-completion search fees, Stamp Duties, etc. The total will be deducted from the money produced on completion day. This amount would probably be not much less than if the buyer used a solicitor of his own who would act on the lender's behalf for free.

- A sheet of requisitions (questions) about your purchase. Lenders don't have a standard form. You will find that the questions are more or less the same as you asked the vendor's solicitor in your Enquiries before Contract.

  Copy off the answers you were given and if there are any you haven't already got the answers to, get on to the vendor's solicitor right away and get the answers back to the lender as quickly as possible, in case they raise supplementaries, as you can do without being harassed by their questions right up to completion day.

  This form will also ask you if you intend to live in the house and to confirm that the whole of the difference between the mortgage advance and the purchase money is being found out of your own resources and without recourse to any other form of borrowing. The lender might also enclose a list of any further documents they require on completion. If they don't, ask them to let you have such a list as soon as possible.

- If applicable, NHBC Form 12 and the NHBC agreement itself.

Vendor: Receive Requisitions on Title – post-exchange questions on title asking about redeeming the mortgage, the completion statement, the payment and purchase monies, etc.

Make up a completion statement as requested, by showing purchase price minus deposit paid. Don't worry about the Council Tax because it is levied on the occupier; simply let the local authority know the date you are moving out and if you have managed to overpay tax they will reimburse you. The purchaser cannot be required to pay for water if you have paid in advance; so ask your water company for an apportioned rebate up to completion date.

Purchaser: Receive replies to Requisitions on Title form and completion statement. If you are buying without a mortgage, you can skip the next bit until we come to Form OS1. About this time you should be in possession of the list of documents your lender will require on completion. They will always require a minimum of:

1. Vendor's Land Certificate (or Charge Certificate if the house is mortgaged). Now Land Certificates and Charge Certificates are no longer produced, an Office Copy Entry should suffice.

2. Vendor's lender's solicitors' undertaking to send you a Land Registry Form DS1 discharging vendor's mortgage.

3. Transfer form TR1 signed by the vendor. Form TP1 if buying from a builder or part of a registered title (i.e. a new title being carved out of an existing larger title), TR2 for a repossession.

   These three forms you will, of course, receive from Skinner on completion. The rest of the documents your lender will ask you to produce are:

4. Mortgage form (Legal Charge) signed by you.

5. They will probably ask you for a copy of the Land Transaction Return, SDLT 1, which is to be provided to the Revenue together with payment of any SDLT which may be due

   Much of the information on the SDLT 1 is provided by means of codes. These codes are to be found in the guidance notes (which are fairly self-explanatory). You need to ask for SDLT 6, which are the guidance notes. Alternatively, the guidance notes may be found on the Stamp Office website: www.hmrc.gov.uk/so.

6. The reply you received to the Form K16, the bankruptcy form (see page 128).

7. Form OS1, Application by Purchaser for official search. Again, a name-and-address job, plus enter the title number and in box 8, 'Search From Date', the date of issue of Office Copy. If you are borrowing money, give the name of the lender and tell the Land Registry it is for a mortgage, so complete box C on the form. If you are not, search in your name and tell the Land Registry you are purchasing and fill in box P. If you search in your own name as the purchaser, your lender cannot rely on the reply and will not accept it. An important form this, which was mentioned in chapter 11, 'The Registers', so we won't labour it again. Suffice to say that you are

enquiring of the Registry whether anyone has registered any dealings in the land since the date the Office Copies were made for you.

There is a fee for this service, currently £4. Don't send this form off until about 10 days before the date agreed for completion, for, as you will see it gives you protection (priority expires box) for 30 working days, 6 weeks, in other words, from the date the application was received in which to complete and register your deal. Though this is a lender's requirement, you should use this form even if you are not taking a mortgage. If you are buying from a landlord who has other properties registered under the same title number or a builder who is developing an area of land, use Form OS2, Search of Part. The Registry needs to know which part, and it is up to the vendor to provide you with sufficient identification (plans, plot no., etc.) to satisfy the Registrar.

8. Form AP1 Application to Change the Register.

9. Form DS1. This is the form that tells the Land Registry to cancel the registration of the vendor's lender's mortgage. Only the vendor can supply this and then not for a week or more after completion. Or not at all if Electronic Notification applies. What the lender will actually want is a cast-iron guarantee that the mortgage will be paid off. Normally, a vendor's solicitors' undertaking will suffice. This will state that the vendor's solicitors will pay off the mortgage from the purchase monies and will forward Form DS1 to the buyer's solicitors when sealed by the lender as evidence that payment has been received.

If the discharge is accompanied by other transactions, the form will be lodged under cover of Form AP1. If stand alone, it is to be accompanied by Form DS2.

The solicitor for the building society will expect you to pay his fees.

You might not be absolutely certain exactly which forms and documents will be 'lodged with this form' as Panel 3 (DS2) requires. Don't worry, you can safely rely on the lender and Skinner to help you out on completion day, because you are not the only party to this deal and matters have gone so far by now, that in 999 cases out of 1,000 your vendor is just as anxious to see the colour of your money as you are to see that of the person who is buying your present abode. So you have them. And as US President

Richard Nixon once said, 'When you have them by the balls, their hearts and minds are sure to follow'!

Vendor: Sign the transfer form and get your partner to sign beside you if the house is in joint names. You will need to sign this in front of an independent, adult witness who should afterwards add his name, address and occupation in the spaces provided. If you have no mortgage to pay off, choose your spot for completion. If you have a mortgage, then as the Charge Certificate and the rest of the papers will have to be sent to your lender's solicitor (if they have one) you will have to use his office. If the lender does not have a solicitor, you are going to have to ask your lender to send the deeds to a solicitor on their panel to act in this capacity, and they might be willing to conduct a completion meeting on site but do not bank on it. They would rather have the money by CHAPS transfer. The lender's solicitor doesn't have much to do, but nevertheless charges the lenders and they in turn charge you by adding the fees on to the outstanding balance of your account with them. His job is to collect and give a receipt for the money and hand over the Charge Certificate to you.

Let your purchaser know the venue and exact time. Also inform him that you will require the balance of the purchase price in the form of a CHAPS payment, which has the advantage over a cheque in that it cannot be stopped and it will not bounce.

In case you are wondering how you would cope with paying off your mortgage in order to lay your hands on the deeds for handing over on completion of a sale, this is how it is done:

Get to know the exact amount of money required on the due date (called a redemption figure). At the same time ask if your lender will give you and the purchaser's solicitor 'the usual' undertaking to send the deeds on to your purchaser's solicitor after completion, in return for a CHAPS payment made payable to your lender, which you will have arranged to be made as part of the purchase money on completion of your sale, to pay off your mortgage with. You are released from the mortgage, and hey presto, the deeds are sent on to your purchaser's solicitor in a short time. The purchaser's solicitor can also give you the balance of the purchase price in the form of a second CHAPS payment; do not be surprised if a fee for this second payment is debited from the sale price, because the purchaser's solicitor may tell his client that since you have no solicitor who could accept one payment and distribute it, why should his client pay for two?

Don't give them the keys of your property until you see the colour of their money.

In practice, do not be too surprised to find no one trusts you or wishes to meet with you at completion, or can say at what time they can complete. So for a more likely scenario, see 'Planning for completion' below.

Purchaser: Receive the completion statement and the request about how the money is to be split. If you don't receive them seven days before completion, gee the other side up – you will soon have plenty of problems coping with crockery and curtain runners, without having uninvited last-minute jobs to do on the financial side.

You have no doubt bought and sold motor cars in the past. Collecting the money on one, paying out on another; paying off the HP on one and obtaining HP on another, are all very fiddly; all on the surface very complicated. Housing transactions are much the same, the big difference being that when the money from the sale of one car is being used to purchase another, both cars can be at the scene of completion. Unless you are moving next door or across the street, this is not possible with housing transactions. So look at the purchase at this stage as being of the title deeds (the Land or Charge Certificate and the transfer form), which represent the house. Anyway, approach the financial side of completion of your purchase as you did swapping cars and you won't go far wrong.

Planning for completion

You now have an interesting dilemma. How to complete? Since you are not a solicitor and since a solicitor will represent everyone or nearly everyone else in the chain, you have a problem. There was a time when you demanded your buyer to come to your property to complete, or if you had a mortgage you would go to the offices of the lender or its solicitors. Here you would swap deeds, cash (or its equivalent) and the keys. This was common 30 years ago, but not now.

The idea that you ask a solicitor to come to your house to complete will cause great merriment. The likelihood is that the solicitor will retell the story at dinner parties to the amusement of all and in time the story will no longer be recognisable. You will have become an urban legend, but for all that, you will receive no visitors at completion. What with electronic cash transfers (often the slowest and most annoying part of the whole process), computerised access to Land Registry records, the ability to search using a computer or the telephone, movement of letters and draft documents by post, fax and email attachments, people do not expect to pay a solicitor to wander around the countryside for completions and so none will. Not that it was ever practicable if there is a long chain that stretched around the country but, here and there, localised completion meetings were once commonplace.

Every case is different, so try to cobble together a completion plan, but the more people there are in the chain the less likely it is that you will be a welcome visitor to the offices of your lender's or your buyer's solicitor, so be prepared to have to pay someone to complete for you. If you are able to make this call, do not be surprised to find out that no one will be able to tell you exactly when they can complete. It can take a long time for money to wander around the country from bank to bank.

Also take your passport with you, in case an objection is raised to handing you a bank draft. In fact, all the solicitors you deal with will insist that you identify yourself, as a safeguard against fraud and as they are required to obtain evidence of identity to comply with their obligations under the money laundering legislation. Your lender's solicitor is given guidance on what to ask for. For those of you on the internet, have a look in section 3 of the CML *Lender's Handbook for England and Wales* on www.cml.org.uk.

Vendor: What are the possibilities?

You are not buying and have no mortgage to pay off. Lucky you. Your buyer's solicitor is not going to call on you and you will not be given any cash until he has all that he thinks he needs. Your best solution is to ask if he will accept from you the deeds and the signed transfer to be held to your order until you are paid. He will not be handing you a box of bank notes or a bank draft and will want to send the money to you by CHAPS transfer to an account nominated by you. You should ask that he undertakes not to part with the deeds until his bank has irrevocable instructions to send the money to you.

You are not buying but have a mortgage to pay off, so ask your lender to nominate a solicitor to represent their interests and ask him to do the same for you as explained in the previous paragraph.

Life becomes fun if you are selling and buying. Your old house is in Devon, the new house is in Essex, your old lender is in Kent and the new lender is in Leeds, and the solicitor who represents your seller is in none of these places. Much the same can be said of your seller and your buyer. Also there are roadworks on the M4 and cones (but no sign of work or workman) on the M25 so flying visits are out. Clearly you are going to have to find a solicitor in the chain to act as your agent.

Do not ask your original lender's solicitors. They have absolutely no interest whatsoever in seeing the matter is completed on the day of your choosing. Next week is as good as this week. Your lender will not be that fussed whether the deal goes through on the day or a week late. After all, the longer it takes the more interest you pay them. Try to persuade someone more closely connected with the transaction, such as the solicitor who represents the people you are borrowing money from, for the new house. They do have an interest in completing the loan since that is what their clients do for a living. Lend money. Or try the solicitor who represents the person buying your house or the solicitor who represents the person you are buying from. He too has clients who will expect 'their man' or 'their women' to get the job done. Again, you will need your chosen solicitor to act as your agent and to hold documents/money to your order until he receives instructions that everything is in place.

Assuming you come up with a workable plan, what next?

You are wearing two hats. You are a vendor and also a purchaser, and the solicitor who is going to do the deed for you will need the relevant deeds, documents, search certificates and so forth. The best thing to do is to ask what he wants. Then if he misses something, it becomes his primary problem. It will also be his task to ensure the correct money comes and goes, to supply any undertakings required and to see you get the residue (if any) due to you.

As the vendor, all you will normally be asked for is the transfer Form TR1 of your house and your Land or Charge Certificate. Your purchaser's solicitors will have typed it, and chances are they will have told you how to sign it.

You may not have the deeds. The bank or building society that has the mortgage over your house have these, and they will have been passed to their solicitors. The solicitors who will be carrying the sale through for you will supply the undertaking the purchaser's solicitors will demand, namely that the mortgage will be paid off and that Form DS1 (the Land Registry's formal release) will be sent on to the purchaser's solicitors when received.

Purchaser: The likely problems and the possibilities are much the same. However, first things first. Arrange with the vendor or his agent for the keys to be available to you or your representative (you can't be in two places at once), for a swift inspection to make sure that everything that was to be left behind is still there, and everyone who was to move out has gone. Make sure you are truly getting vacant possession on completion and if anyone is still there, do not complete, no matter what fanciful explanations or excuses are tried on you. Such a case is one in a million but who wants to be a statistic? This final inspection is made to avoid the greatest calamity of all that can possibly befall a purchaser of a house intended for his own immediate occupation. So whether employing a solicitor or doing your own conveyancing, make sure that no person is left in the house, and also make sure the fixtures and fittings and any extras you are paying for have not been taken.

Now for the possibilities:

You are paying cash and do not need a mortgage. Your seller's solicitor can say where completion is to take place and may just be willing to have you call at his office to complete.

Make sure you have all the identification the solicitor is obliged to see – the money laundering legislation, remember! – and ask how he wishes to receive the money. Do not be surprised if a bank draft is not welcome, but if that is how you wish to pay, insist on this if the contract allows it. However, the fourth edition of the Standard Conditions provides that the balance may only be paid by 'direct credit' – again, to guard against money laundering – so unless you altered it you will have to pay by CHAPS.

When you get to the meeting, check the papers. First, compare the Land or Charge Certificate with the Office Copy of the title you were given, before exchange of contracts. Make sure the transfer has been properly signed by the vendor and witnessed, and make sure anything else you need (which depends on circumstances) is available, for example undertakings to pay off an existing mortgage on the house and to send you Form DS1 when this has arrived in their office.

When all of this is in order, hand over the bank draft in exchange. On the other hand, perhaps you were properly required to pay by CHAPS transfer and so the money may be sitting in their bank account while you are sitting in their chair! Anyway, take up what you want and ask them to telephone the estate agents to release the keys. Then leave!

You are buying and do need a mortgage. In this case, the people you are borrowing money from will have their own solicitor (although you pay normally) and it may be that he has agreed to complete for you (and his own clients). In this case, he will want from you the various papers listed at pages 145–6 as relevant to the transaction.

The probability is that they will have asked you for all these papers before the day of completion and it is extremely unlikely that they will wish to see you at completion, except to the extent necessary to carry out their money laundering checks. In this case, they will be taking up the deeds, checking the transfer and demanding the necessary undertakings for paying off any existing mortgage on the house. They will probably leave it to you to worry about ensuring the keys are released, but you never know. They might just telephone when the transaction was completed.

Whichever option applied, the job is done. You've got yourself a new house!

Cash buyers

For you, there is still work to do. You will need a certificate that you have paid the Stamp Duty Land Tax and the transfer will need to be registered. If you are borrowing on the house, the lender's solicitor may well insist on attending to these formalities, although the Stamp Duty Land Tax Return must be signed by the purchaser. Otherwise, it is down to you. There are two deadlines you should comply with:

Stamp Duty Land Tax

Stamp Duty Land Tax is payable if the cash price stated in the transfer is above £120,000. In the unlikely event that the purchase price was below £120,000, you must still notify the Revenue of the transaction. You get 30 days from the effective date (which is either completion or, if earlier, the date when you were let into possession of the land) to submit the Land Transaction Return, failing which you will be fined £100. HM Revenue &

Customs claim they pocket this money in the interests of fairness, but they would say that, wouldn't they? The form you need to fill in is the SDLT 1. It looks quite formidable at first but it isn't. Rather than supplying a box to fill in that you have purchased the property, you have to fill in 'codes'. These are found in the guidance notes Form SDLT 6. Each SDLT1 has a unique number and photocopies are not acceptable. They can be ordered from the orderline on 0845 302 1472 or alternatively you can fill it in online – www.hmrc.gov.uk/so – then click 'Complete your returns using the online service'. You must send a cheque with the return, but you must not send any other documents other than SDLT 2, 3 or 4, which apply when the transaction is more complicated that the purchase of one house. Not just any office, mind. All Land Transaction Returns must be sent to HMRC SDLT, Netherton, Merseyside, L30 4RN.

Under no circumstances whatsoever should you post the Return to your local tax office! It will confuse them considerably. If you have sent the Return correctly filled in with the right amount of tax, the Revenue will send you a Land Transaction Return Certificate to show you have paid the duty. You will need this when you come to register the purchase.

Registration

A transaction is void if it is not registered within a month. In any event, you should aim to see that your application is with the Land Registry the day before the last day of the priority period noted in your search. You are not the legal owner of your house until you are registered. Double-check your search certificate received from the Land Registry to find that date. The reason for getting your application in before 'the search expires' is to make sure you get there before anyone else – a creditor waiting in the wings, for example. Searches can no longer be extended, but they can be renewed. However, renewal does not afford the same protection, so try to get it right first time. If you slip up, generally it does not matter, but it might, and if it does it could prove to be an expensive mistake because others may register and will then have priority over your interest.

Your application is usually made using Form AP1. Complete the form and send along the transfer Form TR1, the Land or Charge Certificate, a cheque for the fees, Land Transaction Return Certificate and if your vendor had a mortgage you will also send along Form DS1. The DS1 might not be available for days, if not weeks after completion, so if necessary just send it along later. It may even be that there is no DS1 if your vendor's lender is using the recently adopted Electronic Notification of Discharge scheme. If this applies, they tell the Land Registry their mortgage can be cleared from the record rather than issue a DS1 that an applicant can send along. The registration fees change from time to time, so telephone the relevant Land Registry, ask for enquiries and ask for the figure.

A final word on registration: it is very important that you send your Land Transaction Return Certificate (or self certificate if the transaction was exempt from SDLT) together with your AP1 and TR1. If the Land Transaction Return Certificate is not enclosed, the Land Registry will reject your application. The only exception to this is where the Revenue have held on to your Land Transaction Return for 20 days. So check and double-check before sealing the envelope to send off to register your interest!

Builders

If you bought from a builder, the preceding observations are essentially correct, save that the builder's solicitors will have supplied the transfer and plan using transfer form TP1 and the Land Registry application form is called FR1 for 'First registration'. Plus, the documents you send along with the application are listed by you using Form DL and you will also need to tell the Land Registry what the builder's deposit number is (if there is one).

His Land Certificate (if he has one) will be placed on deposit with the Land Registry and they will issue a filing number called a Deposit Number. Your builder vendor will tell you what that number is. Have a look at the standard forms sent to you when you first received the legal papers. It should be there somewhere. If you do not have it, telephone the relevant Land Registry two to three days before completion and ask enquiries if the Land Certificate is on deposit. Tell them the title number and they will tell you the answer. If it is not on deposit, don't worry; since 13 October 2003 the Land Registry has not accepted Land Certificates on deposit, so it is not required for your registration as owner of your new house.

In this chapter and those covering contracts, mortgages and registered land I have covered the typical and some not very typical situations that can arise. The same situations can and do arise with unregistered properties, so they will be covered again in the next chapter. If necessary, refer to that. If you come across anything else that does not yield to common sense, telephone the Land Registry enquiries department. From a buyer saying 'I will', to completion taking place, occupies one or two calendar months, so you need not feel rushed.

Pundits never tire of telling us that buying our first house is the biggest investment of our lives. If you are young, and have a lifetime of buying and selling in front of you, your biggest investment has been in the time spent reading and putting into practice these few pages. Tell everybody!

CHAPTER 14

Conveyancing: the sale and purchase of an unregistered house

In chapter 13, I described all that has to be done to transfer ownership of registered property in England and Wales.

What about unregistered? It is supposed to be more difficult, or so we are told. Judge for yourself.

This is a brief summary to start you off, but do read the whole chapter!

Overview

First, look at your deeds and extract all the conveyances you can find. Find one which is at least 15 years old and that is your 'root of title'. All this means is you contract to prove you and your predecessors have owned the house for at least 15 years. Perhaps you bought more than 15 years ago? If so, your conveyance is your root of title. If not, go back in strict date order and pick the one that is at least 15 years old. Copy all of these to your buyer.

Also send along any Land Charges Department name searches you find with the deeds and look at the conveyance to you to see if there is any reference to covenants in an earlier document. If there is, find your copy

A specimen conveyance

Specimen Conveyance

This Conveyance is made the   day of   20

BETWEEN the Vendors Xavier Lax and Susan Lax his wife both of 14 Plevna Place, Blossomton and the Purchasers Bernard Strong and Ivy Strong his wife both of 127 Lowfield Road, Blossomton.

WHEREAS the Vendor is the estate owner in fee simple in possession of the property hereby conveyed free from encumbrances except as hereinafter mentioned and has agreed with the purchasers for the sale to them of the property for the sum of £20,000 (twenty thousand pounds)

THIS DEED WITNESSETH

1. That in consideration of the sum of twenty thousand pounds now paid by the purchaser to the vendor (the receipt of which the vendor hereby acknowledges) the vendor with full title guarantee hereby conveys to the purchaser ALL THAT land and property known as 14 Plevna Place, Blossomton as shown and outlined in red on the plan attached to a conveyance between Henry Feather and the vendor and dated the first of April 1971 and subject to the covenants therein contained TO HOLD the same unto the purchasers in fee simple as joint tenants in law and equity/tenants in common (decide)

2. With the object of giving the vendor a full and sufficient indemnity but not further the purchasers hereby covenant with the vendors to observe, fulfil and perform the above-mentioned covenants and indemnify the vendor against all actions and claims in respect thereof

3. IT IS HEREBY CERTIFIED that the transaction hereby effected does not form part of a larger transaction or series of transactions in respect of which the amount or value or aggregate amount or value of the consideration exceeds £60,000

IN WITNESS OF WHEREOF the parties have hereunto set their hands and seals the day and year first above written

SIGNED AND DELIVERED as a deed by (vendor)
in the presence of   (witness)

SIGNED AND DELIVERED as a deed by (purchaser)
in the presence of   (witness)

of that deed and make sure your buyer gets a copy, even if it dates from before the conveyance you select as your 'root deed'. You may have the original deed, or you may find you have a copy as part of an 'Abstract of Title'. This is a type written summary of the material contents of the deeds that made up the title at the time the Abstract was typed.

The conveyance or transfer to the buyer is, by custom, typed up by the buyer and it is normally dealt with after exchange of contracts. The buyer can type up another conveyance with the new names and sale price (see the specimen opposite) or he can use a Land Registry Form TR1, provided the property is adequately described. Look, for example, at the description in the specimen conveyance.

This is the main difference between buying and selling registered land and buying and selling unregistered land. The title searches are a little different but see below. As for Stamp Duty Land Tax and registration everything said in the previous chapter applies. On the sale of an unregistered house it must be registered, but in this case the Land Registry application form is called FR1 not AP1 and it must be accompanied by a list of the documents you are submitting called Land Registry Form DL.

Looking more closely at the deeds

Conveyances and transfers are deeds and a deed is an instrument in writing, signed, sealed and delivered; such an instrument of transfer of property, from one person to another, is called a conveyance. If you were the cautious buyer of a second-hand lawnmower, and asked the seller to prove it was his to sell, he would produce the receipt. It is the same with an unregistered house. The first part of any conveyance shows this clearly as you can see from our specimen conveyance opposite.

Like the lawnmower buyer, the purchaser of a house needs to be convinced that what the vendor is offering is his to sell. This is usually done by producing a copy of the conveyance which the vendor obtained when he bought. It will be something like our specimen. A copy of the conveyance referred to will come with the draft contract. If the date on the conveyance, showing the present vendor as the purchaser, is more than 15 years old, he has proved title, because when X Lax moved, his solicitor proved to Strong's solicitor that everything was in order.

It seems to be assumed that if, within 15 years of a person taking possession of a property, no one comes along kicking up a fuss about the ownership, then everything must be in order. But what if the house has changed hands 11 times during the past 15 years? Simple enough, if every transaction was a straightforward sale and purchase; you need to see 11 conveyances, linked in the progression A to B; B to C; C to D; … K to Lax. When you are purchasing an unregistered property that has changed hands a number of times in the past 15 years, apart from wondering why it was so unloved, comfort yourself with this thought about the title: all the purchasers in the chain are likely to have employed highly trained solicitors either to check the title or to supervise their clerks' checking of it. No doubt lenders' solicitors will have satisfied themselves about it, too. If you are taking a mortgage, the lender's solicitor will be giving things the once-over at your expense (plus VAT) and you might feel justified in relying on him. If you have any queries please ask him. Ask nicely; you can only be refused.

It is interesting to play detective with a pile of conveyances, but the important ones are the last one and the one before that which is more than 15 years old. Add a clause to the draft contract saying that copies will be provided which cover the previous 15 years, and ask for them to be forwarded as soon as possible.

I have never met anyone who paid for a house and was subsequently in trouble because one of William the Conquerer's hangers-on hadn't the right to sell. It's the last conveyance that counts and you've met the vendor. You need to check that the person named in the last link of the chain as the purchaser is the same as the one named in your contract; that the address of the house you are buying corresponds; that the plan is the same as the one sent with the draft contract, and that after the words TO HOLD it says 'in fee simple' because these two words define the property as freehold, as opposed to leasehold; if it were leasehold, it would refer to the lease in the section beginning ALL THAT.

If your vendor hasn't owned the property for 15 years or more, you will have to apply all the above checks to the conveyances which take you back over the period required.

As we have said, a conveyance forms what is known as 'good root of title'. It is the most usual because it indicates that an investigation of the title was carried out at the time of its making, and in 99 cases out of a 100 proof of ownership of the average house will be by production of a conveyance, or a series of linked conveyances.

Sometimes, another document is required to forge a link. Obviously, a deceased person cannot pass on ownership by making a conveyance. In such a case a devise (see Glossary) is a good root and the document which forms the link between the deceased owner and the next is a copy of the grant of probate, or letters of administration, issued by the High Court out of the District Probate Registry, which shows who was appointed to administer the deceased's estate. This is often followed by an assent by the personal representatives into the name of a beneficiary.

When the personal representatives ('executors' if there is a Will, 'administrators' if not) have finished administering the deceased's estate, they will wish to transfer the property to a beneficiary. They do this by means of a document called an Assent. It is necessary to appreciate that since 1 April 2000, the beneficiary must register his title and so if you are offered a title with an Assent granted after this date, insist the property be registered before you contract to buy it.

A purchaser need not worry overmuch lest a solicitor fails to tie up all these documents, because in sending you the Law Society's Standard Conditions of Sale contract, he has bound himself to do so. A vendor will expect to find all title documents in his deeds parcel, for the same reason.

If the above last four paragraphs apply to your case (and they normally do), please read them again. After all, you did not fully grasp that two plus two equalled four the first time you heard about it. At the moment, you are dealing with a hypothetical case. Once you have a set of forms and documents on the table before you, it will be that much easier to shuffle them about with the aid of these paragraphs.

In case of difficulty, and if the vendor's solicitor hasn't already sent one, ask for an 'epitome of title', which is a list of the deeds that take you back to the root of title or the deed which created the covenants, or both.

In the rest of this chapter, the information will be divided between that for a purchaser and that for a vendor. But don't eschew the other side's information; it's good to know what the other chap is up to, and in any case, you may well be changing roles in a few years' time.

Vendor: Your first step is to get hold of the deeds. If your house is paid for and you haven't already got the deeds at home, go to wherever they are and get them. If the property is still mortgaged, write to the head office of your lender and ask if they will send the title deeds to their branch office nearest your home, as you are selling the property, acting for yourself, and will need to make copies of the relevant documents. Bear in mind that the title deeds are yours. They are only deposited with the lender as security for the money they have lent you.

The bundle, though referred to as 'the deeds', is made up of all sorts of papers that are and are not deeds. There will be copies of old Land Charges Department search certificates, receipted mortgages and, of course, conveyances, and it is the last with which you concern yourself at this stage. They are typed on stout paper, folded and marked on the outside front:

DATED 8 June 1920

Mr V.A. CATER

to

Mr N. SCONCE

Conveyance

of all that messuage or dwelling house known as
and situated at

14 Plevna Place, in the County of Eden

Skinner, Standing & Still Solicitors
Blossomton

When you look at your deeds, bear in mind the three things your purchaser needs to know about the property at this point:

1.   that you own it;

2.   what, if anything, goes with it – rights of way, etc.; and

3.   what can and cannot be done with it.

If you bought 15 years or more ago, your luck is in. Photocopy the conveyance to yourself, make a copy of the plan if there is one, and copy out the covenants and conditions if they are not 'recited' in your conveyance. But if, during the past 15 years, the house has changed hands a few times, you will need to copy each of the conveyances covering the period that takes you back to the root of title, as given at paragraph 4.2.2 of your Agreement.

But what if the house is built on a plot of land sold off from a larger area of land? In that case, you can only expect to find a written summary of previous deeds on which the builder's solicitor (clerk) will have endorsed something like 'examined against originals at the offices of Messrs Skinner & Stonehart solicitors of that parish'. Copy it.

You will also have to photocopy more than the conveyance to yourself (even if you've been the owner for more than 15 years), if the mention of restrictive covenants in your conveyance confines itself to saying that the benefits, easements and covenants are those 'contained, mentioned or referred to in a conveyance dated ... between So and So and Thingummy'. You root out the conveyance to Thingummy and hopefully the list is set out there of what you HOLD/SUBJECT NEVERTHELESS to. This is the set of capital letters which usually heralds the covenants, restrictions, etc. in a conveyance. Photocopy the whole conveyance. Sometimes it will be easy: a straightforward conveyance to you without a covenant in sight. Sometimes you have to beaver away at the pile.

Hopefully, you will get all that is required at the first go. Even if you only think you have, *that is what matters at this stage*, because you send the lot on to your purchaser's solicitor. And if what you have sent is accepted, you move to the next step. On the other hand, if you have made some mistakes or omissions, Skinner will let you know that you've missed a link in the chain, so off you go to the originals again, this time knowing precisely what you are looking for.

If you are not sure of your purchaser and think the sale might go off, either take two copies of everything (because a solicitor might be on holiday when you request a return) or take one copy and, at this stage: (1) rely on paragraph 4.2.2 of your contract or (2) if there is an epitome of title, copy that and add on short notes regarding transactions since the last one mentioned on it. In your covering letter to Skinner itemise what you are sending, as a reminder for yourself and to avoid disputes later.

But for the present, concern yourself with preparing your draft contract. From the conveyance to you, get the date to answer the question beginning 'root of title/title no.'. If the conveyance to you is less than 15 years old, you have to rummage around to find one that is more, and put the parties and date of that in. Completion date is usually left blank at this stage, but there is nothing to stop you putting a date in if you wish – the purchaser can always ask for an amendment. If you are using the Standard Conditions of Sale, fourth edition, and you wish to include anything in the purchase price that you think needs specifying, there is provision for the cost of chattels and a list of itemised chattels on a separate pre-printed form.

Send two unsigned contracts to Skinner, send along the Fixtures, Fittings and Contents Form and ask Skinner if he will accept a completed Property Information Form or whether he prefers to send you his own preliminary enquiries (see page 112) and send along your epitome of title. This is a form that lists the documents of title. Copies must also be sent along. The list is in columns and contains certain information: date, document name, type, whether you are sending a copy or the original, whether a copy or an original will be handed over on completion, etc. It is not just a list; it is an explanation. Years ago, before the days of photocopies, the practice was for the vendor's solicitors to type out a résumé or abstract of the more important clauses in all the required documents. These are called 'abstracts of title'. No solicitor is going to do this now, but if the property has not changed hands for years or if a very old document is referred to and has to be produced to the purchaser's solicitors, you might be shown an abstract for the relevant title or copy.

If your house is mortgaged, you will have to obtain copy documents from your lender or their solicitors. Ask for a copy of all deeds, all searches, all planning permissions and any other consents.

When you have Skinner's answers on enquiries versus the Property Information Form, act accordingly. As for your answers on either, he will no doubt be fully satisfied with your information, but if he isn't, he will write for more information. In that case, reply as best you can.

Do not part with any original deeds at this stage.

Purchaser: You have viewed the house a couple of times and if you need a mortgage, you have got at least half a promise of one. You have bargained the price down with Feather, told him you are acting for yourself and given him your name and address. Receive the draft contract from your vendor's solicitor, who may well not be as helpful as the vendor (above) and you may only receive the draft contract with a copy. Don't worry, he will give evidence of title later on. If you don't like the look of anything in the contract, give the vendor's solicitor a ring and agree the alterations you require and write them into the draft. The kind of things you are looking for are basically the same as for the purchaser of registered property.

The covenants are included in a conveyance, not necessarily the one to your vendor. His may only give the date and the parties to the conveyance in which the covenants were set out in full. Skinner must either set them out in full in the contract, or supply you with a copy of them and refer to the conveyance from which they came, and if he doesn't, insist, because if you are a surgeon and there is a restrictive covenant against surging in or around the premises, you will not wish to waste further time and money on surveys and such like.

Land Registry: Send off Search Form SIM. Give the address and either cut a piece out of a local street map or sketch a little plan of the surrounding streets (it needn't be to scale) to help with identification, if you think the postal address might not be sufficient. When you get the form back it will reveal if there is a caution against first registration, and whether the land is registered or not (don't take the vendor's word on this – he might not know what he is talking about). If it is registered, you will be given the title number, and your task is much simpler from now on – you take your instructions from the previous chapter, after you first find out why your vendor did not know this! If in reply to Form SIM they give you anything you don't understand, ring the enquiries department.

Land Charges Form K15 Application for an Official Search: Search against the names of all owners to find the root of title. If you cannot extract this information from the copy deeds you have been sent, ask your vendor for a list. He may not have them but ask just in case. When searching for land charges you can only search against names, not against the address of the property so the list of names is important.

Your lender will need to know if you have been bankrupt. So together with your Search Form K15 you can send an application for an Official Search (Bankruptcy Only) K16, provided that completion is not more than a fortnight ahead – lenders need up-to-date information. Put in the name/s of the intending borrower/s, enclose a cheque to the tune of £2 for each of the names to be searched on the K15 and K16 forms, and send them off to the address at Plymouth given on the back of the forms.

It is not strictly necessary to search between the dates they acquired the property and sold it (or died) since you can always search from 1926 to the year of your search. It is a good idea to include the name of the vendor at this time on your Form K15, just in case a nasty turns up, but remember you do need a clear certificate that covers the vendor's name on the date you are actually completing the purchase. The priority period, i.e. when the search expires, will appear on the reply.

For instance, your vendors may not be as lovey-dovey as they appeared when they showed you round 'Shangri-La', and if the house was bought in one name, the partner might have registered a Class F charge to protect matrimonial interests. You need to know about any Class F charge as soon as possible, and certainly before you get too involved. If they have come to some arrangement about sharing the proceeds of the sale, so well and good. However, as soon as you receive your protection period certificate from Plymouth get the cautioner to sign an application to cancel the charge. See chapter 15, 'Matrimonial Homes'. A lender's solicitor will expect you to produce the certificate on completion.

Couples do some barmy things when love turns, at best to indifference, at worst to hate. They often do all they can to make things difficult for the other side. If you had been buying a registered title, the Office Copies would have wised you up on this problem. It is so that you don't get caught in the crossfire that I say: K15 to Land Charges Department as soon as possible and certainly before you sign the contract.

Other things that may turn up following your search are records of various third party rights against the property – these can be anything from second mortgages, to options to purchase, to restrictive covenants. If they are registered, they are binding against you as a purchaser.

It is all very well having a contract that is enforceable, but who wants the bother and expense of enforcement? And what if you came up against someone who thought that they and their case were something special, and it would be unjust for the law to be applied to them?

Such a situation has all the makings of a House of Lords case. *Having rights and asserting them are two vastly different things.* In a word you should take a practical approach and make sure there are not nasty surprises waiting around the corner just after you've signed the contract.

Possession really is nine points of the law! And another thing – always change the locks when you move in, particularly if the house has been standing vacant for any length of time.

'Enquiries of Local Authority Form CON 29' together with 'Search of Local Land Charges LLC1': councils require you to provide two copies of each.

Take them to the council as recommended earlier. CON 29 is in two parts. If you want both parts answering it costs more. You must tick any of the questions in Part 2 to which you need an answer. The kind of questions in Part 2 are such as relate to public footpaths, existing and contemplated, building preservation orders and so on, also questions about registration of houses in multiple occupation. If you tick any of them, look up the fee given on the form and add it to the standard fee.

The LLC1 form is printed in duplicate, one copy for the council to retain, and one to be returned to you with the answers. Use a carbon to complete. The local land charges register is divided into 12 parts, and the first question which faces you on the form is which parts you require searching. Strike out 'Part(s) … of' and you will get the lot. It's much simpler, and costs very little more than picking and choosing. Like a lot of things the prices keep moving up, but mercifully the charges are, in this instance, printed on the back of the form. The reference in the fees section of the form to 'each parcel' means plots, so it does not concern the buyer of a single house.

'Seller's Property Information Form': two copies will normally be volunteered by the vendor's solicitor. If your vendor is a company (has 'Ltd' after the name) you need to be extremely careful that the company is not in the process of being wound up. If you are buying such a house that is not registered, you should make a company search at Companies House, Crown Way, Cardiff CF4 3UZ, tel. 02920 380950, www.companies-house.gov.uk/info/ (check fee), either by calling there, or, if it is too far away, by asking your CAB to give you the address of a land agent or credit reference agency who might help. The trouble here (and a solicitor is just as subject to it as you are) is that it takes time for a note of a winding-up petition to be put on a company's file. Nevertheless, any sale made after winding-up proceedings have commenced is only a purported sale and is null and void unless validated. If this looks like it might be the case, you need to get advice.

As the case where you are likely to come across a company as a vendor is with a newly built house, and it will be on an estate where the Registrar has already agreed to register the property, the chance of your having to cope with this problem is extremely remote. It could occur in the case of a shop and house, because many small shopkeepers have been persuaded to trade as limited liability companies in the last few decades. In such cases, caution is the order of the day.

Vendor: Cope with any amendments to the contract, but don't be bullied into giving undertakings, or adding anything to the contract you don't fully understand. Keep asking for explanations and never be fobbed off with 'it doesn't really mean what it says' or 'it's usual, but doesn't apply in this case'. If it doesn't mean what it says or doesn't apply, it may as well be struck out. On the other hand, if you are asked to take something out and you are told, 'Oh! you don't need that' you can riposte, 'Well, if you know it is doing no harm, you won't object to it remaining'.

Purchaser: Receive the Seller's Property Information Form from Skinner and glean from his answers what you can. Remember that the vendor might not want to buy these forms and send you the answers, in which case it is for you to buy some forms called Enquiries before Contract (or similar) (see page 112). It does not really matter what they are called, since they generally cover about the same issues. If you are not satisfied, or suspect that he knows more than he is telling you, send him a few supplementaries in the form of a letter, but remember he was answering stock questions first time round, so it should occasion little surprise that all you got in return were stock answers. There is a time limit on post-contract requisitions – Condition 4.1.1 of the Standard Conditions – so it is vital to get the title approved before contacts are exchanged, by the solicitor acting for your lender. On the other hand, no one will thank the vendor's solicitor if he refuses to answer sensible questions that might lead to a satisfactory completion.

Using the Seller's Property Information Form as a guide, carry out your inspection of the property and its environs, paying particular attention to the area of land within the fences, any facilities such as drives that are shared, and the neighbours' attitudes towards them.

If, on inspection, it turns out that the road leading to the house is badly potholed, it could be an indication that it is not maintained by the council because it is not adopted by them, so pay attention to Enquiries of Local

Council. If it is a private road, after the description of the property in the contract it should say 'together with a right of way over the road coloured sky blue pink on the said plan'. On the other hand, it might say the words 'and the road has been taken over'. Not to worry: of such redundancies are roots of title made up.

CON 29 and LLC1 will come back from the council with their printed answers. Check them through. If replies on either form cause any head-scratching, ask the person who wrote the replies what he means. Council officials will always explain meanings; what they are not empowered to do is advise what should be done about them. But you never know. A remark such as 'my goodness, I wonder what other people do in such a circumstance' might just elicit a useful hint of how to deal with a problem that is not simply of a technical nature.

Remember also to carry out your water and drainage searches and check out environmental issues. Consider also whether you need to carry out a commons search. See chapter 13 for details of what needs to be done and why.

By now, the Land Registry should also have returned your search of Index Map Form SIM, showing the house to be unregistered, but if there is any kind of entry it is your vendor's problem. Let him know, or to be more accurate, remind him, because he will almost certainly already be aware of the entry.

The reply to your K15 will come to you in the form of a Certificate of Result of Search. Whereas the Land Registry keeps a register of land and the name(s) of the owner(s) of each registered parcel of land, the Land Charges Department keeps a register of interests, which third persons can have in an unregistered house, and which can be registered against the names of **people**. So if your vendor is called Tom Jones, the computer will throw up all the Tom Joneses known to it and you will have to decide which entries belong to your vendor. Luckily, it also gives the addresses where the ubiquitous Joneses lived when the various charges were registered against them. If none of the entries applies to your vendor, he or his solicitor must write on the Certificate of Result of Search words to the effect that it is certified that none of the entries applies to him.

You should, however, search against the name not only of your vendor but also of everyone who has ever owned the land, whose name you know, not just down to the root of title. This is because you will be bound by any land charge that is registered, and if you didn't search against a particular name you may live to regret it.

Obviously, a bankruptcy charge would alert you to the fact that all is not well. More likely than not your reply will show 'no entries'. If there is one, it is likely to be one of the following: C (i) is a second (puisne) mortgage. D (ii) is a splatter of covenants which no doubt you already know of. F is a matrimonial home entry. One of the spouses, not being a joint owner, is protecting rights.

What do you do with any of these in the event of one or all showing up? In the case of C (i) second mortgage, as the reply you get will say no more than that the entry exists, you write, quoting the date and reference number, to the Land Charges Registry, asking for a copy of the details. You will have to take appropriate steps to ensure it will be paid off on completion. Get an undertaking from the vendor's solicitor, or if the vendor is acting for himself, you may be at your lender's solicitors' office at completion. Get the vendor to authorise him to pay off the second charge. He will take up sufficient funds on completion to pay off both debts. Matrimonial Homes Class F we have already dealt with.

You will no doubt already know the contents of a D (ii) entry. The vendor or his solicitor should have put a copy with the draft contract. If he hasn't, ask him to bring the job to the top of the pile of 'things to be done today'.

By now, you have sufficient knowledge to give you confidence to go forward, or back out of the deal.

So let us have a little recap of what a purchaser of an unregistered freehold house in England or Wales will have done up to this point.

He will have:

1. received the draft contract in duplicate with map;

2. called at the local council and deposited LLC1 for information about the council's interests in the property;

3. sent or taken Form CON 29 to the council asking questions about roads, drains and restrictions on use;

4. sent Form SIM to the Land Registry to find out if registered, and if not, any cautions against first registration;

5. received Seller's Property Information Form from vendor's solicitor, with what he knows about any boundary disputes, rights of way, planning consents and such like, or sent his own questions, the Enquiries before Contract, to the vendor's solicitor;

6. carried out a Land Charge search using Form K15 against the name of the vendor and all known owners since 1926;

7. dealt with drainage and environmental issues.

It looks a pretty big list of forms, but you should be able to cope, particularly as nowadays solicitors seem to think nothing of taking two calendar months to get to the stage you are now at – I've seen houses built quicker. If you can deal with this increasingly bureaucratic world, and are in a position mentally and financially to buy a house, the forms should not cause you any difficulty, which with the application of a little logic and common sense, you can't solve for yourself.

Having received satisfactory replies, or your vendor being able to satisfy you on any points raised, you are now ready to exchange contracts, provided you have received a satisfactory mortgage offer from your lender.

Our vendor, doing his own conveyance, has been told to send off copies of the previous conveyances with his draft contract. This seems a sensible way to do things as the buyer's solicitors can then check through all of the documents of title, saving the seller from having to work this out.

Note that in the contract, the covenants will be either set out in full or reference made to their first appearance in the deeds and you should expect a copy of them (written out in full) before you sign the contract. And remember that if the covenants predate your vendor's ownership, there is nothing you can do about them.

However, by now, all things having gone well, you can agree a completion date with the vendor. Enter it into the final copy (engrossed) contract, sign but do not date it, and send to the vendor's solicitor, together with the smallest deposit you have been able to get away with.

For the purchaser, this is also the time to decide if the house needs to be insured before contracts are exchanged or whether insurance can be left to between contract and completion. That is after you have exchanged but before you complete. See further at page 79.

Vendor: Receive the contract signed by the purchaser, and check that the deposit is with a stakeholder or in a joint bank account. Enter the completion date on your copy, sign it, enter the date of your signing and send it off to the purchaser. You have got his part of the contract and he has got yours. Contracts are now said to be 'exchanged'.

If you have not already sent copies of the deeds and documents which prove your title, let Skinner have them now.

If you bought less than 15 years ago, the only link in the title chain before the conveyance to you might be an abstract, and a solicitor will have endorsed it 'Examined against the originals at the office'. This type of endorsed abstract is intended to be used as if it were a set of deeds when you come to sell, and any solicitor would accept it from a brother solicitor.

If in response Skinner sends some obscure requisitions (questions), answer fully, but be ready with the masterpieces:

Question: Who now holds the 1876 indenture?

Answer: I don't know.

Question: Was the plot conveyed in 1975 part of the one conveyed in 1920?

Answer: I suppose so, but form your own view.

If he persists in asking what this or that means, give him 'it means what it says'. Eventually, they give up what they should never have started.

Purchaser: Receive vendor's signed and dated part of the contract. Contracts are now said to be 'exchanged' and the property is at the buyer's risk if the standard conditions of contract have been altered. The standard conditions are frequently deleted or amended so do check that the contract is in the same terms as the one you signed, and if you have not already done so, immediately arrange for the property to be fully insured with the same company as your lender will eventually use.

If you did not receive copies of the deeds (conveyances, etc.), you should expect them now. Check the conveyances, watching for the points at page 160.

An abstract should show, in summary, an unbroken chain of ownership leading to your vendor. It might compress on to three or four pages the meat of a dozen conveyances, mortgage deeds, deeds of gift, probates and Wills. In an abstract, the full names and addresses of parties are not repeated over and over again. When an identical description of a property appeared in a subsequent deed it is referred to as 'all the before abstracted premises'. Exceptions and reservations (e.g. where a vendor had two properties and reserved a right of way over land sold) are similarly treated, and Wills are not set out in full, but only the date of the Will and names of the executors are put in.

Abstracts of title are written in lawyer's speed hand, which consists of abbreviations which are based on omitting vowels. However, Absd does not mean absurd but abstracted. Here are a few more abominations to be going on with:

thereabouts:thrbts, vendor:vndr, property:ppty, hereditaments:hrdmts, indenture:indr, Solicitors:slrs, mortgage:mtge.

You soon get a grsp of it, but be crfl not to let it creep into your gnrl vcblry or it might be thought you need new dntrs.

Requisitions on Title form should now be dispatched.

Vendor: Receive the Purchaser's Requisitions on Title. You only have to prove title going back to the conveyance you agreed to deduce title from, your 'root of title'. Remember that when you and previous owners bought, highly trained solicitors checked out the title so there can't be much if anything wrong with it. That is the theory! However, do your best and give the answers required in relation to providing a completion statement. This is an account showing the precise amount you will require to be paid when you hand the keys over and sign the conveyance. It is sufficient to let your local authority know the date when you are moving out and they will split the Council Tax and anything you have paid in advance will come back to you. Water companies are not always so obliging, so check with them and, if necessary, show in your completion statement how much you need in order to reimburse you for the water rate paid in advance. So make up the bill and send it off with your replies.

Purchaser: In reply to your Requisitions on Title, you receive a list of the documents that will be handed over to you (or your lender) on completion and you are informed who will give a statutory acknowledgement and undertaking for the production and safe custody of any document of title not handed over. The form also asks for receipts for last payments of outgoings. If the previous owner does a moonlight flit leaving the Council Tax unpaid, there is no need to worry because Council Taxes are a personal debt on the occupier, so if they are outstanding for a period before you became the occupier, that debt does not belong to you – the council must look to your predecessor for payment. There is a space for further questions.

If you have raised some questions on the title and feel you haven't altogether got satisfactory answers, bear in mind two things. First, if the conveyance to your vendor looks all right and the person described in there as the purchaser is now your vendor, then it should be all right because a wizard of the law checked out that his predecessors were all that they had cracked themselves up to be. Second, if you are taking a mortgage, the lender's solicitor will make sure that you are getting good title, and will keep on asking questions which you pass on to Skinner until the lender is satisfied. After all, if you default in your payments and they have to sell the house to settle your account, they will only have as good a title (proof of ownership) as you got at this point.

You now prepare a draft of the 'instrument of transfer' you intend to use. As your purchase is subject to compulsory registration use TR1 (TR2 for repossession). If you are buying in joint names and you wish survivor to take all put 'x' in the first box at 11. In layperson's language, the clause now reads: If between now and the next time the house is sold, one of us dies the remaining partner/spouse is entitled to the whole of the sale price, on the strength of the survivor's signature alone. For Consideration put 'x' in the first box and the agreed price. The space for title number you leave blank, because one has not yet been allocated by the Registry.

If you are buying a new house on a development, the builder's solicitor should provide the 'instrument' Form TP1, because only part of the vendor's land is being transferred.

Vendor: Receive and check the draft. Look for any deductions or additions that have been made to the one you got when you bought. If there are any with which you disagree, amend in red ink and bounce it back. Heed previous warnings about 'Oh, it's usual' and 'It doesn't mean what it says'. Make sure that indemnity covenants have been correctly entered. If needed, see page 114. When you are satisfied send it back marked 'approved'. But do not sign it. You do that when you get the money.

Purchaser: When your draft instrument of transfer comes back, look for the red ink. It is extremely rare to find any, but if you do and you understand and accept, so well and good. If you don't accept, argue about it. If you don't understand, ask for an explanation, as you are perfectly entitled to one. When you are satisfied send it to Skinner so that he can have the vendor sign it ready for completion day. (You only need to sign it and have your signature witnessed if you are giving a covenant.)

From now on, your job is basically the same as that handed out to the purchaser of a registered house. What differences there are only arise if you are taking a mortgage, and in relation to what your lender's solicitor will want you to produce just before or on completion.

The lender's solicitor will, no doubt, have written to you asking for the following (even if he hasn't written, get them off to him as soon as you can and ask him if there is anything further required because of the time limit there might be for asking questions on title):

- local authority search forms and replies;

- the results of your enquiries concerning water drainage and environmental issues;

- the Seller's Property Information Forms or your own Enquiries before Contract;

- the contract;

- copy title deeds and the replies to your Requisitions on Title received from vendor's solicitor;

- transfer Form TR1 to yourself (one of your copies);

- replies to your Land Charges searches in Form K15 plus copies of any specific entries you ordered from the Land Charges Registry;

- reply to your bankruptcy search (against you) in Form K16;

- letter from the water company regarding sewers and water mains;

- any indemnity policies, old or new. That is, policies copied to you by the vendor and any policy you have taken out;

- any indemnity insurance obtained by you, etc.;

- he may ask for a copy of the SDLT1 (Land Transaction Return), but this cannot be completed until the date of substantial performance is known and must be signed by you;

- Form FR1 – application to the Land Registry for first registration of a property (below).

As most lenders don't return these documents, it is useful to keep copies for your use in future transactions.

The lender's solicitor will respond by sending you the mortgage deed, an account of fees and Stamp Duties, a sheet of Requisitions on Title and a list of the documents required to be handed over on completion. Deal with them as the purchaser of a registered property was instructed on pages 145–6.

SDLT 1 is the Land Transaction Return, which you have to submit to the Revenue when you pay the Stamp Duty Land Tax. It requires filling in by means of codes – these are found in the Guidance Notes which are in Form SDLT6 available from the Stamp Office or online at www.hmrc.gov.uk/so.

Vendor: Receive the supplementary Requisitions on Title, and root about in the conveyances for answers, not forgetting the time honoured 'I cannot say', 'I presume so', and other such masterpieces. If you have paid for the house, all you are waiting for now is the money and you will have notified your purchaser of a suitable place for him to pay it over. If you still have a mortgage, completion will take place at your lender's solicitors' office whither the actual deeds will have been sent. On your Form of Requisition you told him to whom you wanted the CHAPS payment sending to. If you need the completion money splitting between yourself, mortgage redemption money, or even between you, the redemption money and the vendor of the house you are now buying, say so.

You will also be asked when possession of the property will be given. You answer, 'When I receive the balance of the money by CHAPS payment transfer on completion'. A solicitor acting for a purchaser would be negligent if he sent his client's money off by CHAPS to a private individual, without having the title deeds; expect completion at Skinner's office. If you are also buying a house, you may wish to add a suggested completion date to tie in with your purchase, but see later for more on this subject.

Purchaser: Pass on the vendor's replies to your lender.

You are now geared up for completion. The problems and pitfalls and the completion procedures are essentially the same as those applicable to buying and selling registered land and reference should be made to chapter 13.

Form FR1: First Registration Application. This form is fairly self-explanatory. You must disclose any 'disclosable overriding interests'. These are listed in Schedule 1 of the Land Registration Act 2002, and paragraphs 7–13 of Schedule 12 found at www.uk-legislation.hmso.gov.uk/acts.htm. You should also send along any Land Charges Searches together with your FR1.

A registration fee is normally payable for registering a Legal Charge (mortgage), but when it is done at the same time as a first registration or a transfer for monetary consideration, an abatement of fees applies, i.e. there is no fee to pay for registering the charge. Make sure that no one charges you both for registering your purchase (dealing for value) and for registering a legal charge.

A cash buyer will no longer receive a Land Certificate. However, he may obtain a title information document from the Land Registry. Make sure you put a note of the title number in one or two safe places and put the document under the piano lid ready for the next time.

I do hope you will have noticed that throughout this book the few dire warnings given have been about parting with your money for nothing, or making untested assumptions about what other people who are involved in your house buying and selling will do, won't do, will charge and won't charge.

So maybe a final caution will be acceptable. Your goal is to get the job done – your means are the best and easiest you can find. Your goal is not to do as 'good a job' as solicitors do by aping their style and means. No matter how expert you try to make yourself look, no solicitor I have ever met will recommend you for an honourary law degree. Neither should any layperson conveyancer go lording it over those poor souls who do employ solicitors.

They are, no doubt, already smarting from being smacked in the face by the solicitors' final account.

There are those who are capable but haven't, as yet, tried, and you will get more respect if you tell them what, at the end of the transaction you honestly feel about it as I did years ago, saying, 'I don't know what all the fuss was about, it will be a cakewalk next time!'

CHAPTER 15
Matrimonial homes

Hitherto, care has been taken not to offend half the population by giving the impression that only the male sex is capable of understanding and coping with a property deal. Hence the use of the all-purpose 'person', or 'spouse', and sometimes leaving the reader to decide whether Skinner is Mr, Mrs, Miss or Ms. But in this chapter taking the risk of giving unintended offence, such general terms will be abandoned. It will be assumed that we are dealing with property where the ownership is vested solely in the husband's name, and a claim to have the house treated as the matrimonial home is being made by the wife. This is done for two reasons: first, because clarity demands it, and second, because it corresponds to the situation in the real world. However, any husband who needs to protect his interests in a house that was 'put in the wife's name' will not find it too difficult to transpose the term 'husband' for 'wife', and vice versa as necessary.

A wife might not be certain whether the house was in fact purchased jointly by her and her husband. If there is a mortgage, it's easy – ask the building society. In other cases, ask the solicitor who acted. If you suspect that the solicitor might be afraid of breaching confidence (or is biased in favour of your husband), make the enquiry in writing, because if it is in joint names then as you paid half the solicitors' costs, you have a right to any information in his file. For him to refuse you the information is naughty and he knows it. A wife who knows or learns that the house was bought in joint names is fully protected. In theory, the house cannot be sold or mortgaged without her consent, nor can she be evicted without a court order – such a wife need read no further except out of curiosity and academic interest.

Reference here to 'the Act' will be to the Family Law Act 1996. The purpose of the Act (and earlier legislation) was to protect the right of a spouse (normally a wife) to occupy the matrimonial home if owned by the other spouse. Once a wife registers her right in the appropriate register, all intending purchasers and lenders of money on mortgage will have notice of her rights and they continue negotiations at their peril, until they have the written assurance in the correct form that the wife will agree to withdraw her charge from the register.

But before sending off forms in all directions, the wife needs to establish whether her husband is the freeholder or holds the property on lease. 'Lease', by the way, includes tenancy. In the case of a leaseholder, unless the lease was for more than 21 years when it was granted, it is incapable of registration at the Land Registry, and is a short tenancy. Even so, a wife cannot be evicted without a court order. Following the Land Registration Act 2002, all transfers of leases with not less than seven years left to run are registrable.

Another simple point, but worth making, just in case, is that before a wife can protect her interest in and right to occupy the house, her husband must have a right of occupation. Wives' rights of occupation arise on the latest of the following events:

- the date when the husband acquired the house;

- the date of the marriage; or

- 1 January 1968.

So how does one go about registering a wife's right to occupy? As you have already suspected, it is a matter of form-filling again. It is something you can do, easily and cheaply, for yourself. Where you do not know whether the house is registered or not, send off Form SIM to the Land Registry for your area with 'This search is being made solely for the purposes of the Family Law Act 1996' written across the top, and no charge will be made.

You will get a reply within a day or two telling you whether it is registered or not; if it is registered you will be given the title number. You then send off Form MH1. There is no fee. The Registrar will inform your husband of the registration.

In the case of an unregistered house, the required form is K2, which is sent to the Land Charges Department, Plumer House, Tailyour Road, Crownhill, Plymouth, PL6 5HY, no matter where the house is situated. The fee in this case is £2 and you will be informed within a day or two that a Class F Land Charge has been registered in your name. Your husband will not know unless you tell him.

Where you suspect that dealings are imminent, and the time taken in to-ing and fro-ing outlined above might be too long for safety, I suggest you assume both that it is, and that it isn't registered. Send a Form SIM (no fee) as recommended above, and pin it to a Form MH1. In the box for the title number write 'please supply title number for purpose of Matrimonial Homes Act 1983. URGENT'. At the same time send off a Form K2 with its £2 fee to Plymouth. That's belt and braces for you!

Once you've got a charge on a Register (or both as in the previous paragraph), basically it stays there until death or divorce you do part, and it is known as a charge. Following the abolition of cautions against dealing, the charge is protected as an agreed notice, which will give her priority over a purchaser. Nevertheless, a judge can make what is known as a 'continuation order' of the wife's right of occupation, which can now continue even though the marriage is at an end. But note: though the judge has said so, it does not mean that the whole world has notice. The charge did die with the marriage, so get a copy of the judge's order from the court office quickly and attach it to a Form MH2 in the case of a registered house, or K8 if the house is unregistered. There is no charge for a Form MH2, but the K8 requires a £1 fee and goes to Plymouth. If for any reason you hadn't got a charge on to one of the Registers before the court hearing, then you must get a Form MH1 or K2 off as swiftly as possible, as explained before.

Judges don't always make continuation orders; the reverse may happen – he may order that the right of occupation is at an end. In this case, a copy of the order with a letter form MH4 is sufficient if the property is registered. No fee is required to have the Charge removed at the appropriate Land Registry.

In the case of unregistered land, you need to send the evidence, a covering letter, and a Form K13 together with a fee of £1 to the Land Charges Department, Plymouth, to have the Class F Charge removed from the register.

A wife may apply to have the registration removed at any time, by sending Form MH4 to the Land Registry, or in the case of an unregistered house, Form K13 to the Land Charges Department.

Once a wife's right of occupation is registered, it does no more than ensure that the house is not sold or mortgaged except with her consent or a court order. When a wife is in occupation she can achieve the same end for some time, by simply refusing to show viewers or building society and finance company surveyors round the property. No lender will want to lend, and no purchaser will want to negotiate for a property that has such an unco-operative person living in it.

A wife can only protect her right of occupation in respect of one house; if her husband owns more than one, she will register her right for the one she prefers.

A registration of right to occupy says nothing about how the proceeds will be divided if and when the house is sold. It is essential that the parties try to find a solution between themselves on this point. Recourse to the courts should be the very last resort. Costs can be ruinous, and you might eventually have to pay them yourself, even though you were granted Legal Aid. A person who lodges a caution without reasonable cause is liable in damages to anyone injured as a result.

Earlier in this book, purchasers were advised to treat these entries with grave suspicion, so you will realise that the sooner cautions are removed the better. When an armistice is being arranged, consider putting in a condition that the house be put in joint names (transfer of ownership by way of gift), a little job that you can easily do for yourself.

For a more detailed account, readers with access to the internet should access the Land Registry's homepage, www.landregistry.gov.uk, where two explanatory leaflets can be found – Explanatory leaflet 4 for members of the public and Practice leaflet 10 for legal practitioners. All the Land Registry forms mentioned in this article can also be printed off and completed before printing. This does not apply to the Land Charges Department's K forms but these can be purchased from The Stationery Office, as can the Land Registry MH forms. Readers who do not have access to a computer can obtain the two leaflets from the Citizens Advice Bureau.

CHAPTER 16

Flats

Thus far, this book has concentrated on the sale of houses, which principally have freehold titles. However, a significant number of people, particularly first- or last-time buyers, will probably find that they will be buying flats. This is increasingly the case in areas where space is at a premium and developers, keen to make the most of the buoyant housing market, cram in as many units on their land as possible.

If you do buy a flat, chances are it will be leasehold. The reason for this is that, as we saw in chapter 12, it is almost impossible to enforce positive covenants (i.e. ones that require spending money) against subsequent owners of freehold land. This causes problems in a block of flats where it is necessary to deal with rights/obligations to repair the exterior/common parts, rights of support and so on. The way that this is solved is by giving the flat owners long leases. This not only means that there can be mutual obligations and a consistent regime for enforcing obligations but it also means that the freeholder retains a measure of control over the development. The problem with this is that, no matter how long the lease was at the beginning, leases are wasting assets and do limit, depending on the terms of the lease, the way in which the owner can deal with the property.

The principles of registration searches, etc. are basically the same as for freehold titles. However, there are a number of other things that a purchaser of a flat should look out for when deciding whether or not to sign on the dotted line.

What are the terms of the lease?

The terms of leases vary considerably. The lease governs the relationship between you and the freeholder. If you buy the flat, whatever is written in the lease will be binding on you. There is no real question of varying the obligations. It is therefore important to study it carefully to check you won't be prevented from holding your brass band rehearsals at the property if that's what you intend to do. As always, if you don't understand something, ask!

The basic structure of all leases is similar. It will start off with the name of the parties, the length of the term and the level of ground rent. It will then proceed to detail the obligations of the tenant and then the obligations of the landlord. Usually it will provide that the landlord is to maintain the exterior of the property and the common parts and that the tenant is to pay a proportion (either a fixed percentage or a 'reasonable' proportion) of the costs of such maintenance, repair, etc. as a service charge, usually on a quarterly basis.

Service charges

When purchasing a flat, you should ask the vendor about the level of service charges. This is an ongoing liability that must be budgeted for. If the sum appears very high for the services that the freeholder seems to provide, ask why. It may be that the building is inefficiently managed, which might herald problems later on. You should also ask for copies of the service charge accounts over the last few years, to give you some indication of the consistency and level of charges. Vendors should dig out the service charge accounts over the past few years and have copies ready to give to the purchaser or his solicitor in response to the inevitable question! It is important to check the terms of the lease to see when the service charge is payable. The lease may provide for a regular payment, with a top-up payment once a year. It is important to budget for this and to see how much this is likely to be over a year.

Purchasers should also ask the vendor and his landlord whether there are any proposed 'major works'. These are works which will cost over £1,000 and must be notified to the leaseholders before they can be carried out. It's best to ask this question before you buy so that you don't find yourself landed with a hefty bill for new windows and all the disruption that will inevitably be involved in the work shortly after you move in. The vendor may also be able to give you some idea about how often the freeholder carries out major decorating work (unless it's prescribed in the lease) so you should be able to work out how often you will be faced with a bills for external redecorations and all the paraphernalia which goes with it.

Consents to assignment/subletting

Leases often contain restrictions on assignment (sale) and/or on subletting. Usually the leaseholder is not permitted to assign or sublet without the landlord's consent, such consent not to be unreasonably withheld. There may also be a requirement that a modest registration fee is paid to the landlord when he records the fact that you, Mr Bold, have taken an assignment from Mr Feather. If you intend to let out your new purchase, it is important to be aware of such a restriction and what the landlord will require to be satisfied that he should consent to a subletting.

In the case of any purchase of a lease where the landlord's consent to an assignment is required, this must be obtained before there can be completion. Vendors should make sure that landlords are not allowed to drag their feet and cause the purchase to go off.

Breaches of covenant

It is also important to check whether there have been any breaches of covenant. This is a more immediate problem in the case of a lease than where a purchaser discovers that his vendor has breached a freehold restrictive covenant. The reason for this is that in the case of a lease, the chances are that any breach of covenant renders the lease liable to forfeiture. This means that the landlord can bring the lease to an end and retake possession of the property (albeit with a court order). It is all very well that your vendor promised you that there were no such breaches, but this may not get you too far if you want to live in the flat rather than have to pursue the vendor for damages. It's better to deal with the potential problem before it even arises. A favourite covenant is a covenant against alterations. If it appears that there have been alterations, it is important to ask to see copies of any consents to such alterations and make sure that any conditions have been complied with.

'Share of freehold'

Many flats are advertised as having a 'share of freehold'. This does not generally mean that the flat itself has freehold title; there will still be a lease and the covenants contained in it will have to be adhered to. What it will probably mean is that the freehold on which the block stands is owned by a limited company and the shareholders of that limited company are the owners of the flats in the block. If this is the case, and it is fairly common, the purchaser must ensure that the vendor transfers his share in the limited company to the purchaser on completion of the sale of the property.

Leaseholders who own the freehold of the block through the means of a limited company have more freedom to deal with the flat because if they don't like the lease, they can change it. Usually the leases are longer in blocks with share of freehold. However, even if the flat you are thinking of buying does come with share of freehold, changing the lease might not be so easy, as you are not able to act alone and agreement with your new neighbours would still be required. Dealing with questions of lease extension or purchase of the freehold is beyond the scope of this book. In order to ensure that this is properly dealt with, advice of a specialist solicitor will be required.

CHAPTER 17

Commonhold

It is a fact that people prefer freehold interests to leasehold interests because a lease, which is limited in duration, is a wasting asset. Freehold interests are seen as more marketable. Therefore in 2002 the government passed the Commonhold and Leasehold Reform Act 2002, which provided for a new form of freehold ownership, called commonhold, designed to deal with properties (principally flats) which shared common parts and maintenance obligations. These interests will be freehold interests, i.e. of unlimited duration. The common parts will be owned by a commonhold association. The nature of the commonhold will be determined by the commonhold association's memorandum. The relationship between the association and the unit holders will be regulated by the articles of association. The relationship between the unit holders will be regulated by the commonhold community statement.

Don't be surprised if you hear this term being bandied around by estate agents and the like. Don't let it put you off. It is simply another way of holding land.

Although the provisions creating commonhold are now in force, the early indications are that commonhold will apply to principally new developments. Until one of the units is sold, the common parts will continue to be owned by the developer as was formerly the case. As soon as one of the units has been sold, the common parts will be transferred to a body known as a 'Commonhold Association' in which each of the unit holders in the development (i.e. the owners of the flats or houses) will have a share. The model is similar, although not identical, to the model of the 'shared freehold' mentioned in the previous chapter. However, only one of the unit holders can be a member of the Commonhold Association and if you are buying jointly, you will need to nominate one of you to be the member of your association for your unit.

You will need to carry out a search not only in relation to the unit itself but also relating to the common parts and the property held by the Commonhold Association. A search of the Index Map (using Form SIM) in relation to a commonhold unit will tell you not only the title number of the unit itself but also the title number of the common parts. This will be important and will allow you to obtain the documents relating to the Commonhold Association which will detail the rights and restrictions in relation to the development. An Office Copy entry in relation to the title to the common parts is obtained by serving Form OC1 in the usual way. You should also obtain copies of the Commonhold Community Statement and the articles of the Commonhold Association which you will need to apply for on Form OC2. More details can be found in Practice Guide 12 from the Land Registry at www.landregistry.gov.uk.

Instead of the rights and restrictions of the unit holders being contained in a lease, they are contained in a Commonhold Community Statement. This will let you know what you are getting yourself into and what limits there are on your rights. The main difference between a leasehold and a commonhold interest is that whereas a lease is a wasting asset, a commonhold is a type of freehold and is indefinite in duration. When you buy a commonhold unit, however, you will be bound by the terms of the community statement and the articles of association. It is therefore very important that you ask for copies of these when making enquiries before you sign on the dotted line.

CHAPTER 18

Tricks of the trade for layperson conveyancing

Having read this book, you can assume you know at least as much about conveyancing, particularly your own, as any solicitor or clerk who might be acting for the other side. Because most Skinners are gentlefolk, they will, in the hope of future non-conveyancing business from you, be helpful and treat you kindly. However, if they seek to put you in the wrong, refer back to the book, thank them for their interest and tell them you are working out of the Bradshaw, for sadly, there are people who having heard that conveyancing is only a form-filling job, get a few forms and have a go, and building society managers and solicitors do right to give them short shrift.

Conveyancing is not like fitting a bath panel. You just can't get a pack of forms and hope to 'figure it out on the job'. So please, when recommending layperson conveyancing, make sure the aspirant conveyancer has a guide to work from. Reading someone else's guide and then trying to muddle through will get you wound up into Skinner's wringer.

- If you bought a property before the date when compulsory registration was extended to the area you live in, you are under no obligation to register it now. It will have to be registered by whoever purchases it from you.

- A leaseholder paying an annual rent for the privilege of standing on someone else's land with a lease which has a long time to run can ask the freeholder to sell the freehold interest to the lessees of the building under the Leasehold Reform (Housing and Urban Development) Act 1993, as amended. Offer about a twelve-year purchase; for example, rent £20 per annum times twelve equals £240.

- You must be careful not to get into disputes with your neighbour, particularly about a few inches of a boundary. If your neighbour insists on making trouble, let it be he who traipses off to a solicitor. Let it be he whom the solicitor warns about high costs in such a case. But at least Skinner can get something out of it by sending you one of his bullying letters threatening you with virtual destruction and certain damnation if you don't let Mr & Mrs Angel have all their own way. Treat the letter with a pinch of salt, unless you happen to know that your neighbour is extremely rich. In such a case telephone your CAB for advice.

- While there are no registers from which you can learn who owns vacant land or derelict property, you can ask around. Local parsons and old established doctors are likely sources of information. Alternatively, you could complete an Index Map Search, Form SIM, to find out if the property is a registered title. If it is, you can then find out further details by applying for Office Copies, using Form OC1.

- Quarter days are 25 March, 24 June, 29 September and 25 December. A lease may select some other date such as 1 April, July, October and January.

- You will have fewer questions from Skinner & Probe when you do your sale conveyance if you have already bought out the owner of any 'rent charge' there might be on your property. These are annual charges on freehold land and occur in certain parts of the country. You are entitled to redeem a rent charge (sometimes called 'chief rent' or 'ground rent', depending on the area) for approximately ten times the amount of the annual charge. Get yourself an application form from Rentcharges Unit, Government Office for the North West, City Tower, Piccadilly Plaza, Manchester M1 4BE. Alternatively, it may turn out that a rent charge is necessary because you live in a gated development. If this is the case, it is better to leave well alone.

- Some conveyances do not contain a plan showing the boundaries and rely only on words. Sometimes you get both words and plans and sometimes one clashes with the other. Words are the stronger unless the conveyance says otherwise.

- A survey of estate agents' services boldly suggested that you have a go at selling for yourself for a couple of weeks. If at the end of that time you have had no joy, you should give it to an agent, they say. Surely, if what agents say is true, and they have national link-ups and buyers hanging on the back of the door, the best way is to let them have a go for a fortnight, and if their computers, books and door-hooks are bare, then settle down to the board and advertising routine for yourself.

- Most solicitors will provide your purchase file. Don't fret if they won't. Content yourself by asking them what they have to hide, but if you think there is something in it that is really necessary for you to have, an alternative source could be your lender's records. Keep in mind: the house is yours. The deeds are yours, and those deeds are only deposited with the lender as security for the loan.

- Vendors, do not get too involved with a prospective purchaser's solicitor until a mortgage offer has been issued. Deposits subject to contract are paid today and back tomorrow. £100 paid as a survey fee is lost forever, and therefore more binding.

- Mortgage offer – if the purchase is to be funded by a loan not only never exchange till you have seen and accepted it, but read it very carefully to make sure you can comply with any conditions that appear in the offer. They come in all shapes and sizes and are often long-winded, turgid and badly worded. Also make sure the lender's solicitor is happy with the title, searches and other papers. If you exchange and find you cannot meet a requirement, or he does not like the look of your papers, you will have a serious problem. Remember also the role of the lender's solicitor is to act as the lender's insurer. If the money is advanced and it all goes wrong, he compensates them. On the one hand, he will know that. On the other, he is probably being paid peanuts to deal with the job, so do not be too surprised that he is not going to take any risks or waste too much time helping you out.

- You are in a chain. Your vendor can't complete to contracted date. Write a nice letter to your purchaser, giving the new date. If in reply you receive a snotty letter, use it as a model for a similar one to your vendor, but add a covering note saying where you got the idea from.

- Solicitors sometimes refer to a Land Registry Cover. To be precise, they mean a form for dealing, such as an AP1.

- If a conveyancing clerk asks you for a 'fully attested, certified, adjusted engrossed memorandum free of scrotage, together with vesting and singlet assent to reversion of entailed combination by teazle', ask him for a draft of the wording that would satisfy.

- When you pay your last payment to your lender, write asking for:

  - Registered property: the Charge Certificate and sealed Form DS1 or DS3. You can send it all to the Land Registry (no other form required) and in return you will receive your Land Certificate. No need for a solicitor. The Land Registry makes no charge, and neither should your erstwhile lender.

  - Unregistered property: ask for your deeds and check that the legal charge has something like, 'received all the money intended to be secured herein' signed and sealed on it. Check that the conveyance to you is in the parcel and that it has been stamped by HM Revenue & Customs.

- Master controlled inactivity: just because you get a letter with an official heading, be it from Town Hall or Skinner and Hall, it doesn't mean that you have to answer it immediately, if at all.

- If you are told that there is a delay with the searches, phone the council and find out how long they are taking nowadays to deal with them.

Buying at auction

When the gavel falls, a binding contract between the last bidder and the vendor is made. Don't worry about having a bout of involuntary head nodding. The auctioneer knows the difference between a bidder and a nutter.

Follow the drill outline below. Attend some auctions no matter what the property for sale. If it is obvious that the property is worth £50,000 and the bidding opens at £25,000 make a bid. It's exciting, it's free and you have had a dress rehearsal and prepared yourself for the real thing later.

You prepare by doing what any house buyer should do, or have done for him, before signing a contract:

1. See and approve the contract.
2. Have Enquiries before Contract form answered.
3. Have local authority forms completed and answered.
4. Send search forms to Land Registry/Legal Charges Dept.

A vendor's solicitor should have prepared a set of the above and the agent will have a supply. If all the replies on the forms meet with your approval so well and good. If not, ask questions until you are satisfied or lose interest. So far you haven't spent a penny ... and that is how it should be. If you need a mortgage, leave your enquiries about it as late as possible; others could be in the same position and some anxious soul might already have paid a survey fee to one of the local lenders who can then give you an idea of what could be borrowed. Give them all a chance of not wasting a survey fee for you.

Follow the instructions given earlier about actually visiting the local council offices and gleaning information that other bidders might not hear about, because their hired helps have relied only on the paperwork. You might find out from the officials that 50 years ago there was a proposal to do something nasty in the vicinity. Ask the auctioneer if there is any likelihood of the plan being revived. He will only be able to give a vague reply. You react with a long face for all to see because you will have positioned yourself at the end of the front row where, by sitting sideways-on, you can keep an eye on the whole assembly and know whether the auctioneer is getting genuine bids or taking them off the chandeliers.

Layperson conveyancers should not waste their time trying to find the solicitor Skinner. When I first quarried the person, there was no lawyer by the name of Skinner in a practice that had the name of Skinner in its business name, and even if there were, then or now, we are not referring to him or any person by the name of Skinner who has or has ever had a certificate to practise law.

Postscript

A word about electronic conveyancing

You will have seen the odd reference, as you have been reading this book, to the fact that the law on land registration was altered as from 13 October 2003, when the Land Registration Act 2002 came into force. This new Act basically overhauled the law to ensure that the register was a more accurate reflection of the position on the ground, by reducing the number of overriding interests and requiring registration of those that the vendor is aware of. The idea is to make the purchaser of a registered house even more secure than he is at the moment.

However, the other main reason for the new Act was, in an increasingly technological age, to pave the way for electronic conveyancing. Once electronic conveyancing is possible there can be simultaneous completion and registration; so the headache of ensuring that you get your AP1 to the Land Registry before your priority period expires will disappear (unless, of course, in the unlikely event that you have the patience of a saint and your vendor has managed to drag his feet so much that completion does not take place until your priority period has expired).

E-conveyancing will require a number of trials, regulations and consultations before it can come into effect. A consultation paper has been submitted to the government. It is anticipated that electronic conveyancing will be introduced in phases. There is already automatic registration of charges. It is, however, coming in over a substantial period of time and will not be fully in force until summer 2009 when the provisions regarding DIY conveyancing will be in force. Further details can be found on the Land

Registry website at www.landregistry.gov.uk under the link e-conveyancing, but there is no real indication of when e-conveyancing will come into effect.

However, e-conveyancing is unlikely to mean that the layperson conveyancer will be able to register himself as legal owner from the comfort of his own home – indeed his computer probably should have been packed and in the removal van before time for completion came round! Although the Land Registry has not been persuaded to use the introduction of e-conveyancing as an excuse to deprive laypeople of the right to do their own conveyancing, it seems likely that the layperson conveyancer would have to attend a Registry office or nominated terminal to carry out the conveyancing, but the details have not yet been finalised. When it does come along it will hopefully make the whole process a lot simpler and more painless. However, it is unlikely that paper conveyancing will be phased out completely and wholly replaced by the electronic system. This only affects registration of title and does not affect the carrying out of other searches and obtaining environmental reports, so pen and paper will not be wholly redundant. All that can be said for the moment is watch this space!

Glossary

Absolute title	Highest and most unquestionable title.
Abstract of title	A summary of documents proving title.
Assent	The title of a legatee or devisee is not complete until the deceased's executor/personal representative has completed an assent which then becomes a good root of title.
Assignment	Transfer of benefit of lease.
Attested	Witnessed.
Beneficial owner	Person/s owning land for own benefit.
Beneficiary	One who has the beneficial interest, i.e. receives the rent or is the occupier.
Caution	Means of protecting a right by requiring notice of dealing in land to be given to cautioner; no new cautions were entered after 13 October 2003.
Charge/legal charge	Mortgage.
Commonhold	New type of freehold ownership that principally applies to flats which came into force in 2004.
Conveyance	A written instrument of transfer of real property used when the land is not registered at HM Land Registry.
Counterpart	Lease signed by tenant – the part is signed by landlord.
Covenant	Promise written in deed.

Deed	Is 'signed and delivered'; all transfers of freehold and leasehold property must be.
Demise	Part of property let to a lessee/tenant under a lease.
Devise	A gift by Will of land or other real estate. A bequest is a gift by Will of personal estate.
Easement	Right of one landowner to use another's land for right of way, water, drains, etc.
Equity	(On redemption) the money owing to you after the loan has been paid off.
Escrow	A deed delivered conditionally; it does not become effective until the condition is satisfied, e.g. other party signs his part.
Estate	(a) real: ownership of freehold/leasehold; (b) personal: ownership of effects other than land.
Execute	Sign.
Executor	Person appointed in Will of deceased person to carry out provisions of Will; probate proves entitlement to do so.
Fee simple	Largest estate in land – often equivalent to freehold.
Filed plan	The plan from which Land Registry identifies land.
Flying freehold	(So called) applies to (a) upper parts of buildings where party has an interest unlimited by time; the soil is owned by another; very rarely (b) foreshores and (c) interest in part of area of meadows allocated by annual drawing of lots.
Freehold	Absolute ownership unlimited by time, as opposed to leasehold.
Incumbrance	A mortgage upon either real or personal estate.
Indenture	Deed made by more than one party; conveyance used to be called an indenture.
Intestate	Leaving no valid Will.
Joint and several	Two or more parties who render themselves liable to a joint action against all, as well as to a separate action against each in case the agreement or bond is not kept.

Joint tenants	Co-owners of land with or without buildings on it; survivor takes all (see also tenants in common).
Land	General real estate term, refers to land and all buildings that stand on it.
Notice	Means of protecting a third party interest in registered land.
Overriding interest	The rights of persons other than owners to occupy or receive benefits (i.e. rent/income) from property; also rights of third parties, e.g. to walk over the land or rights under short leases; these rights do not have to be registered at the Land Registry to be effective.
Parcels	The pieces a hitherto single plot has been split into.
Private treaty	Sale not by auction.
Repudiation	Serious breach of contract entitling the other party to treat the contract as at an end ('accept the repudiation'), e.g. failure to complete following service of notice to complete.
Rescission	Unwinding a contract – backing out because you were induced to enter the contract by reason of a misrepresentation.
Restrictive covenant	Promise in a deed restricting use of land.
Root of title	Document from which good title of ownership is proved – at least 15 years old (will become archaic when all land registered); to give good title, there has to be an uninterrupted claim in title from the root to the seller.
Scrotage	A Bradshavian neologism.
Seisen/seised	Possessed of land as freeholders.
Service charges	Money payable to the freeholder of a flat to pay for the general upkeep of the block.
Sitting tenant	Tenant of house or flat; usually, this term means a tenant who has acquired security of tenure and whose tenancy cannot be ended by the landlord giving notice.

Specific performance	Successful completion of contract.
Stakeholder	Holder of deposit which he does not pass to vendor without authority of buyer, or return to buyer without permission of vendor.
Stamp Duty	Payable on some deeds and documents which cannot be used as evidence or registered at the Land Registry unless properly stamped with duty paid, or 'adjudicated' or 'particulars delivered'; now abolished for land transactions.
Stamp Duty Land Tax	Replacement for Stamp Duty. Charged on transactions not documents; no need to submit transfer to the Revenue – simply fill in a Land Transaction Return. Land Registry will refuse to register property without certificate from the Revenue or self certificate.
Tenant for life	Person entitled to benefit of real estate for term of his life, after which it will pass to others as determined by an existing Will or trust.
Tenants in common	The property is owned in shares and each owner can bequeath his part to whom he wishes. Shares do not necessarily have to be equal.
Tenure	The mode of holding or occupying lands. No person except the Sovereign can be the absolute owner of land in England, so the rest of us hold immediately of the crown (freehold) or mediated by a freeholder (leasehold). How far a tenure extends is called the tenant's estate, hence estate in fee simple, etc. Most titles of freehold land are registered with absolute title.
Testimonium	Formal introduction to the attestation clause in a deed.
Title	Evidence which signifies a person's right to enjoyment of land.
Trust	Created when property transferred to a person (trustee) to apply for benefit of another.

Trustees	Where two or more people are entitled to the legal estate they hold the legal title as trustees. Purchasers need receipt for purchase monies on conveyance or Form TR1 (standard Land Registry transfer form) signed by at least two of them unless there are two joint tenants and only one survives; the survivor can then deal with the estate.
Vacating receipt	Receipt written and signed on the Legal Charge showing all monies intended to be secured by the deed to have been paid off.

Appendices

Some of the main forms mentioned in this book are listed below, with completed examples included for guidance on following pages.

You can obtain your forms from HM Land Registry, at their website www.landreg.gov.uk, and legal stationers such as Oyez, website www.oyez.co.uk.

1   **Form OS1 – Application by Purchaser for Official Search**

2   **Form OC1 – Application for Office Copies of Register**

3   **Form K15 – Application for an Official Search**

4   **Form LLCI – Requisition for Search of Local Land Charges**

5   **Form Con 29 – Enquiries of Local Authority**

6   **Form Prop 7 – Completion Information and Requisitions on Title**

7   **Form TR1 – Transfer of Whole of Registered Title(s)**

8   **Form AP1 – Application to Change the Register**

9   **Form FR1 – First Registration Application**

10 **District Land Registries**

Appendix 1: Completed Example Form OS1 – Application by Purchaser for Official Search

Application by purchaser[a] for official search with priority of the whole of the land in a registered title or a pending first registration application

Land Registry

OS1

Land Registry _____ Office

EDENSHIRE, PARKSIDE WAY
BLOSSOMTON
EDENSHIRE EH8 3TG

Use one form per title. If you need more room than is provided for in a panel, use continuation sheet CS and attach to this form.

1. **Administrative area and postcode** if known   EDENSHIRE

2. **Title number** *Enter the title number of the registered estate or that allotted to the pending first registration.*
   EDN 999707

3. **Payment of fee** [b] *Place "X" in the appropriate box.*

	For official use only
[X] The Land Registry fee of £ [4.00] accompanies this application.	Impression of fees
[ ] Debit the Credit Account mentioned in panel 4 with the appropriate fee payable under the current Land Registration Fee Order.	

4. **The application has been lodged by:**[c]
   Land Registry Key No. (if appropriate)
   Name
   Address/DX No.   MR THOMAS BOLD
   1 PROSPECT AVENUE, ORCHARD VALE, BLOSSOMTON,
   EDENSHIRE ED5 7AB
   Reference[d]
   E-mail   tb@email.uk

Telephone No. 01234 567 890	Fax No.

5. If the result of search is to be sent to anyone other than the applicant in panel 4, please supply the name and address of the person to whom it should be sent.

   Reference[d]

6. **Registered proprietor/Applicant for first registration** *Enter FULL name(s) of the registered proprietor(s) of the registered estate in the above mentioned title or of the person(s) applying for first registration of the property specified in panel 10.*

   SURNAME/COMPANY NAME: SMART
   FORENAME(S):   CLINT
   SURNAME/COMPANY NAME: SMART
   FORENAME(S):   CONSTANCE

Appendix 1: Completed Example Form OS1 – Application by Purchaser for Official Search (continued)

7. **Search from date** *For a search of a **registered title** enter in the box a date falling within the definition of search from date in rule 131 of the Land Registration Rules 2003.*[e] *If the date entered is not such a date the application may be rejected. In the case of a **pending first registration** search, enter the letters 'FR'.*

16 MARCH 1997

8. **Applicant** *Enter FULL name of each purchaser **or** lessee **or** chargee.*

MR THOMAS BOLD
MRS PRUDENCE BOLD

9. **Reason for application** I certify that the applicant intends to: *Place "X" in the appropriate box.*

[X] **P** purchase   [ ] **C** take a registered charge

[ ] **L** take a lease

10. **Property details** *Address or short description of the property.*

14 PLEVNA PLACE
BLOSSOMTON ED2 8JD

11. **Type of search** *Place "X" in the appropriate box.*

[ ] **Registered land search**
Application is made to ascertain whether any adverse entry has been made in the register or day list since the date shown in panel 7.

[X] **Pending first registration search**
Application is made to ascertain whether any adverse entry has been made in the day list since the date of the pending first registration application referred to above.

12. **Signature of applicant or their conveyancer** *Thomas Bold*   Date 1 JAN 2006

Explanatory notes

(a) "Purchaser" is defined in Land Registration Rules 2003, r.131. In essence, it is a person who has entered, or intends to enter, into a disposition for valuable consideration as disponee where: (i) the disposition is a registrable disposition (see Land Registration Act 2002, s.27), or (ii) there is a person subject to a duty under the Land Registration Act 2002, s.6, to apply for registration, the application is pending and the disposition would have been a registrable disposition had the estate been registered. An official search in respect of registered land made by a person other than a "purchaser" should be made in Form OS3.

(b) Cheques are payable to 'Land Registry'. If you hold a credit account but do not indicate that it should be debited, and do not enclose a cheque, the registrar may still debit your account.

(c) If you hold a credit account and want the official search certificate sent to an address different from that associated with your key number, enter your key number, reference and telephone number but otherwise leave panel 4 blank. Complete panel 5 instead.

(d) Enter a maximum of 25 characters including stops, strokes, punctuation etc.

(e) Enter the date shown as the subsisting entries date on an official copy of the register or given as the subsisting entries date at the time of an access by remote terminal.

Practice Guide 12 'Official Searches and Outline Applications' contains further information.

Appendix 2: Completed Example Form OC1 – Application for Office Copies of Register

Application for official copies of register/plan or certificate in Form CI

Land Registry **OC1**

Land Registry _____ Office

EDENSHIRE, PARKSIDE WAY
BLOSSOMTON
EDENSHIRE EH8 3TG

Use one form per title. *If you need more room than is provided for in a panel, use continuation sheet CS and attach to this form.*

1. Administrative area if known	
2. Title number if known	EDN 999707
3. Property Postal number or description	14
Name of road	PLEVNA PLACE
Name of locality	
Town	BLOSSOMTON
Postcode	ED2 8JD
Ordnance Survey map reference (if known)	

4. Payment of fee *Place "X" in the appropriate box.*

For official use only

Impression of fees

[X] The Land Registry fee of £ | 4.00 | accompanies this application.

[ ] Debit the Credit Account mentioned in panel 5 with the appropriate fee payable under the current Land Registration Fee Order.

5. The application has been lodged by:
Land Registry Key No. (if appropriate)
Name
Address/DX No.   MR THOMAS BOLD
                    1 PROSPECT AVENUE, ORCHARD VALE, BLOSSOMTON,
Reference   EDENSHIRE ED5 7AB
E-mail   tb@email.uk

Telephone No.	01234 567 890	Fax No.	

6. If the official copies are to be sent to anyone other than the applicant in panel 5, please supply the name and address of the person to whom they should be sent.

Reference

[1] Usually done by phone or online.

Appendix 2: Completed Example Form OC1 –
Application for Office Copies of Register (continued)

7. Where the title number is **not** quoted in panel 2, place "X" in the appropriate box(es).
   As regards this property, my application relates to:

   ☐ freehold estate ☐ caution against first registration ☐ franchise ☐ manor
   ☐ leasehold estate ☐ rentcharge ☐ profit a prendre in gross

8. In case there is an application for registration pending against the title, place "X" in the appropriate box:

   ☒ I require an official copy back-dated to the day prior to the receipt of that application **or**
   ☐ I require an official copy on completion of that application

9. **I apply for:** *Place "X" in the appropriate box(es) and indicate how many copies are required.*

   ☒ _2_ official copy(ies) of the **register** of the above mentioned property
   ☐ ___ official copy(ies) of the **title plan or caution plan** of the above mentioned property

   ☐ ___ a certificate in Form CI, in which case **either**:
   ☐ an estate plan has been approved and the plot number is [   ]
   or
   ☐ no estate plan has been approved and a certificate is to be issued in respect of the land
   shown _____ on the attached plan and copy

10. **Signature of applicant** _____*Thomas Bold*_____ Date ____1 JAN 2006____

Appendix 3: Completed Example Form K15 –
Application for an Official Search (Unregistered Land)

Form K15	Land Charges Act 1972	Payment of fee

APPLICATION FOR AN OFFICIAL SEARCH

NOT APPLICABLE TO REGISTERED LAND

Application is hereby made for an official search in the index to the registers kept pursuant to the Land Charges Act 1972 for any subsisting entries in respect of the under-mentioned particulars.

Payment of fee

Insert a cross (X) in this box if the fee is to be paid through a credit account (see Note 3 overleaf)

IMPORTANT: Please read the notes overleaf before completing this form

For Official Use only			NAMES TO BE SEARCHED (Please use block letters and see Note 4 overleaf)	PERIOD OF YEARS (see Note 5 overleaf)	
STX				From	To
			Forename(s) CLINT		
			SURNAME SMART	1980	2006
			Forename(s) CONSTANCE		
			SURNAME SMART	1980	2006
			Forename(s)		
			SURNAME		
			Forename(s)		
			SURNAME		
			Forename(s)		
			SURNAME		
			Forename(s)		
			SURNAME		

COUNTY (see Note 6 overleaf)	EDENSHIRE
FORMER COUNTY	
DESCRIPTION OF LAND (see Note 7 overleaf)	
FORMER DESCRIPTION	

Particulars of Applicant (see Notes 8, 9 and 10 overleaf)		Name and Address (including postcode) for despatch of certificate (Leave blank if certificate is to be returned to applicant's address)
KEY NUMBER	Name and address (including postcode)	
	MR THOMAS BOLD 1 PROSPECT AVENUE ORCHARD VALE EDENSHIRE ED5 7AB	

Applicant's reference: PLEV0014	Date 7 JAN 2006	FOR OFFICIAL USE ONLY

Appendix 3: Completed Example Form K15 – Application for an Official Search (Unregistered Land) (continued)

NOTES FOR GUIDANCE OF APPLICANTS

The following notes are supplied for assistance in making the application overleaf. Detailed information for the making of all kinds of applications to the Land Charges Department is contained in a booklet entitled "Computerised Land Charges Department: A practical guide for solicitors" which is obtainable on application at the address shown below.

1. Effect of search. The official certificate of the result of this search will have no statutory effect in relation to registered land (see Land Registration Act 1925, s. 59 and Land Charges Act 1972, s. 14).

2. Bankruptcy only searches. Form K16 should be used for Bankruptcy only searches.

3. Fees must be paid by credit account or by cheque or postal order made payable to "HM Land Registry" (see the guide referred to above).

4. Names to be searched. The forename(s) and surname of each individual must be entered on the appropriate line of the form. The name of a company or other body should commence on the forename line and may continue on the surname line (the words "Forename(s)" and "Surname" should be crossed through). If you are searching more than 6 names, use a second form.

5. Period of years to be searched. The inclusive period to be covered by a search should be entered in complete years e.g. 1968-1975.

6. County names. This must be the appropriate name set out in the Appendix to Land Charges Practice Leaflet No. 3. Searches affecting land within the Greater London area should state "Greater London" as the county name. ANY RELEVANT FORMER COUNTY SHOULD ALWAYS BE STATED (see the Appendix to Land Charges Practice Leaflet No. 3 which lists county names).

7. Land description. It is not essential to provide a land description but, if one is given, any relevant former description should also be given (see the guide referred to above).

8. Key number. If you have been allocated a key number, please take care to enter this in the space provided overleaf, whether or not you are paying fees through your credit account.

9. Applicant's name and address. This need not be supplied if the applicant's key number is correctly entered in the space provided overleaf.

10. Applicant's reference. Any reference must be limited to 25 characters, including any oblique strokes and punctuation.

11. Despatch of this form. When completed, send this application to the address shown below, which is printed in a position so as to fit within a standard window envelope.

THE SUPERINTENDENT,
LAND CHARGES DEPARTMENT,
SEARCH SECTION,   (see Note 11 above)
BURRINGTON WAY,
PLYMOUTH PL5 3LP.
DX 8249, PLYMOUTH 3

OYEZ The Solicitors' Law Stationery Society Ltd, Oyez House, 7 Spa Road, London SE16 3QQ   2.98 F34716
5064154
. ★ ★ ★

Appendix 4: Completed Example Form LLCI – Requisition for Search of Local Land Charges

Form LLC1. (*Local Land Charges Rules 1977 Schedule 1, Form C*)

The duplicate of this form must also be completed: a carbon copy will suffice.

For directions, notes and fees see overleaf.

Insert name and address of registering authority in space below

EDENSHIRE COUNTY COUNCIL
HIGH STREET
BLOSSOMTON
ED4 9IJ

fold

Requisition for search
(*A separate requisition must be made in respect of each parcel of land except as explained overleaf*)

Description of land sufficient to enable it to be identified

14 PLEVNA PLACE
BLOSSOMTON
EDENSHIRE ED2 8JD

Name and address to which certificate is to be sent

THOMAS BOLD
1 PROSPECT AVENUE
ORCHARD VALE
EDENSHIRE ED5 7AB

Official Number_____
(*To be completed by the registering authority*)

Register of local land charges

Requisition for search and official certificate of search

An official search is required in *Part(s)*___1-12___of[1]
the register of local land charges kept by the above-named
registering authority for subsisting registrations against the land
[defined in the attached plan and][2] described below.

Signature of applicant (*or his solicitor*)

Thomas Bold

Date
20 JAN 06

Telephone number
(01234) 567 890

Reference

Enclosure
Cheque/Money Order/Postal Order/Giro

Official certificate of search

To be completed by authorised officer

It is hereby certified that the search requested above reveals no subsisting registrations[3]

or the_____registrations described in the Schedule hereto[3] up to and including the date of this certificate.

Signed..

On behalf of...[4]

Date

1 Delete if inappropriate. Otherwise insert Part(s) in which search is required.

2 Delete if inappropriate. (A plan should be furnished in duplicate if it is desired that a copy should be returned.)

3 Delete inapplicable words. (The Parts of the Schedule should be securely attached to the certificate and the number of registrations disclosed should be inserted in the space provided. Only Parts which disclose subsisting registrations should be sent.)

4 Insert name of registering authority.

Reproduced by Law Pack Publishing with the permission of the Controller of HMSO

Appendix 4: Completed Example Form LLCI –
Requisition for Search of Local Land Charges (continued)

Directions and notes

1 This form and the duplicate should be completed and sent by post to or left at the office of the registering authority.

2 A separate requisition for search should be made in respect of each parcel of land in respect of which a search is required except where, for the purpose of a single transaction, a certificate is required in respect of two or more parcels of land which have a common boundary or are separated only by a road, railway, river, stream or canal.

3 'Parcel of land' means land (including a building or part of a building) which is separately occupied or separately rated or, if not occupied or rated, in separate ownership. For the purpose of this definition an owner is the person who (in his own right or as trustee for any other person) is entitled to receive the rack rent of land, or, where the land is not let at a rack rent, would be so entitled if it were so let.

4 The certificate of the result of an official search of the register refers to any subsisting registrations, recorded against the land defined in the application for search, in the Parts of the register in respect of which the search is requested. The Parts of the register record:

Part 1	General financial charges.
Part 2	Specific financial charges.
Part 3	Planning charges.
Part 4	Miscellaneous charges.
Part 5	Fenland ways maintenance charges.
Part 6	Land compensation charges.
Part 7	New towns charges.
Part 8	Civil aviation charges.
Part 9	Opencast coal charges.
Part 10	Listed buildings charges.
Part 11	Light obstruction notices.
Part 12	Drainage scheme charges.

5 An office copy of any entry in the register can be obtained on written request and on payment of the prescribed fee.

Fees

Official search (including issue of official certificate of search)
in any one part of the register £1.90
in the whole of the register £5.00

and in addition, but subject to a maximum additional fee of £13.00, in respect of each parcel above one, where several parcels are included in the same requisition (see notes 2 and 3 above) whether the requisition is for search in the whole or any part of the register 80p

Office copy of any entry in the register (not including a copy or extract of any plan or document filed by the registering authority) £1.40

Office copy of any plan or other document filed by the registering
authority .. .. Such reasonable fee as may be fixed by the registering authority according to the time and work involved.

All fees must be prepaid

OYEZ The Solicitors' Law Stationery Society Ltd, Oyez House, 7 Spa Road, London SE16 3QQ   5.98 F35122
5063019
* * *

LLC1

Appendix 5: Completed Example Form Con 29 Part I – Standard Enquiries of Local Authority

CON 29 Part I STANDARD ENQUIRIES of Local Authority (2002 Edition)

This form and a plan must be submitted in duplicate.

The Law Society

Please type or use BLOCK LETTERS

A.

To [Local Authority address]

EDENSHIRE COUNTY COUNCIL
HIGH STREET
BLOSSOMTON
EDENSHIRE ED4 9IJ

For Local Authority Completion only

Search No. ....
The replies are attached

Signed: ....
Proper Officer

Dated: ....

B.

Enter address of the land/property

NLPG UPRN: 14 PLEVNA PLACE

Address 1:

Address 2:

Street:

Locality:

Town/Village: BLOSSOMTON

County: EDENSHIRE

Post Code: ED2 8JD

C.

Other roadways, footways and footpaths

N/A

D.

Attachments

A plan in duplicate must be attached. This form may be returned if the land/property cannot be easily identified.

Optional Enquiries to be answered: YES/NO
(if so, please attach Con 29 Part II Optional Enquiries of Local Authority form)

Are any additional enquiries attached?   YES/NO
(if so, please attach on a separate sheet in duplicate)

E.

Fees

£ 100   is enclosed/NLIS transfer (delete as applicable).

Signed: Thomas Bold

Dated: 15 JAN 06

Reference: PLEVNA

Tel No: (01234) 567890

Fax No:

E-mail Contact:

Notes.

A. Enter name and address of Council for the area to which this form has been officially submitted. If the property is near a local authority boundary, consider raising certain enquiries (e.g. road schemes) with the adjoining Council.
B. Enter address and description of the property, add the NLPG UPRN (Unique Property Reference Number) where known.
C. Enter name and/or mark on plan any other roadways, footpaths and footways abutting the property (in addition to those entered in Box B) to which a reply to enquiry 2 and 3.6 is required.
D. A duplicate plan is required for all searches. If required, the Optional Enquiries form, ticked where necessary, should be attached along with the relevant fee. Additional enquiries must be attached on a separate sheet in duplicate. An additional fee will be charged for any that the Council is willing to answer.
E. Details of fees can be obtained from the Council or your chosen NLIS Channel.
F. Enter the name and address/DX address of the person or company lodging this form.

F.

Please reply to

THOMAS BOLD
1 PROSPECT AVENUE
ORCHARD VALE, BLOSSOMTON
EDENSHIRE ED5 7AB

DX Address

Oyez 7 Spa Road, London SE16 3QQ
© LAW SOCIETY 2002

6.2002 F39926

5033381
* * * *

Conveyancing 29 Part I **STANDARD ENQUIRIES**

Appendix 5: Completed Example Form Con 29 Part I – Standard Enquiries of Local Authority (continued)

CON 29 Part I STANDARD Enquiries of Local Authority (2002 Edition)

PLANNING AND BUILDING REGULATIONS

1.1. Decisions and Pending Applications
What applications for any of the following (if applicable) have been granted, refused or are now pending?
(a) planning permissions
(b) listed building consents
(c) conservation area consents
(d) certificates of lawfulness of use or development
(e) building regulation approvals
(f) building regulation completion certificates
(g) certificate of compliance of a replacement window, rooflight, roof window or glazed door.
How can copies of any of the above be obtained?

1.2. Planning Designations and Proposals
What designations of land use for the property or the area, and what specific proposals for the property, are contained in any current adopted or proposed development plan?

ROADS

2. Which of the roads, footways and footpaths mentioned in boxes B and C are:
(a) highways maintainable at public expense;
(b) subject to a current legal agreement for adoption and, if so, is the agreement supported by a bond or other financial security;
(c) to be made up at the cost of the frontagers under a current Council resolution;
(d) to be adopted without cost to the frontagers under a current Council resolution.

OTHER MATTERS

Apart from matters entered on the registers of local land charges, do any of the following matters apply to the property? How can copies of relevant documents be obtained?

3.1. Land required for Public Purposes
Inclusion of the property in a category of land required for public purposes within Schedule 13 paras 5 & 6 of the Town & Country Planning Act 1990

3.2. Land to be acquired for Road Works
Inclusion of the property in land to be acquired for an approved scheme of highway construction or improvement.

3.3. Drainage Agreements and Consents
(a) An agreement under the Building Act 1984, s.22 for drainage of any part of the property in combination with another building through a private sewer?
(b) Statutory agreement or consent for a building or extension to a building on the property to be constructed over or in the vicinity of a drain, sewer or disposal main.
Note: The sewerage undertaker for the area should also be asked about 3(b) and drainage generally.

3.4. Nearby Road Schemes
Location of any part of the property within 200 metres of:
(a) the centre line of a new trunk road or special road specified in an order, draft order or scheme notified to the Council by the appropriate Secretary of State; or
(b) the centre line of a proposed alteration or improvement to an existing road, notified to the Council by the appropriate Secretary of State, involving the construction of a subway, underpass, flyover, footbridge, elevated road or dual carriageway (whether or not within existing highway limits); or
(c) the limits of construction of a proposed alteration or improvement to an existing road, notified to the Council by the appropriate Secretary of State, involving the construction of a roundabout (other than a mini-roundabout) or widening by the construction of one or more additional traffic lanes; or
(d) the limits of construction of an approved new road to be constructed by the Council or an approved alteration or improvement by the Council to an existing road involving the construction of a subway, underpass, flyover, footbridge, elevated road or dual carriageway (whether or not within existing highway limits) or the construction of a roundabout (other than a mini-roundabout) or widening by the construction of one or more additional traffic lanes; or
(e) the centre line of the possible route of a new road under proposals published for public consultation by the Council or by the appropriate Secretary of State; or
(f) the limits of construction of a possible alteration or improvement to an existing road involving the construction of a subway, underpass, flyover, footbridge, elevated road or dual carriageway (whether or not within existing highway limits) or the construction of a roundabout (other than a mini-roundabout) or widening by the construction of one or more additional traffic lanes, under proposals published for public consultation by the Council or by the appropriate Secretary of State.
Note: A mini-roundabout is a roundabout having a one-way circulatory carriageway around a flush or slightly raised circular marking less than 4 metres in diameter and with or without flared approaches.

3.5. Nearby Railway Schemes
Location of any part of the property within 200 metres of the centre line of a proposed railway, tramway, light railway or monorail.

3.6. Traffic Schemes
Approval by the Council of any of the following, not yet implemented, in respect of such of the roads, footways and footpaths mentioned in Box B (and, if applicable, Box C) which abut the boundaries of the property:
(a) permanent stopping up or diversion
(b) waiting or loading restrictions
(c) one way driving
(d) prohibition of driving
(e) pedestrianisation
(f) vehicle width or weight restriction
(g) traffic calming works e.g. road humps
(h) residents parking controls
(i) minor road widening or improvement
(j) pedestrian crossings
(k) cycle tracks
(l) bridge construction.

3.7. Outstanding Notices
Current statutory notices relating to the property under legislation relating to building works, environment, health and safety at work, housing, highways or public health, other than those falling elsewhere within 3.1 to 3.13.

3.8. Infringement of Building Regulations
Proceedings authorised by the Council for infringement of the Building Regulations in respect of the property.

3.9. Notices, Orders, Directions and Proceedings under Planning Acts
Subsisting notices, orders, directions, or proceedings, or those which the Council has decided to issue, serve, make or commence in the following categories (other than those which are shown in the Official Certificate of Search or which have been withdrawn or quashed) relating to the property:
(a) enforcement notice
(b) stop notice
(c) listed building enforcement notice
(d) breach of condition notice
(e) planning contravention notice
(f) other notice relating to breach of planning control
(g) listed building repairs notice
(h) order for compulsory acquisition of a listed building with a minimum compensation provision
(i) building preservation notice
(j) direction restricting permitted development
(k) order revoking or modifying a planning permission or discontinuing an existing planning use
(l) tree preservation order
(m) proceedings for breach of a statutory planning agreement.

3.10. Conservation Area
Creation of the area before 31st August 1974 as a Conservation Area or a subsisting resolution to designate the area as a Conservation Area.

3.11. Compulsory Purchase
Inclusion of the property in land which is subject to an enforceable order or resolution for compulsory purchase.

3.12. Contaminated Land
(a) Entry relating to the property in the register maintained under s.78R(1) of the Environmental Protection Act 1990.
(b) Notice relating to the property served or resolved to be served under s.78B(3).
(c) Consultation with the owner or occupier of the property having taken place, or being resolved to take place under s.78G(3) in relation to anything to be done on the property as a result of adjoining or adjacent land being contaminated land.
(d) Entry in the register, or notice served or resolved to be served under s.78B(3) in relation to any adjoining or adjacent land, which has been identified as contaminated land because it is in such a condition that harm or pollution of controlled waters might be caused on the property.

3.13. Radon Gas
Location of the property in a Radon Affected Area.

NOTES:
This form must be submitted in duplicate and should be read in conjunction with the guidance notes available separately.
(1) Unless otherwise indicated, matters will be disclosed only if they apply directly to the property described in Box B.
(2) "Area" means any area in which the property is located.
(3) References to "the Council" include any predecessor Council and also any council committee, sub-committee or other body or person exercising powers delegated by the Council and their "approval" includes their decision to proceed. The replies given to certain enquiries cover knowledge and actions of both the District Council and County Council.
(4) References to the provisions of particular Acts of Parliament or Regulations include any provisions which they have replaced and also include existing or future amendments or re-enactments.
(5) The replies will be given in the belief that they are in accordance with information presently available to the officers of the replying Council, but none of the Councils or their officers accept legal responsibility for an incorrect reply, except for negligence. Any liability for negligence will extend to the person who raised for the enquiries and the person on whose behalf they were raised. It will also extend to any other person who has knowledge (personally or through an agent) of the replies before the time when he purchases, takes a tenancy of, or lends money on the security of the property or (if earlier) the time when he becomes contractually bound to do so.

Reproduced for educational purposes only by kind permission of the Solicitors' Law Stationery Society Limited

Appendix 5: Completed Example Form Con 29 Part II – Optional Enquiries of Local Authority (continued)

CON 29 Part II OPTIONAL ENQUIRIES of Local Authority (2002 Edition)
This form and a plan must be submitted in duplicate. This form may be returned if the land/property cannot be easily identified.

The Law Society

Please type or use BLOCK LETTERS

A.

To [Local authority address]

EDENSHIRE COUNTY COUNCIL
HIGH STREET
BLOSSOMTON
EDENSHIRE ED4 9IJ

For Local Authority Completion only

Search No. ....
The replies are attached

Signed: ....
Proper Officer

Dated: ....

B.

Address of the land/property

NLPG UPRN: 14 PLEVNA PLACE
Address 1:
Address 2:
Street:
Locality:
Town/Village: BLOSSOMTON
County: EDENSHIRE
Post Code: ED2 8JD

C.

Optional Enquiries [please tick as required]

☐	4. Road proposals by private bodies
☐	5. Public paths or byways
☑	6. Advertisements
☐	7. Completion notices
☐	8. Parks and countryside
☐	9. Pipelines
☐	10. Houses in multiple occupation
☐	11. Noise abatement
☑	12. Urban development areas
☐	13. Enterprise zones
☐	14. Inner urban improvement areas
☐	15. Simplified planning zones
☐	16. Land maintenance notices
☐	17. Mineral consultation areas
☐	18. Hazardous substance consents
☐	19. Environmental and pollution notices
☐	20. Food safety notices
☐	21. Hedgerow notices

D.

Fees

£ 100 is enclosed/NLIS transfer (delete as applicable).

Signed: *Thomas Bold*
Dated: 15 JAN 06
Reference: PLEVNA
Tel No: (01234) 567890
Fax No:
E-Mail Contact:

Notes.

A. Enter name and address of Council for the area to which this form has been officially submitted. If the property is near a local authority boundary, consider raising certain enquiries (e.g. road schemes) with the adjoining Council.
B. Enter address and description of property. Please quote the NLPG UPRN (Unique Property Reference Number) where known.
C. Questions 1-3 appear on CON 29 Part I Standard Enquiries of Local Authority.
D. A fee will be charged for any enquiries that the Council is willing to answer. Details of fees can be obtained from the Council or your chosen NLIS Channel.
E. Enter the name and address/DX address of the person or company lodging this form.

E.

Please reply to

THOMAS BOLD
1 PROSPECT AVENUE
ORCHARD VALE, BLOSSOMTON
EDENSHIRE ED5 7AB
DX Address

Oyez 7 Spa Road, London SE16 3QQ
© LAW SOCIETY 2002

Conveyancing 29 Part II OPTIONAL ENQUIRIES

6.2002 F40480
5033383
* * * *

Appendix 5: Completed Example Form Con 29 Part II – Optional Enquiries of Local Authority (continued)

CON 29 Part II OPTIONAL Enquiries of Local Authority (2002 Edition)

OPTIONAL ENQUIRIES FROM BOX C

ROAD PROPOSALS BY PRIVATE BODIES

4. What proposals by others[i], still capable of being implemented, have the Council approved for any of the following, the limits of construction of which are within 200 metres of the property:
   (a) The construction of a new road, or
   (b) The alteration or improvement of an existing road, involving the construction, whether or not within existing highway limits, of a subway, underpass, flyover, footbridge, elevated road, dual carriageway, the construction of a roundabout (other than a mini-roundabout)[ii] or the widening of an existing road by the construction of one or more additional traffic lanes?

(i) This enquiry refers to proposals by bodies or companies (such as private developers) other than the Council (and where appropriate the County Council) or the Secretary of State.

(ii) A mini-roundabout is a roundabout having a one-way circulatory carriageway around a flush or slightly raised circular marking less than 4 metres in diameter and with or without flared approaches.

PUBLIC PATHS OR BYWAYS

5.1. Is any public path, bridleway or road used as a public path or byway which abuts on, or crosses the property shown in a definitive map or revised definitive map prepared under Part IV of the National Parks and Access to the Countryside Act 1949 or Part III of the Wildlife and Countryside Act 1981?

5.2. If so, please mark its approximate route on the attached plan.

ADVERTISEMENTS

Entries in the Register

6.1. Please list any entries in the Register of applications, directions and decisions relating to consent for the display of advertisements.

6.2. If there are any entries, where can that Register be inspected?

Notices, Proceedings and Orders

6.3. Except as shown in the Official Certificate of Search:
   (a) has any notice been given by the Secretary of State or served in respect of a direction or proposed direction restricting deemed consent for any class of advertisement?
   (b) have the Council resolved to serve a notice requiring the display of any advertisement to be discontinued?
   (c) if a discontinuance notice has been served, has it been complied with to the satisfaction of the Council?
   (d) have the Council resolved to serve any other notice or proceedings relating to a contravention of the control of advertisements?
   (e) have the Council resolved to make an order for the special control of advertisements for the area?

COMPLETION NOTICES

7. Which of the planning permissions in force have the Council resolved to terminate by means of a completion notice under s.94 of the Town & Country Planning Act 1990?

PARKS AND COUNTRYSIDE

Areas of Outstanding Natural Beauty

8.1. Has any order under s.87 of the National Parks and Access to the Countryside Act 1949 been made?

National Parks

8.2. Is the property within a National Park designated under s.7. of the National Parks and Access to the Countryside Act 1949?

PIPELINES

9. Has a map been deposited under s.35 of the Pipelines Act 1962, or Schedule 7 of the Gas Act 1986, showing a pipeline laid through, or within 100 feet (30.48 metres) of the property?

HOUSES IN MULTIPLE OCCUPATION

10. Is the property included in a registration of houses scheme (houses in multiple occupation) under s.346 of the Housing Act 1985, containing control provisions as authorised by s.347 of that Act?

NOISE ABATEMENT

Noise Abatement Zone

11.1. Have the Council made, or resolved to make, any noise abatement zone order under s.63 of the Control of Pollution Act 1974 for the area?

Entries in Register

11.2. Has any entry been recorded in the Noise Level Register kept pursuant to s.64 of the Control of Pollution Act 1974?

11.3. If there is any entry, how can copies be obtained and where can that Register be inspected?

URBAN DEVELOPMENT AREAS

12.1. Is the area an urban development area designated under Part XVI of the Local Government, Planning and Land Act 1980?

12.2. If so, please state the name of the urban development corporation and the address of its principal office.

ENTERPRISE ZONES

13. Is the area an enterprise zone designated under Part XVIII of the Local Government, Planning and Land Act 1980?

INNER URBAN IMPROVEMENT AREAS

14. Have the Council resolved to define the area as an improvement area under s.4 of the Inner Urban Areas Act 1978?

SIMPLIFIED PLANNING ZONES

15.1. Is the area a simplified planning zone adopted or approved pursuant to s.83 of the Town & Country Planning Act 1990?

15.2. Have the Council approved any proposal for designating the area as a simplified planning zone?

LAND MAINTENANCE NOTICES

16. Have the Council authorised the service of a maintenance notice under s.215 of the Town & Country Planning Act 1990?

MINERAL CONSULTATION AREAS

17. Is the area a mineral consultation area notified by the county planning authority under Schedule 1 para 7 of the Town & Country Planning Act 1990?

HAZARDOUS SUBSTANCE CONSENTS

18.1. Please list any entries in the Register kept pursuant to s.28 of the Planning (Hazardous Substances) Act 1990.

18.2. If there are any entries:
   (a) how can copies of the entries be obtained?
   (b) where can the Register be inspected?

ENVIRONMENTAL AND POLLUTION NOTICES

19. What outstanding statutory or informal notices have been issued by the Council under the Environmental Protection Act 1990 or the Control of Pollution Act 1974? (This enquiry does not cover notices under Part IIA or Part III of the EPA, to which enquiries 3.12 or 3.7 apply).

FOOD SAFETY NOTICES

20. What outstanding statutory notices or informal notices have been issued by the Council under the Food Safety Act 1990?

HEDGEROW NOTICES

21.1. Please list any entries in the record maintained under regulation 10 of the Hedgerows Regulations 1997.

21.2. If there are any entries:
   (a) how can copies of the matters entered be obtained?
   (b) where can the record be inspected?

NOTES:

This form must be submitted in duplicate and should be read in conjunction with the guidance notes available separately.

(1) Unless otherwise indicated, matters will be disclosed only if they apply directly to the property described in Box B.

(2) "Area" means any area in which the property is located.

(3) References to "the Council" include any predecessor Council and also any council committee, sub-committee or other body or person exercising powers delegated by the Council and their "approval" includes their decision to proceed. The replies given to certain enquiries cover knowledge and actions of both the District Council and County Council.

(4) References to the provisions of particular Acts of Parliament or Regulations include any provisions which they have replaced and also include existing or future amendments or re-enactments.

(5) The replies will be given in the belief that they are in accordance with information presently available to the officers of the replying Council, but none of the Councils or their officers accept legal responsibility for an incorrect reply, except for negligence. Any liability for negligence will extend to the person who raised the enquiries and the person on whose behalf they were raised. It will also extend to any other person who has knowledge (personally or through an agent) of the replies before the time when he purchases, takes a tenancy of, or lends money on the security of the property or (if earlier) the time when he becomes contractually bound to do so.

Appendix 6: Completed Example Form Prop 7 – Completion Information and Requisitions on Title

COMPLETION INFORMATION AND REQUISITIONS ON TITLE

> **WARNING:** Replies to Requisitions 4.2 and 6.2 are treated as a solicitor's undertaking.

Property:

Seller:

Buyer:

1. PROPERTY INFORMATION

Please confirm that the written information given by or on behalf of the Seller prior to exchange of contracts is complete and accurate. (This includes SPIF Parts I and II, SLIF Parts I and II, Replies to Pre-Contract enquiries and correspondence between us).

2. VACANT POSSESSION

2.1 If vacant possession is to be given on completion:–
    (a) What arrangements will be made to hand over the keys?
    (b) By what time will the Seller have vacated the property on the completion date?

2.2 If vacant possession is not being given, please confirm that an authority to the Tenant to pay the rent to the Buyer will be available at completion.

3. DEEDS

3.1 Do you hold all the title deeds? If not, where are they?

3.2 Please list the deeds and documents to be handed over on completion.

3.3 If the land/charge certificate is on deposit, what is the deposit number? If it is not on deposit and will not be handed over on completion, please put it on deposit now and supply the deposit number on completion.

4. COMPLETION

4.1 Will completion take place at your office? If not, where will it take place?

4.2 If we wish to complete through the post, please confirm that:–

    (a) You undertake to adopt the Law Society's Code for Completion by Post, and

    (b) The mortgages and charges listed in reply to 6.1 are those specified for the purpose of paragraph 3 of the Code.

5. MONEY

5.1 Please state the exact amount payable on completion. If it is not just the balance purchase money, please provide copy receipts for any rent or service charge or other payments being apportioned.

Prop 7/1

Appendix 6: Completed Example Form Prop 7 – Completion Information and Requisitions on Title (continued)

Either

5.2 Please give:–
(a) Name and address of your bank.

(b) Sort Code.
(c) Your Client Account Number to which monies are to be sent.

Or

5.3 State in whose favour a banker's draft should be drawn.

6. UNDERTAKINGS

> WARNING: A reply to this requisition is treated as an undertaking. Great care must be taken when answering this requisition.

6.1 Please list the mortgages or charges secured on the property which you undertake to redeem or discharge to the extent that they relate to the property on or before completion (this includes repayment of any discount under the Housing Acts).

6.2 Do you undertake to redeem or discharge the mortgages and charges listed in reply to 6.1 on completion and to send to us Form DS1 or the receipted charges as soon as you receive them?

6.3 If you agree to adopt the current Law Society's Code for Completion by Post, please confirm that you are the duly authorised agent of the proprietor of every mortgage or charge on the property which you have undertaken, in reply to 6.2, to redeem or discharge.

Buyer's Solicitor   Seller's Solicitor

Date...   Date ....

> WARNING: These replies should be signed only by a person with authority to give undertakings on behalf of the firm.

ADDITIONAL REQUISITIONS

Prop 7/2

Oyez 7 Spa Road
London SE16 3QQ

This form is part of The Law Society's TransAction scheme © The Law Society 1994, 2001
The Law Society is the professional body for solicitors in England and Wales.
Oyez is an approved Law Society Supplier

Prop 7

The Law Society

4.2002 F-40315
5065069
* * * * *

Reproduced for educational purposes only by kind permission of the Solicitors' Law Stationery Society Limited

Appendix 7: Completed Example Form TR1 – Transfer of Whole of Registered Title(s)

Transfer of whole of registered title(s)	Land Registry **TR1**

If you need more room than is provided for in a panel, use continuation sheet CS and attach to this form.

1. Stamp Duty

Place "X" in the appropriate box or boxes and complete the appropriate certificate.

☐ It is certified that this instrument falls within category ☐ in the Schedule to the Stamp Duty (Exempt Instruments) Regulations 1987

☒ It is certified that the transaction effected does not form part of a larger transaction or of a series of transactions in respect of which the amount or value or the aggregate amount or value of the consideration exceeds the sum of **£ 250,000**

☐ It is certified that this is an instrument on which stamp duty is not chargeable by virtue of the provisions of section 92 of the Finance Act 2001

2. Title Number(s) of the Property *Leave blank if not yet registered.*

EDN999707

3. Property

14 PLEVNA PLACE
BLOSSOMTON, EDENSHIRE ED2 8JD

4. Date 20 JAN 06

5. Transferor *Give full names and company's registered number if any.*

MR CLINT SMART and MRS CONSTANCE SMART

6. Transferee **for entry on the register** *Give full name(s) and company's registered number, if any. For Scottish companies use an SC prefix and for limited liability partnerships use an OC prefix before the registered number, if any. For foreign companies give territory in which incorporated.*

MR THOMAS BOLD and MRS PRUDENCE BOLD

Unless otherwise arranged with Land Registry headquarters, a certified copy of the Transferee's constitution (in English or Welsh) will be required if it is a body corporate but is not a company registered in England and Wales or Scotland under the Companies Acts.

7. Transferee's intended **address(es) for service (including postcode) for entry on the register** *You may give up to three addresses for service **one** of which **must** be a postal address but does not have to be within the UK. The other addresses can be any combination of a postal address, a box number at a UK document exchange or an electronic address.*

1 PROSPECT AVENUE, ORCHARD VALE
EDENSHIRE ED5 7AB

8. The Transferor transfers the Property to the Transferee

9. Consideration *Place "X" in the appropriate box. State clearly the currency unit if other than sterling. If none of the boxes applies, insert an appropriate memorandum in the additional provisions panel.*

☒ The Transferor has received from the Transferee for the Property the sum of *In words and figures.*

☐ **£155,000 ONE HUNDRED AND FIFTY-FIVE THOUSAND POUNDS**
Insert other receipt as appropriate.

☐ The transfer is not for money or anything which has a monetary value

Appendix 7: Completed Example Form TR1 – Transfer of Whole of Registered Title(s) (continued)

10. The Transferor transfers with *Place "X" in the appropriate box and add any modifications.*

    ☒ full title guarantee   ☐ limited title guarantee

11. Declaration of trust *Where there is more than one Transferee, place "X" in the appropriate box.*

    ☒ The Transferees are to hold the Property on trust for themselves as joint tenants

    ☐ The Transferees are to hold the Property on trust for themselves as tenants in common in equal shares

    ☐ The Transferees are to hold the Property *Complete as necessary.*

12. Additional provisions *Insert here any required or permitted statements, certificates or applications and any agreed covenants, declarations, etc.*

13. Execution *The Transferor must execute this transfer as a deed using the space below. If there is more than one Transferor, all must execute. Forms of execution are given in Schedule 9 to the Land Registration Rules 2003. If the transfer contains Transferee's covenants or declarations or contains an application by the Transferee (e.g. for a restriction), it must also be executed by the Transferee (all of them, if there is more than one).*

    Signed and delivered as a deed by   CLINT SMART   *Clint Smart*

    in the presence of:

    Signature of witness   *George Ross*

    Name   GEORGE ROSS

    Address   6 The Willows
    Blossomton
    Edenshire EH78 1QA

Appendix 8: Completed Example Form AP1 – Application to Change the Register

---

Application to
change the register

Land Registry

AP1

If you need more room than is provided for in a panel, use continuation sheet CS and attach to this form.

1.	**Administrative area and postcode** if known EDENSHIRE – EDEN
2.	**Title number(s)** EDN 999707
3.	If you have already made this application by **outline application**, insert reference number:
4.	**This application affects** *Place "X" in the appropriate box.*

    ☒ the **whole** of the title(s) *Go to panel 5.*

    ☐ **part** of the title(s) *Give a brief description of the property affected.*

---

5. **Application, priority and fees** *A fee calculator for all types of applications can be found on Land Registry's website at www.landregistry.gov.uk/fees*

Nature of applications numbered in priority order	Value £	Fees paid £
1. TRANSFER	155,000	150.00
TOTAL £		150.00

Fee payment method: *Place "X" in the appropriate box.*
I wish to pay the appropriate fee payable under the current Land Registration Fee Order:

☒ by cheque or postal order, amount £ ___150___ made payable to "Land Registry".

☐ by Direct Debit under an authorised agreement with Land Registry.

FOR OFFICIAL USE ONLY
Record of fees paid

Particulars of under/over payments

Fees debited £

Reference number

---

6. **Documents lodged with this form** *Number the documents in sequence; copies should also be numbered and listed as separate documents. Alternatively you may prefer to use Form DL. If you supply the original document and a certified copy, we shall assume that you request the return of the original; if a certified copy is not supplied, we may retain the original document and it may be destroyed.*

LAND CERTIFICATE, FORM TR1

---

7. **The applicant is:** *Please provide the full name(s) of the person(s) applying to change the register.*

The application has been lodged by:	2043311
Land Registry Key No. (if appropriate)	
Name (if different from the applicant)	MR THOMAS BOLD and MRS PRUDENCE BOLD
Address/DX No.	1 PROSPECT AVENUE, ORCHARD VALE, EDENSHIRE ED5 7AB
Reference	
E-mail	tb@email.uk
Telephone No. (01234) 567 890	Fax No.

FOR OFFICIAL USE ONLY
Codes
Dealing

Status

Appendix 8: Completed Example Form AP1 – Application to Change the Register (continued)

8. Where you would like us to deal with someone else *We shall deal only with the applicant, or the person lodging the application if different, unless you place "X" against one or more of the statements below and give the necessary details.*

☒ Send title information document to the person shown below

☐ Raise any requisitions or queries with the person shown below

☐ Return original documents lodged with this form (see note in panel 6) to the person shown below
If this applies only to certain documents, please specify.

Name
Address/DX No.

Reference
E-mail

Telephone No.	Fax No.

9. Address(es) for service of the proprietor(s) of the registered estate(s). The address(es) will be entered in the register and used for correspondence and the service of notice. *Place "X" in the appropriate box(es). You may give up to three addresses for service one of which must be a postal address but does not have to be within the UK. The other addresses can be any combination of a postal address, a box number at a UK document exchange or an electronic address.*

☒ Enter the address(es) from the transfer/assent/lease

☐ Enter the address(es), including postcode, as follows:

☐ Retain the address(es) currently in the register for the title(s)

10. Disclosable overriding interests *Place "X" in the appropriate box.*

☒ This is not an application to register a registrable disposition or it is but no disclosable overriding interests affect the registered estate(s) *Section 27 of the Land Registration Act 2002 lists the registrable dispositions. Rule 57 of the Land Registration Rules 2003 sets out the disclosable overriding interests. Use Form DI to tell us about any disclosable overriding interests that affect the registered estate(s) identified in panel 2.*

☐ Form DI accompanies this application

The registrar may enter a notice of a disclosed interest in the register of title.

11. Information in respect of any new charge *Do not give this information if a Land Registry MD reference is printed on the charge, unless the charge has been transferred.*
Full name and address (including postcode) for service of notices and correspondence of the person to be registered as proprietor of each charge. *You may give up to three addresses for service one of which must be a postal address but does not have to be within the UK. The other addresses can be any combination of a postal address, a box number at a UK document exchange or an electronic address. For a company include company's registered number, if any. For Scottish companies use an SC prefix and for limited liability partnerships use an OC prefix before the registered number, if any. For foreign companies give territory in which incorporated.*

Unless otherwise arranged with Land Registry headquarters, we require a certified copy of the chargee's constitution (in English or Welsh) if it is a body corporate but is not a company registered in England and Wales or Scotland under the Companies Acts.

12. Signature of applicant or their conveyancer _Thomas Bold_ **Date** 20 JAN 06

© Crown copyright (ref: LR/HQ/Internet) 6/03

Appendix 9: Completed Example Form FR1 – First Registration Application

First registration application

Land Registry

FR1

If you need more room than is provided for in a panel, use continuation sheet CS and attach to this form.

1.	Administrative area and postcode if known	EDENSHIRE

2. Address or other description of the estate to be registered

14 PLEVNA PLACE BLOSSOMTON ED2 8JD

On registering a rentcharge, profit a prendre in gross, or franchise, show the address as follows:- "Rentcharge, franchise etc. over 2 The Grove, Anytown, Northshire NE2 9OO".

3. Extent to be registered *Place "X" in the appropriate box and complete as necessary.*

☐ The land is clearly identified on the plan to the
Enter nature and date of deed.

☒ The land is clearly identified on the attached plan and shown   **EDGED IN RED**
Enter reference e.g. "edged red".

☐ The description in panel 2 is sufficient to enable the land to be clearly identified on the Ordnance Survey map
When registering a rentcharge, profit a prendre in gross or franchise, the land to be identified is the land affected by that estate, or to which it relates.

4. Application, priority and fees *A fee calculator for all types of applications can be found on Land Registry's website at www.landregistry.gov.uk/fees*

Nature of applications

in priority order   Value/premium £   Fees paid £
1. **First registration of the estate** 150,000   150
2.
3.
4.
                                TOTAL £150

Fee payment method: *Place "X" in the appropriate box.*
I wish to pay the appropriate fee payable under the current Land Registration Fee Order:

☒ by cheque or postal order, amount £   **150**   made payable to "Land Registry".

☐ by Direct Debit under an authorised agreement with Land Registry.

FOR OFFICIAL USE ONLY
Record of fees paid

Particulars of under/over payments

Fees debited £

Reference number

5. The title applied for is *Place "X" in the appropriate box.*

☒ absolute freehold   ☐ absolute leasehold   ☐ good leasehold   ☐ possessory freehold
☐ possessory leasehold

6. Documents lodged with this form *List the documents on Form DL. We shall assume that you request the return of these documents. But we shall only assume that you request the return of a statutory declaration, subsisting lease, subsisting charge or the latest document of title (for example, any conveyance to the applicant) if you supply a certified copy of the document. If certified copies of such documents are not supplied, we may retain the originals of such documents and they may be destroyed.*

7. The applicant is: *Please provide the full name of the person applying to be registered as the proprietor.*

Application lodged by:
Land Registry Key No. (if appropriate)   2043311
Name (if different from the applicant)   MR THOMAS BOLD
Address/DX No.   1 PROSPECT AVENUE, ORCHARD VALE
                                            EDENSHIRE ED5 7AB
Reference
E-mail   tb@email.uk
Telephone No. (01234) 567890 | Fax No.

FOR OFFICIAL USE ONLY
Status codes

Appendix 9: Completed Example Form FR1 – First Registration Application (continued)

8. Where you would like us to deal with someone else *We shall deal only with the applicant, or the person lodging the application if different, unless you place "X" against one or more of the statements below and give the necessary details.*

☐   Send title information document to the person shown below

☐   Raise any requisitions or queries with the person shown below

☐   Return original documents lodged with this form (see note in panel 6) to the person shown below
If this applies only to certain documents, please specify.

Name
Address/DX No.

Reference
E-mail
Telephone No.   Fax No.

9.   Address(es) for service of every owner of the estate. The address(es) will be entered in the register and used for correspondence and the service of notice. *In this and panel 10, you may give up to three addresses for service one of which **must** be a postal address but does not have to be within the UK. The other addresses can be any combination of a postal address, a box number at a UK document exchange or an electronic address. For a company include the company's registered number, if any. For Scottish companies, use an SC prefix, and for limited liability partnerships, use an OC prefix before the registered number if any. For foreign companies give territory in which incorporated.*

MR THOMAS BOLD and MRS PRUDENCE BOLD
1 PROSPECT AVENUE, ORCHARD VALE
EDENSHIRE ED5 7AB

Unless otherwise arranged with Land Registry headquarters, we require a certified copy of the owner's constitution (in English or Welsh) if it is a body corporate but is not a company registered in England or Wales or Scotland under the Companies Acts.

10.   Information in respect of a chargee or mortgagee *Do not give this information if a Land Registry MD reference is printed on the charge, unless the charge has been transferred.*
Full name and address (including postcode) for service of notices and correspondence of the person entitled to be registered as proprietor of each charge. *You may give up to three addresses for service, see panel 9 as to the details you should include.*

MR THOMAS BOLD and MRS PRUDENCE BOLD
1 PROSPECT AVENUE, ORCHARD VALE
EDENSHIRE ED5 7AB

Unless otherwise arranged with Land Registry headquarters, we require a certified copy of the chargee's constitution (in English or Welsh) if it is a body corporate but is not a company registered in England and Wales or Scotland under the Companies Acts.

11.   Where the applicants are joint proprietors *Place "X" in the appropriate box*

☒   The applicants are holding the property on trust for themselves as joint tenants

☐   The applicants are holding the property on trust for themselves as tenants in common in equal shares

☐   The applicants are holding the property *(complete as necessary)*

12.   Disclosable overriding interests *Place "X" in the appropriate box.*

☒   No disclosable overriding interests affect the estate

☐   Form DI accompanies this application

Rule 28 of the Land Registration Rules 2003 sets out the disclosable overriding interests that you must tell us about. You must use Form DI to tell us about any disclosable overriding interests that affect the estate.

The registrar may enter a notice of a disclosed interest in the register of title.

Appendix 9: Completed Example Form FR1 – First Registration Application (continued)

---

13. The title is based on the title documents listed in Form DL which are all those that are in the possession or control of the applicant.

    Place "X" in the appropriate box. If applicable complete the second statement; include any interests disclosed only by searches other than local land charges. Any interests disclosed by searches which do not affect the estate being registered should be certified.

    ☒ All rights, interests and claims affecting the estate known to the applicant are disclosed in the title documents and Form DI if accompanying this application. There is no-one in adverse   possession of the property or any part of it.

    ☐ In addition to the rights, interests and claims affecting the estate disclosed in the title documents or Form DI if accompanying this application, the applicant only knows of the following:

---

14. *Place "X" in this box if you are NOT able to give this certificate.*   ☒

    We have fully examined the applicant's title to the estate, including any appurtenant rights, or are satisfied that it has been fully examined by a conveyancer in the usual way prior to this application.

15. We have authority to lodge this application and request the registrar to complete the registration.

---

16. **Signature of applicant or their conveyancer** _____ *Thomas Bold* _____   **Date** ___ 15 JAN 06

    Note: Failure to complete the form with proper care may deprive the applicant of protection under the Land Registration Act if, as a result, a mistake is made in the register.

© Crown copyright (ref: LR/HQ/Internet) 6/03

Appendix 10: District Land Registries

Areas served

Administrative area	District Land Registry
England	
Bath and North East Somerset	Plymouth
Bedfordshire	Peterborough
Blackburn with Darwen	Lancashire
Blackpool	Lancashire
Bournemouth	Weymouth
Bracknell Forest	Gloucester
Brighton and Hove	Portsmouth
Bristol	Gloucester
Buckinghamshire	Leicester
Cambridgeshire	Peterborough
Cheshire	Birkenhead (Rosebrae)
Cornwall	Plymouth
Cumbria	Durham (Boldon House)
Darlington	Durham (Southfield House)
Derby	Nottingham (West)
Derbyshire	Nottingham (West)
Devon	Plymouth
Dorset	Weymouth
Durham	Durham (Southfield House)
East Riding of Yorkshire	York
East Sussex	Portsmouth
Essex	Peterborough
Gloucestershire	Gloucester
GREATER LONDON (London Borough)	
Barking and Dagenham	Stevenage
Barnet	Swansea
Bexley	Croydon
Brent	Harrow
Bromley	Croydon

Appendix 10: District Land Registries (continued)

Administrative area	District Land Registry
Camden	Harrow
City of London	Harrow
City of Westminster	Harrow
Croydon	Croydon
Ealing	Swansea
Enfield	Swansea
Greenwich	Telford
Hackney	Stevenage
Hammersmith and Fulham	Birkenhead (Rosebrae)
Haringey	Swansea
Harrow	Harrow
Havering	Stevenage
Hillingdon	Swansea
Hounslow	Swansea
Inner and Middle Temples	Harrow
Islington	Harrow
Kensington and Chelsea	Birkenhead (Rosebrae)
Kingston upon Thames	Croydon
Lambeth	Telford
Lewisham	Telford
Merton	Croydon
Newham	Stevenage
Redbridge	Stevenage
Richmond upon Thames	Telford
Southwark	Telford
Sutton	Croydon
Tower Hamlets	Stevenage
Waltham Forest	Stevenage
Wandsworth	Telford
Greater Manchester	Lytham
Halton	Birkenhead (Rosebrae)
Hampshire	Weymouth
Hartlepool	Durham (Southfield House)

Appendix 10: District Land Registries (continued)

Administrative area	District Land Registry
Herefordshire	Telford
Hertfordshire	Stevenage
Isle of Wight	Portsmouth
Isles of Scilly	Plymouth
Kent	Tunbridge Wells
Kingston Upon Hull	Kingston Upon Hull
Lancashire	Lancashire
Leicester	Leicester
Leicestershire	Leicester
Lincolnshire	Kingston Upon Hull
Luton	Peterborough
Medway Towns	Tunbridge Wells
Merseyside	Birkenhead (Old Market)
Middlesbrough	Durham (Southfield House)
Milton Keynes	Leicester
Norfolk	Kingston Upon Hull
North East Lincolnshire	Kingston Upon Hull
North Lincolnshire	Kingston Upon Hull
North Somerset	Plymouth
North Yorkshire	York
Northampton	Leicester
Northumberland	Durham (Southfield House)
Nottingham	Nottingham (East)
Nottinghamshire	Nottingham (East)
Oxfordshire	Gloucester
Peterborough	Peterborough
Plymouth	Plymouth
Poole	Weymouth
Portsmouth	Portsmouth
Reading	Gloucester
Redcar and Cleveland	Durham (Southfield House)
Rutland	Leicester
Shropshire	Telford

Appendix 10: District Land Registries (continued)

Administrative area	District Land Registry
Slough	Gloucester
Somerset	Plymouth
South Gloucestershire	Gloucester
South Yorkshire	Nottingham (East)
Southampton	Weymouth
Southend-on-Sea	Peterborough
Staffordshire	Birkenhead (Old Market)
Stockton-on-Tees	Durham (Southfield House)
Stoke-on-Trent	Birkenhead (Old Market)
Suffolk	Kingston Upon Hull
Surrey	Durham (Boldon House)
Swindon	Weymouth
Thurrock	Peterborough
Torbay	Plymouth
Tyne and Wear	Durham (Southfield House)
Warrington	Birkenhead (Rosebrae)
Warwickshire	Gloucester
West Berkshire	Gloucester
West Midlands	Coventry
West Sussex	Portsmouth
West Yorkshire	Nottingham (West)
Wiltshire	Weymouth
Windsor and Maidenhead	Gloucester
Wokingham	Gloucester
Worcestershire	Coventry
Wrekin	Telford
York	York

Wales/Cymru

All Areas	Wales/Cymru

Appendix 10: District Land Registries (continued)

Postal addresses and telephone numbers

England

HM Land Registry Headquarters
32 Lincoln's Inn Fields
London WC2A 3PH
Tel: 020 7917 8888
Website: www.landreg.gov.uk

Birkenhead

The address for titles in Cheshire, Halton and Warrington and the London Boroughs of Hammersmith and Fulham / Kensington and Chelsea is:

The Birkenhead (Rosebrae) District Land Registry
Rosebrae Court
Woodside Ferry Approach
Birkenhead
Merseyside CH41 6DU
Tel: 0151 472 6666

The address for titles in Merseyside, Staffordshire and Stoke-on-Trent is:

The Birkenhead (Old Market) District Land Registry
Old Market House
Hamilton Street
Birkenhead
Merseyside L41 5FL
Tel: 0151 473 1110

Coventry

The Coventry District Land Registry
Leigh Court
Torrington Avenue
Tile Hill
Coventry CV4 9XZ
Tel: 024 7686 0860

Croydon

The Croydon District Land Registry
Sunley House
Bedford Park
Croydon CR9 3LE
Tel: 020 8781 9103

Durham (Boldon House)

The Durham (Boldon House) District Land Registry
Boldon House
Wheatlands Way, Pity Me
Durham DH1 5GJ
Tel: 0191 301 2345

Durham (Southfield House)

The Durham (Southfield House) District Land Registry
Southfield House
Southfield Way
Durham DH1 5TR
Tel: 0191 301 3500

Appendix 10: District Land Registries (continued)

Gloucester

The Gloucester District Land Registry
Twyver House, Bruton Way
Gloucester GL1 1DQ
Tel: 01452 511 111

Harrow

The Harrow District Land Registry
Lyon House, Lyon Road
Harrow
Middlesex HA1 2EU
Tel: 020 8235 1181

Kingston Upon Hull

The Kingston Upon Hull District Land Registry
Earle House, Colonial Street
Hull HU2 8JN
Tel: 01482 223 244

Lancashire

The District Land Registry for Lancashire
Wrea Brook Court, Lytham Road
Warton
Lancashire PR4 1TE
Tel: 01772 836 700

Leicester

The Leicester District Land Registry
Westbridge Place
Leicester LE3 5DR
Tel: 0116 265 4000

Lytham

The Lytham District Land Registry
Birkenhead House, East Beach
Lytham St Annes
Lancashire FY8 5AB
Tel: 01253 849 849

Nottingham (East)

The Nottingham (East) District Land Registry
Robins Wood Road
Nottingham NG8 3RQ
Tel: 0115 906 5353

Nottingham (West)

The Nottingham (West) District Land Registry
Chalfont Drive
Nottingham NG8 3RN
Tel: 0115 935 1166

Peterborough

The Peterborough District Land Registry
Touthill Close, City Road
Peterborough PE1 1XN
Tel: 01733 288 288

Plymouth

The Plymouth District Land Registry
Plumer House, Tailyour Road
Crownhill
Plymouth PL6 5HY
Tel: 01752 636 000

Appendix 10: District Land Registries (continued)

Portsmouth

The Portsmouth District Land Registry
St Andrew's Court
St Michael's Road
Portsmouth
Hampshire PO1 2JH
Tel: 023 9276 8888

Stevenage

The Stevenage District Land Registry
Brickdale House
Swingate
Stevenage
Herts. SG1 1XG
Tel: 01438 788 889

Swansea

The Swansea District Land Registry
Ty Bryn Glas
High Street
Swansea SA1 1PW
Tel: 01792 458 877

Telford

The Telford District Land Registry
Parkside Court
Hall Park Way
Telford TF3 4LR
Tel: 01952 290 355

Tunbridge Wells

The Tunbridge Wells District Land Registry
Forest Court, Forest Road
Tunbridge Wells
Kent TN2 5AQ
Tel: 01892 510 015

Weymouth

The Weymouth District Land Registry
Melcombe Court
1 Cumberland Drive
Weymouth
Dorset DT4 9TT
Tel: 01305 363 636

York

The York District Land Registry
James House, James Street
York YO10 3YZ
Tel: 01904 450 000

Wales/Cymru

Cofrestrfa Tir Ddosbarthol Cymru/The District Land Registry for Wales
Ty Cwm Tawe
Phoenix Way
Llansamlet
Swansea SA7 9FQ
Tel: 01792 355 000

Index

This index covers all chapters. An 'i.' after a page number indicates an illustration.